Lectio Divina

CISTERCIAN STUDIES SERIES NUMBER TWO HUNDRED THIRTY-EIGHT

Lectio Divina

The Medieval Experience of Reading

by
Duncan Robertson

α

Cistercian Publications
www.cistercianpublications.org

LITURGICAL PRESS
Collegeville, Minnesota
www.litpress.org

A Cistercian Publications title published by Liturgical Press

Cistercian Publications
Editorial Offices
Abbey of Gethsemani
3642 Monks Road
Trappist, Kentucky 40051
www.cistercianpublications.org

Excerpts from documents of the Second Vatican Council are from *Vatican Council II: The Basic Sixteen Documents,* by Austin Flannery, OP © 1996 (Costello Publishing Company, Inc.). Used with permission.

Scripture texts in this work in Latin are from the Vulgate, *Bibliorum sacrorum iuxta vulgatam clementinam nova editio* (Rome: Typis Polyglottis Vaticanis, 1959).

Scripture texts in this work in English are from the Revised Standard Version of the Bible, copyright 1952 [2nd edition, 1971] by the Division of Christian Education of the National Council of the Churches of Christ in the United States of America. Used by permission. All rights reserved.

Library of Congress Cataloging-in-Publication Data

Robertson, Duncan.
    Lectio divina : the medieval experience of reading / by Duncan Robertson.
      p. cm. — (Cistercian studies series ; no. 238)
    Includes bibliographical references (p.   ) and index.
    ISBN 978-0-87907-238-4 — ISBN 978-0-87907-204-9 (e-book)
    1. Books and reading—Religious aspects—Christianity—History—To 1500.
I. Title.

BR117.R63   2011
248.309'02—dc23   2011032455

For Susan
Amor ipse notitia est

Contents

Abbreviations

CCCM	*Corpus Christianorum: Continuatio Medievalis.* Turnhout: Brepols, 1966–
CCSL	*Corpus Christianorum: Series Latina.* Turnhout: Brepols, 1953–
CF	Cistercian Fathers Series
CS	Cistercian Studies Series
DS	*Dictionnaire de spiritualité ascétique et mystique.* Paris: Beauchesne, 1937–
PG	*Patrologiae Cursus Completus: Series Graeca.* Edited by J. P. Migne. 162 vols. 1857–66.
PL	*Patrologiae Cursus Completus: Series Latina.* Edited by J. P. Migne. 221 vols. 1844–64.
RB	*Rule of Saint Benedict 1980.* Edited by Timothy Fry. Collegeville, MN: Liturgical Press, 1981.
SBOp	*Sancti Bernardi opera*, 9 vols. Edited by J. Leclercq, C. H. Talbot, and H. M. Rochais. Rome: Editiones Cistercienses, 1957–77.
SCh	Sources Chrétiennes. Paris: Éditions du Cerf, 1940–
SC	Bernard of Clairvaux, *Sermones super Cantica canticorum.*

Preface

What does it mean to read? What faculties does this activity involve? What expectations do we bring to it, what limitations do we encounter? The general question has come frequently into the foreground throughout Western cultural history and in our own time—with notable anxiety—among literary critics, neurologists, literacy teachers, and scholars. This book explores an early phase of this history, the "monastic Middle Ages," during which the act of reading remained closely associated with prayer in a practice known as *lectio divina*. My belief is that our ongoing scientific and humanistic investigations of reading have not yet sufficiently taken the medieval religious experience into account; additionally, we have much of value to learn from a review of medieval theory and from a rereading of the texts that put theory into practice.

Lectio Divina

Sit tibi vel oratio assidua vel lectio: nunc cum Deo loquere, nunc Deus tecum ("You should apply yourself to prayer or to reading: at times you speak with God, at times he speaks with you"). This saying, first attributed to Cyprian of Carthage (third century), was repeated throughout the Middle Ages[1] and reaffirmed as recently as 1965 in a decree of the Second Vatican Council.[2] It conveys

---

[1] Cyprian of Carthage, *Ep.* 1.15, PL 4:221; cited in DS 9:473. Cf. Jerome, *Oras, loqueris ad Sponsum; legis, ille tibi loquitur* (Letter 22.25 to Eustochium [PL 22:411]); Ambrose, *Illum alloquimur, cum oramus; illum audimus cum divina legimus oracula* (*De officiis* 1.20.88 [PL16:50]); Isidore of Seville, *Nam cum oramus, cum Deo ipsi loquimur; cum vero legimus, Deus nobiscum loquitur* (*Sententiae* 3.8 [PL 87:670]); Smaragdus of Saint Mihiel, *Nam cum oramus, cum Deo ipsi loquimur; cum vero legimus, Deus nobiscum loquitur* (*Diadema monachorum* 3 [PL 102:597]), etc.

[2] "Let them remember, however, that prayer should accompany the reading of sacred scripture, so that it becomes a dialogue between God and the human

the essence of *lectio divina*, as it has come to be called:[3] an intimate dialogue with a living, present, divine interlocutor who will answer when the reader appeals to him.

Medieval readers of Scripture understood, of course, that communication with the Author could not be completely reciprocal. In the Christian belief system, we are transparent to God, who perceives our thoughts and anticipates our prayers before we utter them. But God is not so clearly visible to us. "For our knowledge is imperfect. . . . For now we see in a mirror dimly, but then face to face. Now I know in part; then [in the next life] I shall understand fully, even as I have been fully understood" (1 Cor 13:9-12). Meanwhile, we have the Scripture to study in which or through which God "speaks" to us. Applying the effort of faith and intelligence to the text, the devout reader recovers God's living presence, however indirectly and intermittently, in Saint Paul's dark mirror of language.

The encounter with the "living word" could prove personally decisive. So Saint Augustine recalls the conversion of Saint Anthony, who happened to enter a church and hear the reading: "Go, sell what you possess and give to the poor . . . and come, follow me" (Matt 19:21). Anthony received the message "as though what was read was being said to him" (*Confessions* 8.12: *tamquam sibi diceretur quod legebatur*), and he proceeded to obey what he had heard. Augustine himself enacts a similar anecdote. Hearing a child's cry in the garden, "*Tolle! lege!*" he opens the Bible and finds himself urgently addressed by the verse, "not in reveling and drunkenness . . ." (Rom 13:13). Saint Francis enlists his first recruit, Bernardo, in like manner. Opening a Bible at random, they find, "Go, sell what you have . . . take up [your] cross, and follow me." Francis

---

reader. For, 'we speak to him when we pray; we listen to him when we read the divine oracles.'" Dogmatic Constitution on Divine Revelation (*Dei Verbum*), article 25; the quotation is from Ambrose.

[3] Mariano Magrassi, *Praying the Bible: An Introduction to* Lectio Divina (Collegeville, MN: Liturgical Press, 1998), 15, cites early occurrences of the term, often synonymous with *sacra pagina or lectio sacra*, in writings by Jerome, Ambrose, and other fourth- and fifth-century patristic authorities. In our time, *lectio divina* has come to signify a systematic reading-prayer exercise, as set forth in a number of modern manuals (see below, pp. 25–26 and p. 25, n. 48)

concludes, "That is the counsel that Christ gives us. So go and do perfectly what you have heard."[4] Throughout the Christian tradition, readers are similarly called upon to "listen to" the sacred text, that is to say, to receive it obediently, as though it were spoken to one directly and personally. One has then to engage the text in prayer and apply it in action.

Beyond the drama of conversion, medieval religious readers sought the integration of reading-reception into a way of life. The early theorists of *lectio divina* all stress the need for assiduity, persistence, and commitment. Disciplined application will develop into a true mutuality of response between the reader and the text over time. John Cassian, in the *Conferences* (fifth century),[5] foresees a progressively deepening dialogue: "As our mind is increasingly renewed by this study, the face of Scripture will also begin to be renewed, and the beauty of a more sacred understanding will somehow grow with the person making progress."[6] *Etiam scripturarum facies incipiet innouari*; what does Cassian mean by the "face" of Scripture? Something, perhaps, like what we call the "interface," the locus of contact between writing and reading. He seems mysteriously to suggest (and Gregory later confirms) that the Scripture itself will be renewed, that it could indeed change as the person studying it changes.

In the Monastery

In practice, the spiritual development prescribed by Cassian would require the shelter of a stable institution. From the fifth century onward, the cultivation of *lectio divina* became primarily associated with the monastery. Literacy was a prerequisite for admission, and further instruction was offered in intramural classes. The Rule of Saint Benedict (RB 48) schedules times for "meditation

[4] Saint Francis of Assisi, *The Little Flowers of St Francis of Assisi*, trans. Roger Hudleston (New York: Heritage Press, 1965), chap. 2.

[5] Jean Cassien, *Conférences*, ed. E. Pichéry, SCh 42, 54, 64 (Paris: Éditions du Cerf, 1955–59). John Cassian, *The Conferences*, trans. Boniface Ramsey (New York: Paulist Press, 1997).

[6] Casssian, *Conferences*, 14.11.1; Ramsey, 515; SCh 54:197.

or reading" in alternation with manual labor according to seasonal needs.[7] Other early rules make similar provisions.

Reading in the early monastic environment was normally performed out loud. Early medieval authorities testify, and modern studies of the manuscripts have shown, that from the second century CE onward, the spaces and *interpuncta* which had been placed between words disappeared, leaving the reader to contend with unseparated text (*scriptura continua*). In the era of Saint Benedict, a monk making his first approach to a text needed to vocalize in order to decipher the writing. Pronunciation remained necessary at all subsequent stages of the reading process, particularly in the work of memorization, which formed the basis of the monastic *meditatio*.

In the early monastic rules, as in classical usage, *meditatio* chiefly means repetition, memorization, and recitation. The term refers to the process of learning texts by heart, and also to psalmody and recitation performed while the monk is at work, away from the written page. When the reader returns to the book, *meditatio* ensures that he will be able to "read" it more easily, as children learning to read today do with texts they have previously memorized. "Reading needs the aid of memory," Isidore of Seville notes, "and even if memory is sluggish, it is sharpened by frequent *meditatio*, and recovered by assiduous reading."[8] Strictly construed, *meditatio* is the continuation of reading and is all but synonymous with reading in Saint Benedict's phrase, *meditare aut legere* (RB 48.23).

Did the constant recitation of Scripture lead to the ethical internalization that Cassian describes? Often enough, the documents warn against mechanical, thoughtless repetition and hint at a daily struggle against boredom. To some extent, the emphasis on orality was imposed by practical necessity; books were scarce as well as difficult to read. Yet even in later centuries, among educated people in situations where material and social constraints have largely disappeared, reading aloud and recitation continue to occupy a central place in the religious environment. Reading aloud transforms reading into prayer. Pronouncing the words under one's

---

[7] *Rule of Saint Benedict 1980*, ed. Timothy Fry (Collegeville, MN: The Liturgical Press, 1981), 252–53.

[8] Isidore of Seville, *Sententiae* 3.14.7–8 (PL 83:689).

breath, one quite literally "tastes" them in the mouth, and more profoundly, *in ore cordis*, "in the mouth of the heart." Sounding words out loud (*voce magna*, or *clare legendo*) engages the sense of hearing and opens the ethical dimension of the listening attitude. By these means, the reader discovers the emotional inflections contained in the meaning of the words and acts out the protagonist's role. Memorization, finally, realizes an elementary form of Pauline spiritual freedom: singing/reciting Scripture *submoto libro*, "with the book put aside," at work or wherever one may find oneself, one is liberated from servitude to the "custodian" (Gal 3:25)—the *littera*, the law, the written text. Having memorized the texts and having placed them in the context of one's own experience, the reader re-authors them and makes them, in effect, his or her own.

Intellectual comprehension in this culture is secondary. That would come late in the course of the reading experience, if at all, as a gift of the Holy Spirit—in sleep perhaps, as Cassian suggests (Conf 14.10.4)—but never completely, of course, in this life. The scriptural text is conceived to be inexhaustible and capable of conveying different meanings to different readers, or to the same reader at different stages of spiritual maturation. Understanding (*intellectus spiritualis*) would result less from any synthesis of ideas than from a patient frequentation, a familiarity grown from long acquaintanceship, as though the Bible were a language which could only be learned by living in the country where it is spoken. Accordingly, theorists and teachers of *lectio divina* concern themselves more with the process of reading than with its result. Reading, like prayer, is an activity performed mainly in the present tense; indeed, one could never finally "have read" the Scripture.

Reading and Exegesis

Where the disciplines of *lectio divina* focus on subjective experience, biblical exegesis springs from the contrasting, complementary belief that the scriptural text has one or more objective meanings to be discovered. That fundamental assumption spans various systems of interpretation and underlies the vast literature of commentary extending from late antiquity through the Middle Ages. Exegesis and *lectio divina* develop, as it were, in tandem throughout this period. The two disciplines overlap, however, whenever (as often happens) an interpreter assumes the role of a preacher addressing an audience orally or in writing. The discourse in the form of a sermon begins with the reading of a passage from Scripture— a reading "out loud" to other present readers. Exposition then emerges from an implied dialogue. In Augustine's sermons on the psalms, in Gregory's *Moralia on Job* and his *Homilies on Ezekiel*, in Bernard of Clairvaux's *Sermons on the Song of Songs*, the real or imaginary audience is constantly invoked. In the process, reading attitudes derived from *lectio divina* are focused upon the work of interpretation; the meaning of the text is sought in the dialectic between knowledge and experience—*scientia* and *sapientia*—and ideally is found at their point of convergence.

As the literature proliferated, an increasing need was felt for consolidation. From the sixth century onward, there appears a number of patristic anthologies and digests—*florilegia, sententiae, excerpta*—which transmit the teachings of Augustine, Gregory, and other authorities in accessible form. These compilations facilitate the application of reading to moral and liturgical life. They offer practical instances of the reading-reception that Cassian had theorized. In such volumes, we find biblical and patristic sources freely quoted, excerpted, and combined, often without attribution to their original authors. The materials are frequently organized under topical headings, such as justice, faith, patience, envy, idleness, discipline, prayer, and reading itself.

Another kind of compilation is exemplified by Benedict of Aniane's *Concordia Regularum*, which follows the Rule of Saint Benedict chapter by chapter, listing for each chapter the stipulations found in all the other available rules. Still another kind of compilation is that of the prayer books, which were composed for prominent laity from the eighth century onward; these collections assemble psalm texts and collects, along with patristic excerpts, to be used by individuals or groups in prayer. In a further development of the compilation genre, John of Fécamp's *Confessio theologica* (mid-eleventh century) and its various revisions offer what may be described as original "meditations" on sacred writings, quoted at length and focused through extended first-person prayers. In these works, reading flows into writing, the quotations into the quoting texts, in an unbroken continuum.

In religious writing at the turn of the twelfth century, we note an increasing theoretical consciousness expressed in introductory statements and in instructions to real or ideal readers. Saint Anselm warns the reader that his *Prayers and Meditations* should be read not hurriedly or in a turmoil but quietly and thoughtfully, a little at a time; the reader should not even strive to read all of the book, "but only as much as, by God's help, she finds useful in stirring up her spirit to pray."[9] The writings of Hugh of Saint-Victor, particularly the *Didascalicon* (written in the 1120s), bring basic formulations concerning exegesis together with considerations of *lectio divina* as moral instruction.

Hugh confirms a widening of the concept of "meditation," already apparent in Anselm, as extending beyond the retention of the sacred text emphasized by the ancients. "Meditation takes its start from reading, but is bound by none of reading's rules or precepts; for it delights to range along open ground" (Did 3.10).[10] Meditation remains integral to the whole reading-prayer process, which Hugh outlines in five steps: reading (proper), meditation, prayer, action, and contemplation. The term also recurs with extended connotations in the titles of collections of original writings; for example, the gnomic *Meditationes* of the Carthusian prior, Guigo I, or the *Meditativae orationes* of William of Saint-Thierry.

It remained for another Carthusian prior, Guigo II, to formulate a complete summary, "after the fact" as it now appears, of the *lectio divina* process. The steps of Guigo II's *Ladder of Monks* are four: *lectio* (the first reading), *meditatio* (repetition and reflection), *oratio* (prayer), and *contemplatio* (rest in the presence of the Spirit). Action, which Hugh of Saint-Victor had proposed as a fifth term, remains implicit throughout Guigo II's treatise. Each stage is carefully defined and illustrated with reference to the gospel verse, "Blessed are the pure in heart, for they shall see God" (Matt 5:8). Prescriptive as well as descriptive, Guigo II's outline anticipates the

---

[9] Saint Anselm, *The Prayers and Meditations of Saint Anselm*, trans. Benedicta Ward (Harmondsworth, Middlesex, UK: Penguin Books, 1973), 89.

[10] Hugh of Saint Victor, *The Didascalicon of Hugh of St. Victor: A Medieval Guide to the Arts*, trans. Jerome Taylor (New York: Columbia University Press, 1961), 92.

systematic prayer methods of the following centuries, those that will be summarized in the *Spiritual Exercises* of Ignatius of Loyola.

Turning from theory to practice, we find in the twelfth century an outpouring of works illustrating *lectio divina* in process. The various commentaries on the Song of Songs produced during this period inflect exegesis toward tropology, that is to say, toward moral psychology and individual spirituality. On the horizon there appears a new convergence of objective and subjective interpretation, which is exemplified *par excellence* by the *Sermons on the Song of Songs* by Bernard of Clairvaux. Bernard's conviction, repeatedly restated throughout the *Sermons*, is that the Song cannot be read or heard from the "outside"; only in a personal *experientia* can one apprehend its meaning. He seeks not only to translate the love poem into religiously meaningful terms, as traditional commentators had done, but also to participate directly and actively in the text as a protagonist, ultimately as the Bride in the dialogue. Beyond exegesis, his line-by-line analysis chronicles a day-to-day struggle to realize this objective and to transcend the limitations of the human reader's role.

With Guigo II's didactic outline of *lectio divina*, and even more definitively with Bernard of Clairvaux's exhaustive exploration of its possibilities, we reach a terminus in the development of reading culture. Accordingly, the year 1200 will serve as the limit of the present study. That date marks the beginning of a sea change. In the following years, the dominant monastic tradition yielded to the scientific theology taught in the nascent universities. Developments in reading and writing technology led to improved legibility, enabling silent and individual reading, releasing readers from a live and present audience environment, and eventually releasing them altogether from the pedagogy of memorization. The thirteenth-century proliferation of books allowed more readers to gain access to the texts, and also to exploit the freedom to turn their pages at will. The heritage of *lectio divina* survived, however, along with the yearnings and instincts associated with it—the reciprocities linking reading, experience, and writing—in vernacular spiritual writings from the beginning of the twelfth century onward. Women religious, whose vocations had typically been hampered by the lack of clerical Latin education, took an increasingly significant role in this movement, introducing the later medieval flowering of religious poetry and prose in all the European tongues. These thirteenth-century developments lie beyond the scope of the present study, which is concerned with the earlier monastic reading culture and with the writing that sprang from it.

Reading beyond Reading

Modern reading-theorists have rediscovered certain transcendent dimensions of the act of reading that were altogether familiar to medieval readers. As one scholar notes, "Reading is a thoughtfull activity. . . . It is creative and constructive, not passive and reactive."[11] Moving away from a passive, mechanical text-reception model, we have come to recognize the ways in which reading *overflows* itself in all directions and at every moment. The process begins with expectations and predictions that precede contact with the text; it proceeds through the perception of letters and words, continues through the visualizations, inferences, and syntheses that orchestrate comprehension, and, at last, quite possibly takes leave of the written page altogether. Reading is surrounded always by an extratextual, experiential context, an aura integral to the essence of the act. In this concentric zone is located the creativity of the reader's response, his or her contribution to creating the text that is read, and also the conditioning, virtual presence of other readers—the "interpretive community,"[12] or, in medieval culture, the church—with whom the reader remains in constant communion.

The historical study of reading, like the act of reading itself, tends to overflow scholarly boundaries as we become aware of the modern intellectual, spiritual, and even political contexts in which this study has come of age. The first chapter of this book offers orientations; I recall the pioneering work of Jean Leclercq and Henri de Lubac in relation to the *ressourcement* movement preceding the Second Vatican Council. I also summarize more recent medievalist

---

[11] Frank Smith, *Understanding Reading: A Psycholinguistic Analysis of Reading and Learning to Read*, 6th ed. (New York: Routledge, 2011), 27.

[12] Stanley Fish was among the first to develop this concept, in "Interpreting the Variorum," *Critical Inquiry* 2 (Spring 1976), 465–85.

research and developments in academic literary theory—notably the reader-response criticism of the 1970s—and in reading-cognition theory. Chapters 2 through 7 study the medieval history of reading and offer discussions of pivotal authors and texts presented in an approximate chronological order. This study extends from the third century through the twelfth. Rather than attempting a comprehensive history of this populous field, I have chosen to offer readings of writings—readings of readings—undertaken each for its own sake and ideally on its own terms, with attention to individual complexities and nuances. A final chapter, *in libro experientiae*, summarizes reflections on reading experience, both medieval and modern.

Medieval commentaries on Scripture teach us to "taste" the texts in their own order, rather than rearranging references in a critical synthesis in the modern academic manner. In following medieval expositions, I am conscious of imitating at times the reading methodology that I purport to describe. In this spirit, I have not resisted the temptation to quote liberally in Latin and French as well as in translation in order to allow my readers to taste the beauty of these writings for themselves. There is an indefinable benefit to be gained from the contact with original texts in their own languages; we need to approach their *presence* reverently, as closely as intervening manuscript traditions will allow us to do. As Cassian comments, we feel the power of the texts even before we understand them intellectually (Conf 10.11.5). Augustine, Gregory, and Bernard wrote with urgency and elegance in Latin, as did Henri de Lubac and Jean Leclercq in modern French prose. The aesthetic value of their writings cues us to a deepening process of appreciation that should not be cut short. I do systematically translate all quotations, referring to published English translations whenever they are available, occasionally emending these for clarity. The Bible is quoted in Latin from the Vulgate, *Bibliorum sacrorum iuxta vulgatam clementinam nova editio* (Rome: Typis Polyglottis Vaticanis, 1959), and in English from *The New Oxford Annotated Bible with the Apocrypha. Revised Standard Version* (New York: Oxford University Press, 1973). With other texts where no reference is made, the translation is my own.[13]

---

[13] I follow also the great example of Henri de Lubac in *Exégèse médiévale: Les quatre sens de l'écriture*, 4 vols. (Paris: Aubier, 1959–64). In *Mémoire sur l'occasion*

It is a pleasure to acknowledge at this time the help and advice received from colleagues east and west in the course of this study. I have derived particular encouragement from the scholars and priests who have created the Institute of Cistercian Studies, under the leadership of E. Rozanne Elder, at the annual Congress on Medieval Studies at Western Michigan University in Kalamazoo, MI. Several chapters in this book originated as papers given at that forum. I also wish to thank Fr. Luke Anderson, Marsha Dutton, Martha Krieg, Br. Simeon Leiva, Thomas Renna, John R. Sommerfeldt, and especially Fr. Mark Scott, the executive editor of Cistercian Publications, and Eric Christensen of the Liturgical Press. Closely associated with this group are the memories of two extraordinary scholar-priests whom I can no longer thank in person: Fr. Louis Bouyer (1913–2004) and Fr. Chrysogonus Waddell (1930–2008). I have been aided also over many years by medievalist teachers and friends: the directors of my studies at Princeton, Alfred Foulet (1901–1987) and Karl D. Uitti (1934–2003); and among others, Gabriel Bianciotto, Renate Blumenfeld-Kosinski, Peter Dembowski, Ángel Gómez Moreno, Catherine Jones, Barbara Newman, Mary Speer, and Jocelyn Wogan-Browne. I also wish to thank my patient colleagues at Augusta State University, including especially Jana Sandarg and Lillie B. Johnson, the chair of the English and Foreign Languages department, who obtained released time from teaching for me during a critical phase of the project. The most joyous debt I have to acknowledge is to my wife Susan. To her this book is dedicated.

---

de mes écrits (Namur, Belgium: Culture et Vérité, 1989), 86–87, de Lubac comments, *On m'a aussi quelquefois reproché d'abuser des citations latines. La part faite à la négligence, ou à la hâte excessive, je dirai pour ma défense que j'ai souvent conservé le latin des textes, en raison de leur singulière beauté, que toute traduction efface* ("I have been criticized sometimes for excessive use of Latin quotations. Admitting some negligence or haste on my part, I will say in my defense that I have often kept the Latin of the texts for the sake of their striking beauty, which translations obscure").

Chapter One

Scholarly Contexts:
Ressourcement and Research

Ressourcement

The modern rediscovery of medieval literary spirituality has been led by an extraordinary group of scholar-theologians affiliated with the Catholic Church. A race of giants they now seem, including Henri de Lubac, Jean Daniélou, Hans Urs von Balthasar, Karl Rahner, Louis Bouyer, Marie-Dominique Chenu, and, especially important to the study of medieval reading, the Benedictine Jean Leclercq. They became associated during the 1950s with the movement of church renewal known as *ressourcement*. The term means "return to the source," or rather *sources* in the French sense—wellsprings, fountainheads of tradition; it means also a return to the ultimate Source of Christian religious culture, Jesus Christ. As scholars working individually on very different projects, occasionally disagreeing sharply with each other, they shared a frustration with the neoscholastic orthodoxy that was established in the seminaries at the time. "Their common instinct was a paradox: in order to go forward in theology, one has first to go backward."[1] They endeavored to return not only to Thomas Aquinas himself but also to the patristic and medieval authors that preceded him; this program is embodied in the *Sources Chrétiennes* collection founded by de Lubac and Daniélou, published by Éditions du Cerf, which now includes more than four hundred volumes. "What the *ressourcement* theologians sought, then, was a spiritual and intellectual communion with Christianity in its most vital moments as transmitted to us in its classic texts, a

---

[1] Marcellino D'Ambrosio, "*Ressourcement* Theology, *Aggiornamento*, and the Hermeneutics of Tradition," *Communio* 18 (Winter 1991), 3. Available online: http://www.crossroadsinitiative.com.

communion which would nourish, invigorate, and rejuvenate twentieth-century Catholicism."[2]

Despite initial censure by church authorities, the *ressourcement* movement gained influence in the discussions leading up to the Second Vatican Council. De Lubac, Daniélou, Congar, and other scholars were appointed as theological expert advisors *(periti)* to the preparatory commissions. Their ideas were eventually incorporated into the publications of the council, most notably the Dogmatic Constitution on Divine Revelation *(Dei Verbum)*, promulgated by Pope Paul VI in 1965.[3] In the carefully calibrated language of that document, the initiated could read a summary of years of often highly politicized debate and a provisional resolution in favor several basic themes: Catholics were invited and required to read the Bible, "too long left to the Protestants";[4] reading would be guided by tradition and also by an awareness of the historical circumstances and the literary forms governing the scriptural writings; the reading process would reaffirm, finally, the continuity linking the Old Testament inseparably to the New.

---

[2] D'Ambrosio, "*Ressourcement,*" 4.

[3] *Dei Verbum* (Dogmatic Constitution on Divine Revelation), in *Vatican Council II: The Basic Sixteen Documents*, trans. Austin Flannery, OP (Northport, NY: Costello Publishing Co., 1996).

[4] As Louis Bouyer puts it in *Introduction à la vie spirituelle: Précis de théologie ascétique et mystique* (Paris: Desclée, 1960), 30: *Trop longtemps les Catholiques ont tendu à penser que la Bible devait être laissée aux Protestants. Cette pensée, ou plutôt ce préjugé, doit être déraciné. L'erreur des Protestants n'a nullement été de croire que la Bible est la Parole de Dieu et qu'elle doit être reçue comme telle. Ceci n'est point du tout une erreur : c'est la pure vérité Catholique, attestée par toute la tradition de l'Église. Leur erreur a été de vouloir revenir à la Bible en se débarrassant de tout ce qui est nécessaire pour la garder vivante : pour qu'elle ne se réduise pas pour nous à une lettre morte que l'Esprit ne vivifierait plus* ("For too long now Catholics have tended to think that the Bible should be left to Protestants. That thought, or rather that prejudice, must be uprooted. The mistake of the Protestants has not at all been their belief that the Bible is the Word of God, and that it should be received as such. This is not a mistake; it is the pure, Catholic truth, attested by the whole tradition of the church. Their error has been their attempt to return to the Bible while getting rid of all that is necessary to keep it alive, so that it might not be reduced for us to a dead letter, no longer vivified by the Spirit").

Those things revealed by God which are contained and presented in the text of sacred scripture have been written under
the inspiration of the holy Spirit. For holy mother church,
relying on the faith of the apostolic age, accepts as sacred and
canonical the books of the Old and the New Testaments, whole
and entire, with all their parts, on the grounds that, written
under the inspiration of the holy Spirit (see Jn 20:31; 2 Tim
3:16; 2 Pet 1:19-20; 3:15-16), they have God as their author, and
have been handed on as such to the church itself. To compose
the sacred books, God chose certain men who, all the while
he employed them in this task, made full use of their powers
and faculties so that, though he acted in them and by them, it
was as true authors that they consigned to writing whatever he
wanted written, and no more. . . .

For in the context of the human situation before the era of
salvation established by Christ, the books of the Old Testament
provide an understanding of God and humanity and make clear
to all how a just and merciful God deals with humankind. These
books, even though they contain matters which are imperfect
and provisional, nevertheless contain authentic divine teaching.
Christians should accept with reverence these writings, which
express a lively sense of God, which are a storehouse of sublime
teaching on God and of sound wisdom on human life, as well
as a wonderful treasury of prayers; in them, too, the mystery of
our salvation is implicitly present.

God, the inspirer and author of the books of both Testaments,
in his wisdom has so brought it about that the New should be
hidden in the Old and that the Old should be made manifest
in the New. For, although Christ founded the New Covenant
in his blood (see Lk 22:20; 1 Cor 11:25), nevertheless the books
of the Old Testament, all of them given a place in the preaching of the Gospel, attain and display their full meaning in the
New Testament (see Mt 5:17; Lk 24:27; Rom 16:25-26; 2 Cor
3:14:16) and, in their turn, shed light on it and explain it. (*Dei
Verbum* 11, 15–16)

The implementation of the council's proclamations in the
following decades has satisfied few in the Catholic world. That
troubled history lies beyond the scope of the present study. The
legacy of the *ressourcement* movement has included, however, a number of scholarly masterworks which remain standard references for

all who study medieval literature today, in the university as well as in the church community. Two books have had a particular relevance to the study of reading: *L'amour des lettres et le désir de Dieu* by Jean Leclercq (1957), familiar throughout the English-speaking world in the translation by Catherine Misrahi;[5] and *Exégèse médiévale* (four volumes, 1959–64), by Henri de Lubac, partially translated by Mark Sebanc and others.[6] Any approach to this field must necessarily take these two foundational studies into careful account. In the following pages I propose to recall the intellectual and spiritual context in which they were written, in an effort to discover where our steps beyond their sphere of influence might presently lead.

Jean Leclercq

The presence of Jean Leclercq (1911–93) remains pervasive throughout the world of medieval studies today. Looking over his bibliography,[7] which includes over a thousand items at the last count, one takes note of his major works: the seven-volume critical edition of the writings of Bernard of Clairvaux (1957–77), prepared in collaboration with Charles H. Talbot and Henri M. Rochais; the studies of Bernard collected in the three-volume *Recueil d'études* (1962–69) and in *Nouveau visage de Bernard de Clairvaux* (1976); the studies of John of Fécamp (1946), Peter of

---

[5] Jean Leclercq, *L'amour des letters et le désir de Dieu. Initiation aux auteurs monastiques du moyen âge* (Paris: Éditions du Cerf, 1957); *The Love of Learning and the Desire for God: A Study of Monastic Culture*, trans. Catherine Misrahi (New York, NY: Fordham University Press, 1961).

[6] Henri de Lubac, *Exégèse médiévale: Les quatre sens de l'Écriture*, 4 vols. (Paris: Aubier, 1959–64); *Medieval Exegesis: The Four Senses of Scripture*, trans. Mark Sebanc and others, 3 vols. (Grand Rapids, MI: Eerdmans, 1998–2009).

[7] The most complete bibliography of his writings is by Michael Martin, in E. Rozanne Elder, ed., *The Joy of Learning and the Love of God: Studies in Honor of Jean Leclercq*, CS 160 (Kalamazoo, MI, and Spencer, MA: Cistercian Publications, 1995), 414–98. For an assessment of the major themes in his writings, see Bernard McGinn, "Jean Leclercq's Contribution to Monastic Spirituality and Theology," *Monastic Studies* 16 (1985): 7–23. See also Leclercq's own *Memoirs: From Grace to Grace* (Petersham, MA: St. Bede's Publications, 2000), and the short biography by Louis Leloir in *Bernard of Clairvaux: Studies Presented to Dom Jean Leclercq*, CS 23 (Washington, D.C.: Cistercian Publications, 1973), 1–17.

Celle (1946), Peter the Venerable (1946), Peter Damian (1960), and other individuals; the *History of Christian Spirituality*, 3 vols. (1961–66), coauthored with Louis Bouyer and François Vandenbroucke, especially part 1 of volume 2 on the Middle Ages, "De saint Grégoire le Grand à saint Bernard," which was written by Leclercq alone; the studies of monastic "vocabulary"(1963); and finally *The Love of Learning and the Desire for God.*

Beyond these references, one becomes aware of the general atmosphere that his studies have generated: a way of feeling as well as thinking about the material that identifies his "school" and its distinctive discourse. Especially in the introductory *Love of Learning*, one finds a scholarly style which includes notes of warmth, enthusiasm, and reverence—a seductive manner, highly attractive to researchers new to the field as well as to the monastic novices of Sant' Anselmo to whom it was first directed.

Leclercq did not pursue scholarship for its own sake. He exemplifies the "overflow" of reading that I have alluded to above (see p. xix). He sought throughout his career to apply the findings of research to present, active religious life. He had confronted the "studies problem," that is, the reconciliation of learning with contemplation in his own experience, before discovering the traditional solutions proposed by Peter of Celle and other medieval authors.[8]

As a Benedictine monk and literary scholar, Jean Leclercq made valuable contributions to the *ressourcement* movement. He was not a prelate; he did not place himself on the polemical-political edge with de Lubac and Daniélou. His role, not at all a secondary one, was to open the "sources"—that is to say, the whole province of medieval monastic literature—to the theologians, activists, and contemplatives who sought them. In the 1960s he participated in the work of Aide à l'Implantation Monastique (AIM), an international Benedictine organization devoted to monastic renewal. Leclercq traveled widely through Africa and Asia and participated as a consultant in the creation of new foundations. He published many articles during this period, applying insights drawn from medieval writings to various modern social and geographical contexts, in

---

[8] Leclercq, *Memoirs*, 20–21.

relation to the decrees of the Second Vatican Council. He remained all the while in close personal contact with many of the major figures in the church. His correspondence with Thomas Merton, for instance, has been published.[9] A full account of his relations with others has yet to be written, but their constant references to him convey the presence that de Lubac acknowledges in the dedication of his own work, *Exégèse médiévale: À Jean Leclercq, O.S.B., dont la science et l'amitié me furent d'un égal secours.*

Several leading themes emerge from Leclercq's oeuvre. "Monastic theology" is among the most important. In response to those who had relegated the monastic authors to the category of unscientific piety, Leclercq took stock of the complementarity that developed in the twelfth century between the cloisters and the schools, and he valorized the monastic emphasis on practical, spiritual experience, which is illustrated by Bernard's *credo ut experiar* in contrast to Anselm's *credo ut intelligam.*[10]

"Monastic theology" widens in Leclercq's studies into "monastic culture," which is oriented toward literary study, as opposed to the dialectical methodology of *disputatio* fostered by the medieval cathedral schools. In the interpretation of medieval monastic writings, Leclercq demonstrated the relevance of literary–critical analysis as a necessary complement to theological questioning and historical research. Particularly in the case of Bernard, Leclercq showed how the cultivation of grammar and rhetoric, as well as the development of the *sermo* as a compositional genre, could decisively inflect the development of doctrinal ideas. For Bernard, as we shall see, the impetuous poetic *style* of the Bride's utterance in the Song of Songs is an all-important key to his understanding of the love of God.

The activity of reading is found at the very heart of monastic culture. In memorable pages of *Love of Learning*, Leclercq describes the physical, emotional, and spiritual dimensions of *lectio divina*:

---

[9] *Survival or Prophecy? The Correspondence of Jean Leclercq and Thomas Merton,* ed. Patrick Hart (Collegeville, MN: Cistercian Publications, 2008).

[10] Bernard McGinn summarizes Leclercq's writing on monastic theology in "Jean Leclercq's Contribution," 13–21.

Au sujet de la lecture s'impose ici une constatation fondamentale: au moyen âge, comme dans l'antiquité, on lit, normalement, non comme aujourd'hui, principalement avec ses yeux, mais en prononçant ce qu'on voit, en le parlant, et avec ses oreilles, en écoutant les paroles qu'on prononce, en entendant, comme on dit les *voces paginarum*. On se livre à une véritable lecture acoustique : *legere* signifie en même temps *audire* ; on ne comprend que ce qu'on entend, comme nous disons encore : « entendre le latin », c'est-à-dire le « comprendre ». Sans doute la lecture silencieuse, ou à voix basse, n'est-elle pas inconnue : elle est alors désignée par des expressions comme celles de S. Benoît : *tacite legere* ou *legere sibi*, et celle de S. Augustin : *legere in silentio*, par opposition à *clara lectio*. Mais le plus souvent, quand *legere* et *lectio* sont employés sans spécification, ils désignent une activité qui, comme le chant et l'écriture, occupe tout le corps et tout l'esprit. . . . La *lectio divina* était nécessairement une lecture active. C'est par là qu'elle était très proche de la *meditatio*. . . . Pour les anciens, méditer c'est lire un texte et l'apprendre « par cœur » au sens le plus fort de cette expression, c'est-à-dire avec tout son être : avec son corps, puisque la bouche le prononce, avec la mémoire qui le fixe, avec l'intelligence qui le prononce, avec la volonté qui désire le mettre en pratique.

With regard to reading a fundamental observation must be made here: in the Middle Ages, as in antiquity, they read usually, not as today, principally with the eyes, but with the lips, pronouncing what they saw, and with the ears, listening to the words pronounced, hearing what is called the "voices of the pages." It is real acoustical reading; *legere* means at the same time *audire*; one understands only what one hears, as we still say: "entendre le latin," which means to "comprehend" it. No doubt, silent reading, or reading in a low voice, was not unknown; in that case it is designated by expressions like those of St. Benedict: *tacite legere* or *legere sibi*, and according to St. Augustine: *legere in silentio* as opposed to the *clara lectio*. But most frequently, when *legere* and *lectio* are used without further explanation, they mean an activity which, like chant or writing, requires the participation of the whole body and the whole mind. . . . In this way reading is very close to the *meditatio*. . . . For the ancients, to meditate is to read a text and to learn it "by heart" in the fullest sense of this expression, that is, with one's whole being: with the body, since the mouth pronounced it, with the memory which fixes it, with the intelligence which understands its meaning, and with the will that desires to put it into practice.[11]

Méditer, c'est s'attacher étroitement à la phrase qu'on se récite, en peser tous les mots, pour parvenir à la plénitude de leur sens : c'est s'assimiler le contenu d'un texte au moyen d'une sorte de mastication qui en dégage la saveur ; c'est le goûter, comme S. Augustin, S. Grégoire, Jean de Fécamp et d'autres le disent d'une expression qui est intraduisible, avec le *palatum cordis* ou *in ore cordis.*

To meditate is to attach oneself closely to the sentence being recited and weigh all its words in order to sound the depths of their full meaning. It means assimilating the content of a text by means of a kind of mastication which releases its full flavor. It means, as St. Augustine, St. Gregory, John of Fécamp and others say in an untranslatable expression, to taste it with the *palatum cordis* [with the palate of the heart] or *in ore cordis* [in the mouth of the heart].[12]

Once the relationship of monastic reading to spirituality is understood, it becomes possible to appreciate the unsystematic, digressive, and repetitive meditations of writers like Gregory, whom earlier modern commentators (Adolf Harnack and even Beryl Smalley) had seriously undervalued. It becomes possible also to conceive the essential conservatism of monastic culture in positive terms, and not merely as a fearful resistance to the philosophical speculation introduced by Abelard and other pre-Scholastics, or as an intolerant reaction to the "pagan" transmission of Aristotle. It was indeed the monastic culture, founded on reading as Leclercq demonstrates, that assured the continuity between the patristic age and subsequent generations.

Reflection on this tradition constitutes a major strand in Leclercq's thinking and links his work directly to the *ressourcement* movement. His early study of John of Fécamp (1946) opens this pathway by directing attention to the freedom with which

---

[11] Leclercq, *L'amour des lettres*, 21–23; *Love of Learning*, 19–22.
[12] Leclercq, *L'amour des lettres*, 72; *Love of Learning*, 90.

John quotes the Bible, the fathers, and the liturgy. John quotes at length, inexactly and from memory, generally without attribution to sources. He "frequents" or "inhabits" the literature, which he recalls spontaneously, "naturally," disclaiming originality with a slogan that Leclercq frequently quotes in turn: *dicta mea dicta patrum* ("my words are the words of the fathers"). From John's example and others Leclercq concludes, in *Love of Learning*:

> Ainsi en usait-on avec une grande liberté à l'égard des sources les plus respectées, des autorités les plus hautes : dans des compilations qui avaient un but pratique, et non littéraire ou scientifique, on se permettait de transformer, d'adapter, de gloser les documents qui devaient servir de règle de vie ; c'est souvent sous une forme ainsi élaborée—mais pas toujours améliorée—que les textes monastiques parviennent jusqu'à nous. Encore les manuscrits de ces diverses formes d'un même texte offrent-ils des variantes qui ne sont pas toutes des bévues des copistes. Mais cette divergence même des témoins d'une même traduction prouve le caractère mouvant—et vivant—de ces anciens textes monastiques. . . . Le texte sur lequel [les copistes] travaillaient ne se présentait pas à eux comme fixé une fois pour toutes, mais continuait à vivre et à se transformer.

Thus great freedom was exercised in the use of the most respected sources and highest authorities. In compilations whose purpose was practical, not literary or scientific, [monastic copyists] felt free to transform, adapt or gloss documents which were to serve as a rule of life. It is often in such an elaborated—but not always improved—form that the monastic texts of antiquity have come down to us. Furthermore, the manuscripts of these different forms of the same text present variants which are not all due to copyists' gross mistakes. But the very divergency among manuscripts of the same translation proves the changing, and living, character of these ancient monastic texts . . . . [The copyists] did not consider the text they were working on as having been established once and for all; it continued to live and to change.[13]

The medieval monastic tradition was very much alive as far as Leclercq was concerned: as a Benedictine monk, he himself

---

[13] Leclercq, *L'amour des lettres*, 92; *Love of Learning*, 118.

participated in the continuity that he had undertaken to observe. His conception of the "life" of monastic texts includes, and in fact requires as essential, a nontextual or posttextual dimension, which is that of "experiential transmission":

> Il ne faut point méconnaître le rôle qui revient, dans la conti-nuité qui relie le monachisme occidental au passé de l'Église entière, à ce qu'on peut appeler la tradition vivante. On affirme souvent que le monachisme a maintenu la tradition en copiant, en lisant, en expliquant les ouvrages des Pères, et cela est exact ; mais il l'a fait aussi en vivant de ce que ces livres contenaient. Il y a là un procédé de transmission qu'on peut dire expérimental.

> The part played by what can be called the living tradition in the continuity linking Western monasticism to the past of the whole church must not be underestimated. It is often affirmed that monasticism maintained tradition by copying, reading and explaining the works of the Fathers, and that is correct; but it did so also through *living* by what these books contained. This might be called an experiential mode of transmission.[14]

Under Leclercq's pen, the history of medieval monastic culture flows imperceptibly into the description of timeless spiritual "reali-ties," and from there into prescriptions of belief and behavior. *Love of Learning* contains many such didactic affirmations, in keeping with the stated introductory and formative purposes of the work.[15] Reading Leclercq today, the literary historian will need at times to disentangle these different discourses. Leclercq himself consistently maintained the flow of scholarly reading into affective experience and practical activity, in the search for a wholeness of understanding.

---

[14] Leclercq, *L'amour des lettres*, 105; *Love of Learning*, 135.

[15] For example, in the concluding chapter of *Love of Learning* on page 328, he writes, "St. Bernard thinks the angels will help him [to communicate] since they also are servants of the word. They 'administer' to the mind beautiful conceptions and the images which make them perceptible. But while images express God they likewise conceal him. This radical defect in everything the mystic tries to express succeeds in detaching him from his literary pursuits and removing any self-satisfaction he might take in what he writes. Literature, he knows, with all its formalities and necessary laws, is an example of the impotence of our condition, its limitations and of the inadequacy of what we say to represent what gives us life."

In later writings he turned to psychology, evoking Freud, Jung, gestalt concepts, and even behaviorism as keys to medieval spirituality.[16] These experiments seem today less convincingly rigorous than his earlier work. They do illustrate his lively curiosity and continuing intellectual growth. Throughout his varied career, *lectio divina* remained a central concern, not merely as an object of historical research, but as a hermeneutic that informed all of his studies. He made full use of the meditative freedom it provides—freedom in the Pauline, spiritual sense—to appropriate the medieval texts into personal participation, and to inscribe his own writings among them.

Henri de Lubac

The abundant and at times controversial writings of Henri de Lubac (1896–1991) have received more thorough study than those of Jean Leclercq.[17] De Lubac was principally a theologian. Like Leclercq, he did not undertake scholarship for its own sake, as merely an academic enterprise. It was rather in response to needs perceived in the church in his own time that de Lubac turned to medieval and patristic texts and to the insight that they might provide. With others in the *ressourcement* movement, he deplored the separations then prevailing among theology, scriptural exegesis, ecclesiology, and moral teaching. The church since the sixteenth century had lost touch with its own foundational history, he found, and needed to rediscover the unity of religious reflection that had governed the earlier phases of its growth. De Lubac's scholarship followed from this urgent conviction, and from a self-consistent intellectual conservatism that his contemporaries did not always correctly understand. Not without conflict with the ecclesiastical

---

[16] See especially the essays in Jean Leclercq, *Monks and Love in Twelfth-Century France: Psycho-Historical Essays* (Oxford: Clarendon Press, 1979).

[17] For biographies of de Lubac, see Jean-Pierre Wagner, *Henri de Lubac* (Paris: Éditions du Cerf, 2001); and Rudolf Voderholzer, *Meet Henri de Lubac*, trans. Michael J. Miller (San Francisco: Ignatius Press, 2008). For an authoritative theological study, see Hans Urs von Balthasar, *The Theology of Henri de Lubac: An Overview*, trans. Joseph D. Fessio and others (San Francisco: Ignatius Press, 1991). De Lubac's own *Mémoire sur l'occasion de mes écrits* (Namur, Belgium: Culture et vérité, 1989) presents a summary narrative and copious documentation concerning the more conflictual phases in his career.

authorities was he able to publish the body of work that continues to influence medievalists in both the church and the university today.

For summaries of de Lubac's formation and early teaching career as an ordained priest in the Jesuit order, I refer the reader to the published biographies cited above (n. 17). In 1938, at the age of 42, he was appointed Professor of Fundamental Theology at the Catholic University of Lyons. He took up residence at the Jesuit preparatory college on the hill of Fourvière nearby and became associated with the school of theology known thereafter by that name. At this time, his major writings began to appear, although they were interrupted by delays in publication during the war: *Catholicisme: Les aspects sociaux du dogme* (1938); *Corpus mysticum: L'eucharistie et l'église au moyen âge* (1944); *Le drame de l'humanisme athée* (1944). In 1941, de Lubac and Jean Daniélou began publishing the Sources Chrétiennes series, which now comprises over four hundred volumes.

Following the fall of France in 1940, Lyons became the "capital" of the *résistance*. De Lubac joined other Fourvière Jesuits Gaston Fessard and Pierre Chaillet in developing an intellectual and spiritual movement of opposition to Nazi anti-Semitism. Their views were articulated in the publication of the *Cahiers clandestins du témoignage chrétien*.[18] De Lubac's orientation, in keeping with Jesuit principles, remained religious rather than political or paramilitary in nature. He and his colleagues nevertheless risked capture at any moment by the Gestapo (Yves de Montcheuil was in fact arrested and executed in 1944).[19] They struggled, moreover, with policies of collaboration set forth by members of the ecclesiastical hierarchy. De Lubac's *Lettre à mes supérieurs* (1941) conveys the urgency of his engagement in characteristically compelling prose:

> En face d'une situation aussi tragique, comment ne pas s'étonner de ne percevoir que si peu de signes d'inquiétude dans les milieux catholiques et même ecclésiastiques ? . . . Beaucoup

---

[18] De Lubac's wartime writings have been republished by Éditions du Cerf as Volume 34 in the series of his complete works: Henri de Lubac, *Résistance chrétienne au nazisme. Sous la direction de Jacques Prévotat* (Paris: Éditions du Cerf, 2006).

[19] Wagner, *Henri de Lubac*, 18.

de prêtres sont dans une ignorance extrême de la situation, ou se montrent sceptiques sur les faits qui sont pourtant, hélas ! les mieux établis ; l'horreur même de ces faits les enfoncent parfois dans leur scepticisme. . . . Au reste, ne nous y trompons pas : l'antisémitisme actuel n'est plus celui qu'ont pu connaître nos pères ; outre ce qu'il a de dégradant pour ceux qui s'y abandonnent, il est déjà de l'antichristianisme. C'est à la Bible qu'on en veut, c'est à l'Évangile aussi bien qu'à l'Ancien Testament, c'est à l'universalisme de l'Église, à ce qu'on appelle « l'Internationale romaine » ; c'est à tout ce que Pie XI revendiquait comme nôtre à la suite de saint Paul, le jour où il s'écriait : « Spirituellement, nous sommes des Sémites ! »

Facing such a tragic situation, how can one not be surprised to perceive so few signs of concern in Catholic and even in ecclesiastical milieus? . . . Many priests remain in total ignorance of the situation, or else show themselves skeptical concerning facts which are, alas! very well established; the very horror of these facts reinforces sometimes their skepticism. . . . Moreover, let us not deceive ourselves: the present anti-Semitism is not that which our fathers knew; beyond the degradation that it brings to those who yield to it, it is already anti-Christianism. It is the Bible that is being attacked; it is the Gospel as well as the Old Testament, it is the universalism of the Church, what they call the "Roman International"; they are attacking all that Pius XI claimed as our own, following Saint Paul, on the day that he cried out: "Spiritually, we are all Semites!"[20]

The above passage is directed not only against Nazi anti-Semitic propaganda, but also against a tendency, found in certain Catholic

---

[20] De Lubac, *Résistance chrétienne*, 116, 120. De Lubac refers here to an incident that occurred on September 6, 1938, when the pope thanked a group of Belgian pilgrims for the gift of an ancient prayer book. Reading aloud a passage in which God is asked to accept the altar gifts with the same graciousness with which he once received Abraham's sacrifice, the pope commented, «Whenever I read the words: The sacrifice of our Father Abraham, I cannot help being deeply moved. Mark well, we call Abraham our Patriarch, our ancestor. Anti-Semitism is irreconcilable with this lofty thought, the noble reality which this prayer expresses.» And, with tears in his eyes, he concluded: «Anti-Semitism is inadmissible; spiritually, we are all Semites.» Reported by Luigi Sturzo, *Church and State* (London, 1939), 524.

milieux at the time, to minimize the importance of the Jewish heritage within the Christian tradition. De Lubac's wartime writings repeatedly insist that anti-Semitism is indeed anti-Christianism; militating against any attempt to create an "Aryan" Christianity, he had begun to reflect on the essential continuity linking the Old Testament to the New. The essay, "Un nouveau « front » religieux," concludes:

> Nous repousserons comme une sottise autant que comme un blasphème cette contradiction qu'on essaie d'établir entre un « Ancien Testament sémite » et un « Nouveau Testament aryen ». De l'un à l'autre de nos deux Testaments, nous maintiendrons le lien indissoluble, interprétant toujours en fin de compte l'Ancien par le nouveau, mais fondant aussi toujours le Nouveau sur l'Ancien.

> _____

> We will reject as foolishness as well as blasphemy the contradiction that some are seeking to establish between a "Semite Old Testament" and an "Aryan New Testament." We will maintain the unbreakable bond that unites our two Testaments to each other, interpreting always the Old by the New, but also founding the New upon the Old.[21]

This theme continued to inform his scholarship through the following decades, and it underpins the four volumes of *Exégèse médiévale*.

Surnaturel: Études historiques (1946)[22] sparked an immediate controversy. The modest subtitle of this work conceals a challenge to a point of doctrine received since the sixteenth century, namely, the notion of *natura pura*: the supposition that man in his natural state could only desire a fulfillment corresponding to that human nature; the desire to see God could come then only from God, as a gift a grace. In asserting this "extrinsistic" concept, de Lubac argues, baroque scholasticism departed from earlier authoritative teaching. Augustine and Thomas Aquinas had conceived that the desire for the beatific vision informs man's experience from the beginning, as affirmed in the opening statement of the *Confessions*:

---

[21] De Lubac, *Résistance chrétienne*, 189.
[22] Henri de Lubac, *Surnaturel: Études historiques* (Paris: Aubier-Montaigne, 1946).

"You made us for Yourself, and our hearts can find no peace until they rest in You."[23]
De Lubac's argumentation proved vulnerable to misunderstandings, which he found himself obliged to clarify in subsequent publications.[24] Critics asserted that his theses tended to compromise the absolute gratuity of God's gift of grace, which could in no way arise from or depend upon any inherent predisposition in human nature. An influential 1946 article by the Dominican Réginald Garrigou-Lagrange, "La nouvelle théologie où va-t-elle?"[25] associated de Lubac's book with an emergent *nouvelle théologie*, whose hallmarks were philosophical relativism, skepticism, and a questioning of the *magisterium*—a resurgence of modernism to be rejected in accordance with the established orthodoxy. What de Lubac later recalls, in his *Mémoire sur l'occasion de mes écrits* (1989), is a climate of suspicion and distortions of his position, and in 1950, he and four colleagues were silenced by the Father General of the Jesuit order, forbidden to teach theology or publish theological writings. In the same year, Pope Pius XII published the encyclical *Humani generis* denouncing "False Opinions Which Threaten to Undermine the Foundations of Catholic Doctrine." This document contains a phrase which many took to refer to de Lubac: "Others destroy the gratuity of the supra-natural order, since God, they say, cannot create intellectual beings without ordering and calling them to the beatific vision."[26] De Lubac, refraining from protest, accepted

---

[23] Saint Augustine, *Confessions*, trans. R. S. Pine-Coffin (New York, NY: Penguin Books, 1961), 21.

[24] Henri de Lubac, "Le mystère du surnaturel," *Recherches de science religieuse* 36 (1949), 80–121. His book with the same title, *Le mystère du surnaturel* (Paris: Aubier-Montaigne, 1965; republished by Éditions du Cerf, 2000), summarizes the issues most fully.

[25] Réginald Garrigou-Lagrange, "La nouvelle théologie où va-t-elle?" *Angelicum* 23 (1946): 126–45; this article is available on the internet at http://www.salve-regina.com. It has been translated into English as "Where is the New Theology Leading Us?" at http://cfnews.org/gg-newtheo.htm. See also John Milbank, *The Suspended Middle: Henri de Lubac and the Debate Concerning the Supernatural* (Grand Rapids, MI: Eerdmans, 2005). Other references are provided by Wagner in his bibliography, 249–50.

[26] *Humani generis*, paragraph 26, available on the internet: http://newadvent.org.

obediently the decisions of his superiors and went into an "exile" that lasted most of the following decade.

At the present time, the *nouvelle théologie* controversy has receded into distant memory, and de Lubac's courageous stand against anti-Semitism has been completely vindicated. The two issues are related, since it is possible that the measures imposed by the authorities against de Lubac and others in 1950 were determined by conflicts which had arisen previously during the war.[27] De Lubac's opposition to anti-Semitism belongs, in any case, to the modern historiography of reading. His statements followed, as I have noted, from his scholarly and religious conviction concerning the indispensable continuity of the Old and New Testaments. Duly rehabilitated in the 1960s, de Lubac participated in the work of the Second Vatican Council and was appointed cardinal in 1983.

While in "exile" during the 1950s, forbidden to teach or publish theology, he turned to historical studies, as though seeking a way to do theology by other means. His study of Origen, *Histoire et esprit*, appeared in 1950.[28] This important work rehabilitates the great Alexandrian exegete and theologian, whose writings had lain under a cloud of suspicion ever since the fourth century. Focusing upon Origen's hermeneutics and upon his extant Biblical commentaries, de Lubac clarifies Origen's attitude toward what we now identify as the literal reading of the scriptural text (not to be confused with the "proper" meaning of the words, as we shall see later on pp. 46–48). In this work and in others, we recognize de Lubac's characteristic strategy, one of circling behind present conventionally established notions in order to perform fresh readings of the primary sources. He carefully questions the meanings

---

[27] Garrigou-Lagrange and other opponents of *nouvelle théologie* had supported the policy of collaboration with Vichy adopted during the war by many French bishops and also by Norbert Boynes, S.J., the assistant general of the Jesuit order. Voderholzer comments, "At any rate, some of the driving forces among de Lubac's opponents were the same men who had accused him of disloyalty toward Marshall Pétain during the Occupation. Father Garrigou-Lagrange had gone so far in his defense of Pétain as to characterize any form of support for de Gaulle as mortally sinful" (*Meet Henri de Lubac*, 66–67).

[28] Henri de Lubac, *Histoire et esprit: L'intelligence de l'Écriture d'après Origène* (Paris: Aubier-Montaigne, 1950).

of terms, looking beneath surface systems to seek out the deeper principles that govern them; in this case, it is the whole process of spiritual interpretation—the basis of the allegorical methodology discarded by modern historical–critical exegesis—that de Lubac undertakes to reconceive and recover. This is, again, an *étude historique*, asserting by implication the relevance of theological history to the practice of theology at the present time.

Did de Lubac identify personally with Origen? There are perhaps parallels to be drawn between the latter's struggles with authorities and those of de Lubac himself. He maintains in this book the stance of the objective historian, and in the *Mémoire sur l'occasion de mes écrits* (1989) he denies (with some disingenuousness?) ever having adopted Origen's ideas as his own: "I will observe simply that I do not adopt as my own the theories and procedures of Origen. . . . I have never treated on my own behalf the question of the 'spiritual sense,' neither in my classes nor in writing."[29] He does conclusively reinstate Origen as a founding father of Christian hermeneutics, one whose influence, acknowledged or not, pervaded the entire Middle Ages. It is this long history that de Lubac explores through the four volumes of *Exégèse médiévale.*

Cet acte complet qu'est l'ancienne exégèse chrétienne est une très grande chose. What de Lubac understands by "exegesis" is a much broader concept than that which governs the historical- and text-critical study of the Bible today: "Now this 'complete act' that is ancient Christian exegesis is a very great thing. . . . It defines the relationship between historical reality and spiritual reality, between society and the individual, between time and eternity. It contains, as one might say today, a whole theology of history, which is connected with a theology of Scripture."[30] The patristic and medieval practice of scriptural interpretation included, as he notes, a whole Christian reflection on Revelation as transmitted by the sacred texts, including theology, history, ecclesiology, morality, and spirituality as well. His hope, as he later recalled, was that his

---

[29] De Lubac, *Mémoire sur l'occasion,* 314.
[30] De Lubac, *Exégèse médiévale,* 1.1:16–17; *Medieval Exegesis,* trans. Sebanc, 1:xix.

historical study might initiate a reunification among these presently separated disciplines.[31]

Exégèse médiévale continues accordingly to the history of scriptural interpretation begun in his book on Origen. De Lubac differentiates critically between Christian typology and the "pagan" philosophical allegory associated with Philo Judaeus, and he reaffirms the continuity of the two Testaments, linked by the absolutely singular, pivotal event: *la nouveauté prodigieuse, le Fait du Christ*. He proceeds then to trace the evolution of the fourfold interpretive model, comprising the following: *historia*, the literal reading; *allegoria*, the doctrinal exposition; *tropologia*, its moral or ethical implications; and *anagogia*, the prophetic sense, oriented toward the heavenly life to come.

De Lubac's exposition opens into a labyrinthine meditation, exhaustively footnoted, including repetitions, digressions, and revisions of leading ideas, supported throughout by Latin quotations—lacking, however, as one might object, any single, unifying organizational plan. *Felix culpa*. He follows, it appears, several different plans simultaneously, corresponding to the need to survey the field thematically as well as chronologically. The first two volumes (that is, *première partie, tomes* 1 and 2) present essays on foundational ideas, such as *disciplina*—the sensed need for orderly procedure; Scripture and revelation; theology as "Queen of the arts"; the concord of the two Testaments; and many others. He compares, then, the various medieval lists of the levels of interpretation, with careful attention to their number and order. Concurrently, he follows the chronological sequence of authors, beginning with Origen, and tracing the *postérité origénienne* through the twelfth century. In the four chapters that conclude the *première partie, tome* 2, he provides critical and historical discussions of each of the four levels in turn. The *seconde partie, tome* 1, provides further studies

---

[31] "I had nourished indeed a vague hope that this large work, however formless and how little methodical it remained (there reigns in it a whimsical composition, an arbitrariness in developments or omissions . . .) a hope that this sort of Purana might provide a basis, or at least an occasion, for the installation of a desirable exchange among exegetes, theologians (dogmatitians) and religious. My timid hope was disappointed" (De Lubac, *Mémoire sur l'occasion*, 85).

of individual authors: Berno of Reichenau, Paschasius Radbertus, Rupert of Deutz, Hugh of Saint-Victor and his school, and Joachim of Flore. The final volume (*seconde partie, tome* 2) extends the survey through the thirteenth century and beyond.

De Lubac notes that by the beginning of the fifth century the fourfold system appears complete in Cassian's fourteenth Conference.[32] But the consensus that defined the four terms, and the order in which they follow each other, was reached only after many different schemes had been put forward. Clement of Alexandria (ca. 150–ca. 215) had divided "Mosaic philosophy" into four aspects: history, legal precepts, liturgy, and theology.[33] Origen had posited three levels of reading: the literal, the moral, and the spiritual, corresponding to the human body, soul, and spirit.[34] Augustine, in *De utilitate credendi*, defended the Old Testament against the Manichaeans by proposing yet another fourfold distinction: history, aetiology (for what cause something was done or said), analogy (typology), and allegory (figurative interpretation).[35]

In sorting through these early systems, de Lubac dismisses as secondary the question of the number of levels, three or four, depending on whether allegory and anagogy were treated together or separately.[36] More important for de Lubac is the order of the terms, reflecting two contrasting understandings: a "philosophical" order (history, tropology, allegory) and a "theological" one (history, allegory, tropology). The "philosophical" order, which is that of

---

[32] De Lubac, *Exégèse médiévale*, 1.1:190–93; *Medieval Exegesis*, trans. Sebanc, 1:134–37. E. Ann Matter, in *The Voice of My Beloved: The Song of Songs in Western Medieval Christianity* (Philadelphia, PA: University of Pennsylvania Press, 1990), 54 and passim, refers to Cassian's scheme as authoritative throughout the Middle Ages, although his presentation is tentative and unsettled, as other commentators have noted. See below, pp. 82–83 and n. 18.

[33] De Lubac, *Exégèse médiévale* 1.1:172–77 ; *Medieval Exegesis*, trans. Sebanc, 1:117–23.

[34] See below, pp. 45–46.

[35] Augustine, *De utilitate credendi* 5–8, PL 40:68–70; *On the Profit of Believing*, trans. Whitney J. Oates, *Basic Writings of St. Augustine*, 2 vols. (New York, NY: Random House, 1948), 1:402–04.

[36] De Lubac, *Exégèse médiévale* 1.1:171–207; *Medieval Exegesis*, trans. Sebanc, 1:117–50. Jerome and Gregory the Great follow Origen's trichotomy; Bede, Rhabanus Maurus, and Honorius of Autun develop a four-level construction.

Origen, follows the Platonic model of the human person, comprised of body, soul and spirit. The "theological" order, followed by Gregory, and more authoritative in de Lubac's view,[37] gives precedence to the allegorical exposition of Christian doctrine and provides for moral instruction to follow from it logically as a third term.

Another contrast is to be observed between the understanding that different levels of reading may be appropriate to different types of biblical texts, and the perception that a given biblical text may be read on several different levels, or on all of them together. Scripture addresses various classes of readers, ranging from the least instructed to the most adept. In Paul's metaphor, the novice's mind is nourished with "milk," easy to digest, while "solid food" is offered to the spiritually mature (1 Cor 3:2; cf. Heb 5:13-14). Accordingly, Scripture offers a variety of texts. Some, Augustine stresses, are to be read literally, others figuratively. "Some things are taught for everyone in general; others are directed toward particular classes of people, in order that the medicine of instruction may be applicable not only to the general state of health but also to the special infirmities of each member."[38] Different readers find their needs met, and the given reader is urged to progress from the simple texts and first-level readings to those which are more complex, higher, and deeper. Following Origen, however, commentators tend to superimpose the different levels of reading, literal and figurative, upon each given text; this approach governs the deepening exercise of *meditatio*, and it is developed with especial richness in the interpretation of the Song of Songs, as we shall see.

De Lubac emphasizes how fluid and various was the application of the fourfold system throughout the Middle Ages.[39] The

---

[37] De Lubac, *Exégèse médiévale*, 1.1:146–69; *Medieval Exegesis*, trans. Sebanc, 1:96–115.

[38] Augustine, *De doctrina christiana*, 3.17, CCSL 32:93; *On Christian Doctrine*, trans. D. W. Robertson (Upper Saddle River, NJ: Prentice Hall, 1958), 94.

[39] See also the more recent history by Manlio Simonetti, *Biblical Interpretation in the Early Church: An Historical Introduction*, trans. John A. Hughes (Edinburgh: T. and T. Clark, 1994). For a more concise summary, see Peter R. Ackroyd and others, *The Cambridge History of the Bible: Volume 1, From the Beginnings to Jerome*, (Cambridge: Cambridge University Press, 1963–1970), 412–89. Fourfold exegesis

modern reader will find that it is not necessarily realized successfully where it is most methodically or mechanically applied. Conversely, the impulse to seek out a spiritual interpretation will often be most keenly felt beneath or beyond systematic interpretation, if only in the reverent, intuitive sense of *something* hidden, situated beyond the grasp of understanding. For as Origen puts it, "Even those who cannot understand what is concealed in these writings yet understand clearly that something is concealed there" (*manifeste ab his, qui intellegere non possunt quid in ea latet, intellegitur tamen quia latet quid*).[40]

Concerning de Lubac's later undertakings—his participation in the Second Vatican Council, his defense of Teilhard de Chardin, his resumption of theological inquiries, and his books on Pico de la Mirandola and Joachim of Flore—the reader is referred to the bibliography cited above (n. 17, p. 11). In the trajectory of this generous career, *Exégèse médiévale* takes a central position as a compelling statement on behalf of historical study as de Lubac conceived it. That assertion takes the form of a paradox (as does much else in his thinking). On the one hand, as in his study of Origen, he proposes to work as a historian; he does not personally assume the theories or espouse the doctrines under review as his own, *à son compte.* "The present work," his preface to *Exégèse médiévale* begins, "is not an allegorical or spiritual study of Scripture. Instead, it is a work that endeavors to be an historical and literal study of the ancient commentators on Scripture."[41] He makes, however, no claim to objectivity. On the contrary: "In fact, as the author, I am far from taking a step back and engaging in

---

has proven to be dangerous territory for modern scholars. Mary Carruthers, in *The Book of Memory: A Study of Memory in Medieval Culture* (Cambridge: Cambridge University Press, 1990), 186 and passim, cites confused references to Augustine made by students of D. W. Robertson, whose application of patristic exegesis to Chaucer stirred controversy during the 1960s and 70s. More recent recuperations of Augustine on behalf of post-structuralist literary theory have not clarified matters, in my view.

[40] Origen, *On First Principles*, 4.2; Origène, *Traité des principes*, ed. Henri Crouzel and Manlio Simonetti, vol. 3, SCh 268:306; trans. G. W. Butterworth (Gloucester, MA: Peter Smith, 1973), 274. The Latin rendering is by Rufinus.

[41] De Lubac, *Exégèse médiévale* 1.1:11; *Medieval Exegesis*, trans. Sebanc, 1:xiii.

objective science, thus placing myself in opposition to my object in some way. Rather, I am deliberately preserving those links with the object that render me bound up with it."[42] Without denying the insights achieved by modern historical-critical biblical scholarship, de Lubac continues to insist on the pertinence of patristic and medieval commentary to modern religious life. Making no attempt to revive ancient, "precritical" methodologies, he makes apology for their valid basis or essence, namely the principle of spiritual interpretation, founded upon the concordance of the two testaments. He firmly rejects antiquarianism, however, and—as yet in the midst of his personal struggle with church authorities—he resists any impulse to take refuge in nostalgia.

> Nous n'y avons mis, faut-il le redire, aucun archaïsme, aucun désir d'arrêter le temps ou d'en remonter le cours—quoique l'effort même de reconstruction du passé puisse quelquefois en donner l'apparence. Rien n'est plus vain que ces tentatives de retourner à quelqu'une de ces anciennes étapes que l'histoire nous fait connaître, de s'y fixer, de s'y enfermer comme dans un rêve. Même si elles n'entraînaient pas une attitude incompatible avec la Foi, elles seraient condamnées d'avance. Elles ont quelque chose de puéril et de lâche. Si donc nous ne consentons à traiter aucun des vingt siècles chrétiens comme « un univers préhistorique », nous n'en considérons aucun non plus comme « un paradis perdu. »

I have not introduced, it must be reiterated, any sort of archaism, any sort of desire to arrest time or stem its flow—although the very effort of reconstructing the past can sometimes give the appearance of being just such an enterprise. Nothing is more vain and fruitless than such attempts to return to one of these ancient stages of growth that history makes it possible for us to know, to settle down in it, to ensconce ourselves in it as in a dream. Even if attempts like this did not involve an attitude that is incompatible with faith, they would stand condemned under a heading that is even more basic. They have something of the childish and fainthearted about them. If, then, I am loath to treat any of the twenty centuries of Christianity as a "prehistoric universe," I am no more inclined to envision any of them as a "paradise lost."[43]

---

[42] De Lubac, *Exégèse médiévale* 1.1:20; *Medieval Exegesis*, trans. Sebanc, 1:xxii.
[43] De Lubac, *Exégèse médiévale* 1.1:19; *Medieval Exegesis*, trans. Sebanc, 1:xxi.

De Lubac's engaged scholarship, his solidarity with the authors he studies—or rather, we should say, his sense of communion with them—offers a challenging alternative to the scientific deontology that governs academic historical studies today. The subject of reading offers, I believe, a fertile ground for dialogue. For the present, we will need to survey the research on reading that has gone forward since the 1960s, comparing "sacred" and "secular" inquiries in order to highlight the zone of convergence between them.

Research and Practice

The field of studies related to medieval literary spirituality has grown exponentially since the 1960s. The definitive critical edition of the works of Saint Bernard, prepared by Jean Leclercq, C. S. Talbot, and H. M. Rochais, was completed by 1977. New critical editions of other authors have steadily appeared since then in the *Corpus Christianorum* and the *Corpus Christianorum: Continuatio Mediævalis* series; the Sources Chrétiennes series has published many of these same works and others in an elegant format with facing-page French translations. These texts replace those of Migne's *Patrologia Latina*, notoriously unreliable. English translations, notably those published in the Cistercian Fathers series, have made the literature accessible to a widening readership. Historical and theological studies have multiplied, especially in the United States, led by the Cistercian Studies group based at Western Michigan University in Kalamazoo, Michigan. That location has become the focus of an ongoing cultural exchange between monks and university-based scholars at an annual international congress which has become the obligatory rendezvous of the entire medieval studies profession.

Recent researchers have cast new light on the social and material conditions that attended the activity of reading. Paleographical studies by Malcolm Parkes[44] and Paul Saenger[45] highlight the

---

[44] Malcolm B. Parkes, "The Contribution of Insular Scribes of the Seventh and Eighth Centuries to the 'Grammar of Legibility,'" in *Scribes, Scripts and Readers: Studies in the Communication, Presentation, and Dissemination of Medieval Texts* (London and Rio Grande: The Hambledon Press, 1991), 1–18.

[45] Paul Saenger, *Space Between Words: The Origins of Silent Reading*, 2nd ed. (Stanford, CA: Stanford University Press, 1997).

problem of the legibility of early medieval manuscripts and clarify the comments on reading made by Augustine, Cassiodorus, Isidore of Seville, and other early authorities. Mary Carruthers's *Book of Memory* focuses on techniques of memorization, an integral dimension in reading throughout the Middle Ages. Broad studies of "literacy" and "orality"[46] have led to reconceptions of these basic terms, allowing for more nuanced descriptions of the various *semiliterate* strategies—listening to reading, memorization and recitation, rereading of memorized texts—that enabled medieval literary experience. Brian Stock's concept of "textual communities," originally formulated to describe eleventh and twelfth-century heretical groups, applies to the earliest Christian monasteries as well: "[Textual communities are] microsocieties organized around the common understanding of a script. . . . These textual communities were not composed entirely of literates. The minimal requirement was just one literate, the *interpres*, who understood a set of texts and was able to pass his message on verbally to others."[47] M. T. Clanchy's study of legal and business documentation in England from 1066–1307 leads to a description of the growth of the "literate mentality" over that period. Clanchy shares with Stock a determination to "avoid being prejudiced in favour of literacy" (Clanchy, 7) and an abiding interest in the "interdependence" of oral and written communication. The general concepts derived from their researches allow us now to fill in the outline of reading culture drawn by Leclercq. It is now more possible to gauge the degree to which material and social constraints—notably the scarcity of texts and difficulty of reading them—shaped the early

---

[46] Walter J. Ong, *Orality and Literacy: The Technologizing of the Word* (London and New York, NY: Routledge, 1982); Michael T. Clanchy, *From Memory to Written Record: England 1066–1307* (London: Edward Arnold, and Cambridge, MA: Harvard University Press, 1979; 2nd ed. Oxford and Cambridge, MA: Blackwell, 1993); Brian Stock, *The Implications of Literacy: Written Language and Models of Interpretation in the Eleventh and Twelfth Centuries* (Princeton, NJ: Princeton University Press, 1983); Brian Stock, *Listening for the Text: On the Uses of the Past* (Baltimore, MD: Johns Hopkins University Press, 1990).

[47] Stock, *Listening for the Text*, 23. The sixth-century Rule of the Master provides an example of an early textual community (see below p. 92). See also Stock's discussion of the term in reference to early Christianity in *Listening for the Text*, 148–58.

practice of *lectio divina*, and we can now more confidently assess the persistence of the associated spiritual culture (e.g., in Bernard of Clairvaux's sermons and in Guigo II's *Ladder of Monks*) long after the original constraints had been eased.

Lectio divina persists indeed in active religious practice today. Interest in meditative reading was rekindled during the postwar years in association with the *ressourcement* movement and with the renewal of mystical contemplation that accompanied it. At the present time, publications, workshops, and organized retreats at monasteries in the United States and Europe all testify to the continuing vitality of this traditional discipline among clerics, monks, and laity. There are many short, didactic summaries now available.[48] These handy small-format paperbacks, intended mainly for lay readers, generally outline *lectio divina* as a devotional method, specifying prayer procedures and offering lists of scriptural and patristic texts to use. This kind of modernizing program filters *lectio divina* through the late-medieval prescriptive systems that culminated in the *Spiritual Exercises* of Saint Ignatius of Loyola. One might object, as does Michael Casey, to a certain "medicine chest" approach to Scripture offered by some of these manuals, reminiscent of the Gideon Bibles found in hotel rooms.[49] Historicity is not, of course, their primary concern. Bibliographical references and footnoting are in most cases kept to a minimum.[50]

---

[48] I find no fewer than six of these publications on my desk: Enzo Bianchi, *Praying the Word: An Introduction to* Lectio Divina, CS 182 (Kalamazoo, MI: Cistercian Publications, 1998); Michael Casey, *Sacred Reading: The Ancient Art of* Lectio Divina (Liguori, MO: Liguori/Triumph, 1996); Charles Dumont, *Praying the Word of God: The Use of* Lectio Divina (Oxford: SLG Press, 1999); Thelma Hall, *Too Deep for Words: Rediscovering* Lectio Divina (New York, NY: Paulist Press, 1988); Mariano Magrassi, *Praying the Bible: An Introduction to* Lectio Divina (Collegeville, MN: Liturgical Press, 1998); M. Basil Pennington, Lectio Divina: *Renewing the Ancient Practice of Praying the Scriptures* (New York, NY: Crossroad, 1998). Raymond Studzinski offers much longer lists of articles and books on *lectio divina* published since the 1970s, in *Reading to Live: The Evolving Practice of* Lectio Divina, CS 231 (Collegeville, MN: Cistercian Publications, 2009), 194–95, nn.56–60.

[49] Michael Casey, *Sacred Reading*, 12.

[50] Exceptionally, Mariano Magrassi's *Praying the Bible* supplies copious references to primary sources, especially Rupert of Deutz, and integrates program statements from the Second Vatican Council.

Even so, the academic scholar will find valuable insights in these publications that challenge one to relive the medieval reading experience and to resolve the anachronisms that arise.

Particularly welcome, in this context, is the recent study by Raymond Studzinski, *Reading to Live: The Evolving Practice of* Lectio Divina.[51] Studzinski's short but inclusive survey spans the history of Christian religious reading from the first century CE through the twentieth-century revival. Necessarily, in view of the long "eclipse" of *lectio divina* from the thirteenth century through the early modern period, Studzinski's most careful attention is focused on the beginning and end of the story, notably on the writings of Origen and Augustine and on the present rediscovery of meditative reading practice, threatened perhaps by the development of computer technology. Along the way, Studzinski carefully cites recent secondary literature, including, for example, Karen Jo Torjesen's studies of Origen, Brian Stock's *Augustine the Reader*, and Ivan Illich's provocative reading of Hugh of Saint Victor, *In the Vineyard of the Text*.[52] Studzinski also refers glancingly to modern novels such as Chaim Potok's *The Chosen*, John Updike's *Pigeon Feathers*, and Bernard Schlink's *The Reader*; wider literary–theoretical perspectives are provided by references to George Steiner, Paul Ricoeur, and Michel Foucault.[53]

[51] Raymond Studzinski, *Reading to Live: The Evolving Practice of* Lectio Divina, CS 231 (Collegeville, MN: Cistercian Publications, 2009).

[52] Karen Jo Torjesen, *Hermeneutical Procedure and Theological Method in Origen's Exegesis* (Berlin: de Gruyter, 1986); Brian Stock, *Augustine the Reader: Meditation, Self-Knowledge, and the Ethics of Interpretation* (Cambridge, MA: Harvard University Press, 1996); Ivan Illich, *In the Vineyard of the Text: A Commentary to Hugh's Didascalicon* (Chicago, IL and London: University of Chicago Press, 1993).

[53] George Steiner, "The End of Bookishness?" in *Times Literary Supplement*, 8–16 July, 1988, 754; Paul Ricoeur, *Hermeneutics and the Human Sciences*, ed. and trans. John B. Thompson (Cambridge: Cambridge University Press, 1981); Michel Foucault, "Technologies of the Self," in Luther H. Martin and others, eds, *Technologies of the Self: A Seminar with Michel Foucault* (Amherst: University of Massachusetts Press, 1988), 16–39. From Illich and Steiner, Studzinski derives a view of reading history that places the beginning of the era of "bookish reading" in the middle of the twelfth century; from that moment on, books became more available than they were before, less expensive to reproduce, and more legible; indexes and headings on chapters and subsections were introduced, further increasing ease of reference. These observations are doubtless correct. Confusingly, however, Studzinski and

Implications for Literary Theory

We expect as a matter of course that modern scholarly research could illuminate aspects of past cultures that had previously been imperfectly understood. In the area of literary theory, however, one might well seek to reverse the direction of inquiry; medieval literature (especially as Leclercq has taught us to understand it) offers exemplary responses to many general questions that we now pose—sometimes naively—concerning the nature and epistemological status of texts; the roles of authors, performers, and audiences; and the possibilities for interaction among them. In particular, medieval reading theory offers powerful insights into the question of reader-response taken up by academic critics in America and Germany during the 1970s. That question remains open and unresolved, as I shall argue, at least in part because of a lack of consideration of the medieval tradition and a lack of reference to modern Catholic scholarship.[54]

Let me recall briefly the main lines of the modern reader-response debate made familiar through anthologies and summaries.[55] The point of departure, acknowledged by theorists who disagreed

---

Illich conceptualize the changing relationship between a text and the physical page of writing as follows: "With these twelfth-century innovations, the text could rise off the page and be visualized in the mind without the page. The text had acquired autonomy and did not need the page as it once did. In fact, what was written on the page could now be seen simply as a shadow of the text, whose existence transcended the concrete page" (Studzinski, 12; cf. Illich, 116–19). In fact, the perception of the text as "lifted off" the page "into autonomous existence" (Illich, 119) appears better suited to the earlier culture of "monastic reading"—that of Cassian and the early rules (discussed in chapter 3, pp. 81–103 below)—than it is to twelfth and thirteenth-century scholasticism. Of necessity, the earlier monks relied upon memorization and meditation *submoto libro*, "with the book put aside." It was only later, as books became more available and more legible, that the need for memorization eased and texts descended, so to speak, from the space of virtuality to the page of writing. The word "text" as Illich uses it seems to refer to the discussion of ideas (*disputatio*) as practiced by the scholastics.

[54] The remainder of this chapter appeared in an abbrieated form as Duncan Robertson, "*Lectio divina* and Literary Criticism from John Cassian to Stanley Fish," CSQ 46 (2011): 83–93.

[55] See especially Jane Tompkins, ed., *Reader-Response Criticism: From Formalism to Post Structuralism* (Baltimore, MD, and London: Johns Hopkins University Press, 1980); Susan R. Suleiman and Inge Crosman, eds., *The Reader in the Text:*

on almost all else, was a revolt against the then-prevailing Formalist/ New Critical view of the literary text as an autonomous, freestanding, objective entity cut off from the author's intention and also from the reader's personal experience of it. The New Critics had rejected the "Intentional Fallacy," that is, the supposition that the author's intention determined the meaning of the work. They had similarly rejected the "Affective Fallacy" as a "confusion between the poem and its *results* (what it *is* and what it *does*)." The "poem itself," according to the New Critics, should be the focus of "specifically critical judgment"; its meaning should be sought within it, as manifested by its observable formal and thematic features.[56]

In a 1970 essay, "Literature in the Reader: Affective Stylistics,"[57] Stanley Fish launched an attack on the New Critical doctrine. He argues that meaning is indeed not contained in the text and that it is not something to be "extracted" by interpretation, but is rather to be identified with the effect of the text upon the reader. The operational question would not be "What does this sentence mean?" but, "What does this sentence do?"[58] Where New Critics tended to read the literary text, especially poetry, as a whole, perceived in simultaneity as though in space (e.g., as a "well wrought urn"), Fish proposes to follow the "developing responses of the reader in relation to the words as they succeed one another in time."[59] He would discuss the process of reading rather than the result; his method would "*slow down*" reception,[60] forestall the premature closure of interpretation, and intentionally delay as long as possible the moment of "coming to a point."[61]

Essays on Audience and Interpretation (Princeton, NJ: Princeton University Press, 1980); Andrew Bennett, ed., *Readers and Reading* (London and New York, NY: 1995). For a summary of the German theorists, see Robert C. Holub, *Reception Theory: A Critical Introduction* (London and New York, NY: Methuen, 1984).

[56] William Wimsatt, Jr., and Monroe C. Beardsley, *The Verbal Icon: Studies in the Meaning of Poetry* (Lexington: University Press of Kentucky, 1954).

[57] Stanley Fish, "Literature in the Reader: Affective Stylistics," *New Literary History* 2, no.1 (Autumn 1970): 123–62, reprinted in Tompkins, *Reader-Response Criticism*, 70–100. For the sake of convenience, I refer to Fish's essays as they appear in the Tompkins anthology.

[58] Fish, "Affective Stylistics"; Tompkins, 72.

[59] Fish, "Affective Stylistics"; Tompkins, 73.

[60] Fish, "Affective Stylistics"; Tompkins, 74 (Fish's emphasis).

[61] Fish, "Affective Stylistics"; Tompkins, 89.

Fish's argument evolved over time—his essays offer a criticism in process and in ongoing self-revision, reflecting his theory of reading—as it became apparent that his emphasis on reader-reception had not in fact dislodged the objective status attributed the text, conventionally supposed to exist prior to and independently of the reader's encounter with it. In "Interpreting the *Variorum*" (1976),[62] he takes a further step: it is the reading experience, he argues, that constitutes and creates the formal features of the text and the perceived authorial intention, as well as the form of that experience itself.

From this point on, Fish and other commentators turned to circumscribing the apparently limitless freedom they had awarded to the reader. There was, it would seem, a palpable fear of "interpretive anarchy" to be allayed.[63] Accordingly, critics sought order in descriptions of various readers' roles as they may be inscribed in or evoked by the literary text; among these were the "informed reader,"[64] the "implied reader,"[65] the "ideal reader," the "virtual reader," and the "narratee."[66] All of these theoretical roles were distinguished from the actual or real readers whose interpretive activities could be observed, for example, in college English classes and studied empirically.[67]

Fish, at this time, focused attention on the necessary participation of readers, both theoretical and actual, in "interpretive communities" defined by a sharing of the strategies that constitute texts and acknowledge intentions.[68] This construct allows for the formation of consensus among readers of a given text, based on communal

[62] Fish, "Interpreting the *Variorum*," *Critical Inquiry* 2 (Spring 1976): 465–85, reprinted in Tompkins, 164–84.

[63] Fish, "Interpreting the *Variorum*"; Tompkins, 182.

[64] Fish, "Affective Stylistics"; Tompkins, 86.

[65] Wolfgang Iser, *The Act of Reading: A Theory of Aesthetic Response* (Baltimore, MD and London: Johns Hopkins University Press, 1978), 34–38.

[66] Gerald Prince defines these three terms in "Introduction to the Study of the Narratee," *Poétique* 14 (1973), 173–96, translated by Francis Mariner and reprinted in Tompkins, 7–25 (see especially p. 9).

[67] See especially David Bleich, *Subjective Criticism* (Baltimore, MD, and London: Johns Hopkins University Press, 1978); and Norman Holland, *5 Readers Reading* (New Haven, CT: Yale University Press, 1975).

[68] Fish, "Interpreting the *Variorum*"; Tompkins, 182.

interests and beliefs which precede the individual encounter and guide interpretation. Jonathan Culler further developed the communal dimension of reading in the course of identifying a number of literary conventions and codes through which the community makes its presence felt, orienting the individual.[69]

In the 1980s and 90s, the reflection on community led to interventions by critics involved in the feminist movement and in the field of cultural studies who were concerned with exposing the political and cultural power-relations that govern groups and individuals.[70] Political analysis became the seemingly inevitable next step; there was a sense that the reader-response critics had escaped the Formalist/New Critical trap—that of the objectification of the literary text—only to fall into another one, that of an individualistic, aestheticist consumerism, harshly criticized by leftist, socially conscious ideology.[71] And that critique effectively brought the reader-response movement to an end.

The movement had not, in my estimation, gone far enough. Rereading the reader-response discussion today, I note that the theoretical concepts developed by Fish and others were constricted by the narrow field of literature they surveyed, mainly American and English poetry and fiction taught in the freshman-sophomore curriculum.[72] Occasional allusions are made to the continental Eu-

---

[69] Jonathan Culler, *Structuralist Poetics: Structuralism, Linguistics, and the Study of Literature* (Ithaca, NY: Cornell University Press, 1975).

[70] Judith Fetterley led this trend with *The Resisting Reader: A Feminist Approach to American Fiction* (Bloomington, IN: Indiana University Press, 1978). She argues that the female reader must resist identification with the male point of view that is predominant in Western literature and in the academic institutions founded upon it.

[71] *Sed contra*, Roland Barthes, *Le plaisir du texte* (Paris: Editions du Seuil, 1973), 91, responds in defense of aesthetic pleasure: *À peine a-t-on dit un mot, quelque part, du plaisir du texte, que deux gendarmes sont prêts à vous tomber dessus : le gendarme politique et le gendarme psychanalytique : futilité et/ou culpabilité, le plaisir est ou oisif ou vain, c'est une idée de classe ou une illusion* ("Hardly has one said a word, somewhere, about the pleasure of the text, when two policemen are ready to fall on one: the political policeman and the psychoanalytic policeman: futility and/or guilt, pleasure is either idle or vain; it is a class idea or an illusion").

[72] Fish could have introduced wider perspectives drawn from his study of Milton; Gerald Prince and Michael Riffaterre cite occasional examples from

ropean tradition, but almost none at all to works composed before 1500 CE. Jane Tompkins's concluding essay, "The Reader in History: The Changing Shape of Literary Response,"[73] skips blithely from Plato to the Renaissance without pause for the Middle Ages and without considering religious approaches. In the context of a discussion of reading, these omissions constitute a serious oversight, not only because a millennial accumulation of pertinent theory and examples is thereby neglected; the further consequence has been that the failure to take note of medieval reading theory has demonstrably hobbled the reader-response exploration and contributed to its premature closure.

Between medieval and modern theories of reading, several areas of concordance invite further attention. In the insistence that the meaning of a text is "experienced" by the reader over time, and with the call to "*slow down*" the activity of interpretation, Fish reinvents, as it were, the ruminative meditation prescribed by the church fathers. The medieval writers, we recall, conceive the activity of reading in alimentary metaphors; the reader "tastes" the words of Scripture on the "palate" of the heart, or indeed literally in the mouth as he or she pronounces them; one has then to "chew" the text thoroughly and "digest" it, that is so say, proceed toward interpretation and personal appropriation. These formulations take into account the affective, even visceral, responses that precede understanding and eventually accompany and follow it. The reader, according to Cassian, should feel the "power" of the words before attempting to grasp their meaning.[74] Understanding would come later (if ever) as a gift of the Spirit at some unguarded moment (e.g., during sleep).

French writings. Hans Robert Jauss was, in fact, a medievalist who had studied the French *Roman de Renard*, but his writings on reader-response make no reference to medieval reading theory.

[73] Tompkins, *Reader-Response Criticism*, 201–32.

[74] *Prius dictorum virtutem quam notitiam colligente*, ("We first take in the power of what is said, rather than the knowledge"). Cassian, *Conferences* 10.11.5; SCh 54:92; Ramsey, 384.

Fish does not enter into this territory. Other modern theorists have somewhat timidly ventured to specify pre-intellectual responses. David Bleich posits three steps: perceptions, affects, and associations, leading eventually to interpretive recapitulation.[75] Gerald Prince allows for (but denigrates) free associations and fantasies in the early, "minimal" (precritical) reading stage. The medieval spiritual writers, by contrast, highly value incidents of reverie or distraction; they counsel the reader to remain open at all times to the unforeseeable interventions of the Spirit, who often answers prayers before they are completed, and who frequently turns a reading, meditation, or exposition in a seemingly tangential direction, beyond rational human control. Modern critics, and especially modern literature teachers, do not usually appreciate interruptions. Nor do they explore such notions as faith, patience, and humility. These terms (perhaps all too familiar in church discourse) denote pre-interpretive *disciplines* governing the intensive work of rereading[76] and *meditatio*, vitally important in religious reading pedagogy (e.g., in the *Didascalicon* of Hugh of Saint-Victor).

Fish assigns, as we have noted, a creative role to the reader in constituting ("writing") the formal features of the text and even in the authorial intention realized in them. Wolfgang Iser similarly conceives a "partnership" between reader and text in which the reader "participates both in the production and the comprehension of the work's intention."[77] This aspect of modern reading theory is anticipated to some extent by the medieval masters who construed the given passage from Scripture as having various levels or depths of meaning to be realized by the reader in accordance with the level of his or her spiritual maturity. In Saint Gregory's terms (see below, p. 65) there are beginners, "little" readers (*parvuli*), and there are more advanced or greater ones (*magni*); the text, infinitely variable, can

---

[75] David Bleich, *Readings and Feelings: An Introduction to Subjective Criticism* (Urbana, IL: National Council of Teachers of English, 1975). In another work, *Subjective Criticism*, 97, Bleich offers this definition: "Generally response is a peremptory perceptual act that translates a sensory experience into consciousness."

[76] Matei Calinescu's recent *Rereading* (New Haven, CT, and London: Yale University Press, 1995), fills an important niche in the bibliography but does not discuss the medieval period in detail.

[77] Iser, *The Act of Reading*, 24.

mean different things to different readers, or to the same reader at different developmental stages. Meaning is indeed created by the dialogue between the reader and the Author who replies to him or her; there is not only a "reader-response" but also an "author-response," which the medieval religious theory takes fully into account.

The communal dimension of reading, introduced by Fish in his consideration of "interpretive communities," has been of course a matter of highest importance in religious theory through the ages. Within the church community, traditionally received doctrine orients the understanding of Scripture and forestalls "interpretive anarchy." Saint Augustine directs the reader of Scripture to attempt to first discern the intention of the writer; where that is hidden, the reader should be guided by the context (*circumstantia Scripturae*) and by the prescriptions of "sound teaching" (*sana fides*), which is the final authority.[78] Elsewhere, Augustine specifies the building up of charity as the ultimate aim and meaning of all the Scripture (*De doctrina Christiana* 1.36).[79] Restrained from error by doctrine and authority, the reader derives positive inspiration from the communion with the congregation, which remains virtually present to him, even when he finds himself geographically distant from it or reading in physical solitude. In the sharing of intellectual and affective devotion (*intenta mentium devotio*), the many become one.

Granting that the spiritual dimension of the community may be inaccessible to many modern, secular academic critics—typically church-averse, for political reasons, especially in America[80]—I would argue that spirituality is a domain into which the activity of reading naturally leads, and that this movement effectively transcends aestheticist self-absorption. "Spirituality," according to one succinct definition, is a mode of introspection that brings one into communication with something beyond oneself; that "something" becomes, in religion, "Someone."[81] Christian theory finds

[78] Augustine, *De Genesi ad litteram* 21 (PL 34:262).

[79] Fish cites this passage in "Interpreting the *Variorum*," Tompkins, 181.

[80] See, for example, Jonathan Culler, "Political Criticism: Confronting Religion" in *Framing the Sign: Criticism and its Institutions* (Norman, OK, and London: University of Oklahoma Press, 1988), 69–82.

[81] Louis Bouyer, *Introduction à la vie spirituelle* (Paris: Desclée, 1960), 6, writes, *Nous n'atteignons la « vie spirituelle » que lorsque cette « vie intérieure » se développe*

that entity or person, located beyond individual consciousness, as a presence evoked by the liturgical celebration: "For where two or three are gathered in my name, I am there in the midst of them" (Matt 18:20). The attendance of the community together with the priest constitutes the presence of God; it is the precondition for the reception of Scripture as a "living word." "The Word is living when the speaker is present and it is actually coming from his mouth. Only the presence of Christ prevents the Word from becoming a purely historical document. The church can claim this presence because it is identified with Christ."[82]

Communal reading institutes a live dialogue among readers/hearers and with the Author of the text, an interaction in which all participants are able respond to one another. Gregory, Bernard, and other church fathers routinely describe the activity of preaching in these dialogic terms: they emphasize that the expositor of the Scripture must remain alert to the reactions of the congregation through which the Spirit himself communicates inspiration. Through the monastic centuries, in church or in other locations, reading took place normally out loud and in groups. Solitary, individual reading—an exceptional situation in the age of Augustine and Gregory—has become, of course, the norm in modern life. Reading aloud is now conceived in religious practice as an extension of liturgical hearing, as its preparation or continuation. The community, and therefore God as well, remains present to the solitary reader; the reader, conversely, remains present to God, who is aware of him or her, and responds. As the ancient formula puts it, you speak to God in prayer; in reading, God speaks to you.

---

non pas dans l'isolement, mais au contraire dans la conscience d'une réalité spirituelle, de quelque manière qu'on l'entende, qui déborde la conscience de l'individu . . . . Si toutefois l'« esprit » que la « vie spirituelle » connaît est reconnu non seulement comme « quelque chose » mais comme « Quelqu'un », la « vie spirituelle » sera en même temps « vie religieuse » comme telle ("We attain 'spiritual life' only when the 'interior life' is developed, not in isolation, but on the contrary in the awareness of a spiritual reality, however one understands it, which overflows individual awareness. . . . If, however, the 'spirit' that 'spiritual life' acknowledges is recognized not only as 'something' but as 'Someone,' 'spiritual life' will be also 'religious life,' as such").

[82] Mariano Magrassi, *Praying the Bible*, 3.

In modern literary criticism the supposition of authorial presence has acquired the status of heresy and has been repeatedly attacked over the past half century. I have alluded above to the New Critics' rejection of the "intentional fallacy" (that is, the presumption that the intention of the author could determine what the work of literature *now* means). In *De la Grammatologie* (1967), Jacques Derrida generalized this critique into an attack on the "metaphysics of presence" inherent in the "phonocentric" conception of language.[83] Derrida argues that writing, as a representation of speech, necessarily implies the absence of the writer; speech itself, as representation, is also absent from or detached from its "originary meaning," which will always already differ from itself, in an infinite regress of representation of representation, never actually reaching a fixed point of departure at which a meaning would be fully "present to itself." The supposition of a stable originary meaning is, of course, theological: *Ce logos absolu était dans la théologie médiévale une subjectivité créatrice infinie : la face intelligible du signe reste tournée du côté du verbe et de la face de Dieu* ("This absolute logos was an infinite creative subjectivity in medieval theology: the intelligible face of the sign remains turned toward the word and the face of God").[84] Derrida concedes that this notion has governed much of our intellectual history, but he then denounces it as a delusion violently imposed. Proceeding to "deconstruct" the dependence of writing on a previous meaning thought or spoken or intended by an author, Derrida sets the written text free from (supposedly oppressive) author-ity, free to play, as it were, with unintended meanings such as puns. "Deconstructionists" celebrated that release and looked forward to analogous liberations from social constructs, such as gender and racial roles. Traditionalists once again expressed fear of interpretive anarchy and moral relativism. One might rather have remonstrated that Derrida's argument returns the text to the merely objective existence assigned to it by the Formalists and New Critics: writing on paper, unanswerable to the

---

[83] Jacques Derrida, *De la grammatologie* (Paris: Éditions de Minuit, 1967).

[84] Derrida, *De la grammatologie*, 25; Translated by Gayatri Chakravorty Spivak as *Of Grammatology* (Baltimore, MD, and London: Johns Hopkins University Press, 1974), 13.

(supposedly absent) writer and unresponsive to the reader, unable then to mediate intersubjectivity between them.

The *sequellae* of Derrida's analysis—the post-structuralist or postmodernist movement and the debates it has occasioned—lie beyond the concerns of the present summary. I note in passing that the concept of the text as opaque or impenetrable has been warmly welcomed by various critics concerned with the Old French vernacular literature. Paul Zumthor, as early as 1972, developed the notion of the "alterity," the otherness of the Middle Ages, shrouded in the "night of time," inaccessible to our view.[85] We recognize the ancient notion of the "dark ages" outfitted in postmodernist sheep's clothing. More recently, a spokesman for the "New Philology" movement proclaimed that "the Old French text is as richly complex, as contrived and perverse, as self-contradictory and problematic, as deceptive and falsely seductive, as opaque, and thus as needy of interpretation, as any literary work of any age."[86] A practical instance of textual opacity, perversity, and so on was found in the study of manuscript variation behind which, it was asserted, the author (for example, Chrétien de Troyes) could not be discerned or recovered.[87]

The attack on authorial presence and the resolve to complicate reader accessibility have proceeded on many different fronts with

---

[85] Paul Zumthor, Essai de poétique médiévale (Paris: Éditions du Seuil, 1972), 19–20, writes, *Une première évidence éclate aux yeux : l'éloignement du moyen âge, la distance irrécupérable qui nous en sépare. . . . La poésie médiévale relève d'un univers qui nous est étranger. . . . Lorsqu'un homme de notre siècle affronte une œuvre du XIIᵉ siècle, la durée qui les sépare l'un de l'autre dénature jusqu'à l'effacer la relation qui, ordinairement, s'établit entre l'auteur et le lecteur par la médiation du texte* ("One thing is immediately obvious: the distance of the Middle Ages from us, the unrecoverable distance that separates us from it. . . . Medieval poetry belongs to a universe that is foreign to us. . . . When a man of our century confronts a work of the twelfth century, the time distance that separates the one from the other denatures and practically erases the relationship that ordinarily is established between the author and the reader through the mediation of the text").

[86] R. Howard Bloch, "New Philology and Old French," *Speculum* 65 (1990): 46.

[87] In the case of the *Chevalier de la charrette* romance, Karl D. Uitti and Alfred Foulet argued on the contrary that the style of the poet and his intention are to be discerned and respected, and that an egregious fault in the base manuscript should be corrected on that basis. See Karl D. Uitti, "On Editing Chrétien de Troyes: Lancelot's Two Steps and their Context," *Speculum* 63 (1988): 271–92.

an enthusiasm that I find puzzling. Where taken seriously, this critical tendency has unnecessarily restricted the respective roles of author and reader and imprisoned the text in inert objectivity. I would like to suggest, however, that a more lively understanding of reading experience could yet be reopened and that medieval religious theory, broadened into an exploration of literary spirituality in general, might serve as a key.

Chapter Two

The Interpretation of the Scriptures

Letter and Spirit

The religious experience of reading begins with the concept of the Scripture as inspired writing dictated directly by the Holy Spirit to patriarchs, prophets, evangelists, and apostles. It was inspired in the original event of composition, and it remains so, the church believes, in an abiding presence: "The breath of the Spirit animates it still."[1] Modern studies have refined this article of faith, the respective roles of the divine and human ("instrumental") authors have been reapportioned, and the biblical books have been situated in historic periods and literary genres. Where today scholars perceive a collection of writings reflecting the diversity of ancient cultures, the early church fathers saw a totality, a unified composition containing all of revealed truth, all of theology. "All Scripture is inspired by God and profitable for teaching, for reproof, for correction and for training in righteousness" (2 Tim 3:16). All of Scripture, it follows, is true and meaningful; "Every jot and tittle," every crumb, as it were, of the textual bread, like that of the Eucharist, is to be gathered up in study. The depth of Scripture is infinite, inexhaustible, admitting of numberless rereadings and interpretations. Its writing reflects the artistry of the Holy Spirit,

---

[1] de Lubac, *Exégèse médiévale*, 1.1:128: *Ce ne sont pas seulement les écrivains sacrés qui furent inspirés, un jour : les livres sacrés eux-mêmes sont et demeurent inspirés. . . . L'Écriture n'est donc pas seulement divinement garantie : elle est vraie divinement. L'Esprit ne l'a pas seulement dictée : il s'est comme enfermé en elle. Il y habite. Son souffle l'anime toujours.* Medieval Exegesis, trans. Sebanc, 1:81–82: "It is not only the sacred writers who were inspired one fine day. The sacred books themselves are and remain inspired. . . . Thus Scripture is not merely divinely guaranteed. It is divinely true. The Spirit did not merely dictate it. The Spirit immured himself in it, as it were. He lives in it. His breath animates it still."

replete with figures and allegories. *Mira profunditas!* The devout reader will seek meaning beneath or beyond the textual surface, but an impious, slothful, or arrogant reader will be baffled by obscurities and excluded from the textual communion. Guided, however, by the magisterium of the church, the reader discovers that the Scripture interprets itself. Explicitly and by implication, it directs its own exegesis and orients the reader's role, both as an individual and as a participant in the interpretive community.

For the earliest Christians, Scripture meant the Old Testament. The psalms continued to form the basis of Christian prayer, public and private. Jesus himself constantly recalled the Old Testament prophecies and acted deliberately to fulfill them, as the gospels record. But the textual culture of the "law" inherited from Judaism would be subjected to repeated questioning in Christian teachings, which proposed simultaneously to fulfill it exactly and to transcend, if not transgress, its detailed prescriptions. Over against Jewish textualism, the early Christians asserted the authority of tradition, that is to say, the living memory of Jesus's life and teachings. In the course of the second century, however, as the last eyewitnesses died out, tradition was necessarily confided to writing, and, in the process, the New Testament canon emerged. Received then as authentic Scripture, the Christian writings claimed theological and legal authority on a par with the Old Testament. They also claimed a more direct access to the divine, as well as a new explicitness and immediacy. They demanded a new way of reading that involved a mixture of textual and supratextual receptive modes. Beginning with the New Testament and continuing in their re-reading of the Old, Christians developed a distinctive reading methodology which included both a devotion to the sacred page and a prescient alertness to what might lie beyond the wording.

Saint Paul's letter to the Galatians (4:22-26) accordingly identifies the two sons of Abraham (Gen 16:15) conceived respectively by the slave and the free woman. "Now this is an allegory: these women are two covenants" (Gal 4:24). Hagar is from Mount Sinai and bears children for slavery; thus, Paul asserts that she corresponds to the present Jerusalem. "But the Jerusalem above is free, and she is our mother. . . . So, brethren, we are not children of the slave but of the free woman" (Gal 4:26, 31). Generalizing from such examples, the early patristic exegetes interpreted Old Testament persons, things, and events "spiritually," that is, as allegorical figures, or "types," foreshadowing those in the New. "The law has but a shadow of the good things to come instead of the true form of these realities" (Heb 10:1). Thus Jonah's three days in the belly of the whale are taken to prefigure Christ in the tomb; the four major prophets, Isaiah, Jeremiah, Ezekiel, and Daniel, likewise prefigure the four evangelists; and Jesus refers to the brazen serpent of Moses as a type of himself, since "as Moses lifted up the serpent in the wilderness, even so must the Son of man be lifted up" (John 3:14).

In 2 Corinthians 3 and in Galatians 3–4, Paul brings the Christian act of reading Scripture into a dimension of transcendence. We are called to be "ministers of a new covenant"—he refers to Jeremiah 31:31-34—"not in the letter, but in the Spirit; for the letter kills, but the Spirit gives life" (2 Cor 3:6), and "where the Spirit of the Lord is, there is freedom" (2 Cor 3:17). Freedom means, ultimately, the vision of the glory of the Lord shining directly into the human heart (2 Cor 4:6). As yet, in this life we continue to depend upon the mediation of texts. But we are mandated to read them with "confidence," with "great boldness" (*fiducia* [2 Cor 3:4 and 3:12; Eph 3:12]). With the coming of Christ, the veil of Moses has been lifted, allowing a clear and transparent understanding of what was concealed in Old Testament figurative language. It is time to "give up childish ways" of thinking (1 Cor 13:11), and among these are literal ways of reading; one must now accept an adulthood of interpretation, throwing off the tutelage of the law as one might discharge a "custodian" or "disciplinarian" (*paedagogus* [Gal 3:24]). To read spiritually would mean to assume the inheritance and authority that were promised to one upon coming of age. The fourfold system of exegesis described in detail by de Lubac (see above, pp. 18–21) functions ideally as an exercise in freedom, one that may take the form of a muscular human intervention into the scriptural text.

In patristic commentaries, the first level of reading is normally designated by the term *historia*, denoting a factual history whose truth is never denied. The events recounted in the Bible "really" happened, and they have a sacred character. History is the foundation or the root to which all superstructures must remain secured;

typology, in particular, depends absolutely upon history as its initial term. Thus, de Lubac forcefully argues that it would be a mistake to see a negation of history in the many medieval expressions which signify the refusal to *limit* exegesis to the historical reading alone.[2] *Servata quippe veritate historiae* ("saving the truth of history"), exegesis includes history and reaches beyond it, following Paul's mandate.

The same first level is referred to by the term *littera*, "writing," analogous in Paul's formulation to the "law" transcended by grace. *Littera* denotes, first, the written words (*verba, voces*) and phrasing, and, second, their logical or narrative sequence (*prosecutio verborum, consequentia litterae* or *historiae*). Insofar as the concept of *littera* includes both *signifiant* and *signifié*, it is roughly equivalent to the modern term "text." As such, it mediates—as a translation or intrusion—between the Word of God and the "listening" reader. Its meaning is seldom transparent. The authors of Scripture use figurative expressions and tropes of rhetoric, as Augustine points out in numerous examples. Metaphors abound, of course, in the psalms; for example: "He drew me up from the desolate pit, out of the miry bog, and set my feet upon a rock" (Ps. 39 [40]:2). Metaphors recur also in Paul's letters: "If your enemy is hungry, feed him; if he is thirsty, give him drink; for by doing so you will heap burning coals upon his head" (Rom 12:20; cf. Prov 25:21–22). Necessarily, the concept of literal reading must be extended to include the *intended meaning* of such figures. With "burning coals," Augustine explains that Paul means to evoke the shame of the penitent enemy, directing the reader to discover the "intention of the human author through whom the Holy Spirit created the Scripture" (*De doctrina Christiana* 3.38), and this inclusive definition of the *littera* will eventually be confirmed by Thomas Aquinas.[3] In short, the "literal reading" includes the understanding of figures and tropes, and there is no necessary equivalence between "figurative" and "spiritual" interpretation.[4]

[2] Henri de Lubac, *Exégèse médiévale*, 1.2:439.

[3] *Summa Theologiae* I, q. 1, aa. 9–10; cf. *Quodlibet* 7, q. 6.

[4] Denys Turner, in *Eros and Allegory: Medieval Exegesis of the Song of Songs*, CS 156, (Kalamazoo, MI: Cistercian Publications, 1995), 92–108, labels "metaphoricism" the confusion found in many authors (as in Origen) between metaphors deployed on the literal level of the text and allegories requiring a spiritual interpretation.

As the reader moves from the literal/historical reading to the spiritual, the first step taken (following the "theological" order) will be that of allegory. This term refers generally to the truth of faith, that is to say, *the* (Catholic) faith, or the understanding of doctrine which is "sought by faith" (*fides quaerens intellectum*). More specifically, the allegory will be expounded primarily with reference to the nature and function of the church; early commentaries on the Song of Songs give especial prominence to this ecclesial reading of the bride's role in the dialogue.

Where modern summaries distinguish carefully between allegory and typology—the prefiguration in the Old Testament of events disclosed in the New[5]—the two modes of interpretation are often closely associated, as in Paul's paradigmatic example in Galatians 4:22-31 concerning the two sons of Abraham conceived respectively by the slave and the free woman. Allegory, ultimately, may be extended to subsume the fourth term, anagogy—the prophetic vision of the "last things" and of the kingdom of heaven to come—as in Paul's reference to the Jerusalem above. In the cases of Gregory's commentaries on Job and Ezekiel and Bernard of Clairvaux's *Sermons on the Song of Songs*, the result is a tripartite division: history/*littera*, allegory/anagogy, and tropology.

Tropology, the final step, translates the exposition of doctrine in the allegory into moral teaching expressed in general or communal terms, which are ultimately focused upon the conduct of the individual. Gregory's *Moralia* on Job leads the medieval shift in emphasis in this direction, which will be consummated in the writings of the twelfth-century Cistercians, Bernard of Clairvaux, William of Saint-Thierry, Aelred of Rievaulx, and others.

It would appear that the reader's role implied in exegesis is mainly limited to the discovery of inherent meanings, conceived as residing "in" an objective text. However, the description of the sacred text and the instructions on how it is to be read intertwine with a conception of the reader's own experience and a summons to creative intervention. In the following pages, I will study three classic instances. Origen, in *On First Principles*, describes the method

---

[5] See, for example, J. N. D. Kelly, *Early Christian Doctrines* (San Francisco, CA: Harper Collins, 1978), 69–75.

of spiritual interpretation of the sacred text; he develops a more personalized view of the reader in his *Homilies on the Song of Songs* (see below, chap. 6, pp. 163–70). Augustine, wary of reinstating textual servitude, views reading as a means, not an end; in *On Christian Doctrine*, he describes reading as just one of the many different pathways that may be taken toward the ultimate goal of all Christian religious activity: charity. Gregory's *Moralia* and *Homilies on Ezekiel* adapt the Augustinian sermon form (e.g., in the *Enarrationes* on the Psalms) to dramatize the scriptural reading, interpreted by the preacher and the congregation in the interplay of dialogue.

Origen's *On First Principles*

"More than any other figure in the fields of hermeneutics, exegesis, and spirituality, he would be the grand master."[6] Origen (185–253), the outstanding figure of the Alexandrian school, was a pioneer in developing the allegorical methodology that would govern Biblical commentary throughout the Middle Ages and beyond.[7] His vast scholarly works included textual criticism, commentary on almost every book of the Bible, and theological treatises. When his orthodoxy came under attack after his death, a large proportion of his writings was destroyed. Among the most important of his surviving works are three and a half books of his *Commentary on the Song of Songs*, translated into Latin by Rufinus, and two *Homilies* on the Song, translated by Jerome; I will return to these texts in chapter 6. Commentaries on the gospels of Matthew and John have also survived, along with homilies on other Scripture. There are two major works extant: the apologetic *Against Celsus*, in Greek, and

[6] Henri de Lubac, *Exégèse médiévale*, 1.1:219; *Medieval Exegesis*, trans. Sebanc, 1:159.

[7] For authoritative studies of Origen, see Henri de Lubac, *Histoire et esprit: L'intelligence de l'Écriture d'après Origène* (Paris, Aubier-Montaigne, 1950); Henri Crouzel, *Origen*, trans. A. S. Worrall (San Francisco, CA: Harper and Row, 1989); and Karen Jo Torjesen, *Hermeneutical Procedure and Theological Method in Origen's Exegesis* (Berlin and New York, NY: Walter de Gruyter, 1986). Raymond Studzinski, *Reading to Live: The Evolving Practice of Lectio Divina*, CS 231 (Collegeville, MN: Cistercian Publications, 2009), 28–58, summarizes Origen's hermeneutics with particular reference to his homilies on Genesis, Jeremiah, Joshua, and Leviticus, as well as his *Commentary on John*.

On First Principles (dated before 231 CE), in Greek fragments and in the complete, free Latin translation by Rufinus. *On First Principles* is an ambitious attempt to present the whole of Christian doctrine in a unified system composed of four books devoted, respectively, to God and the trinity, the world in relation to God, man and free will, and the Scriptures. This fourth book situates Origen's hermeneutics in a doctrinal context and effectively introduces the discussion of reading as a necessary constituent of textual analysis.[8]

The following summary is based on Rufinus's Latin translation, the text in which Origen's treatise was received in the West throughout the Middle Ages. Rufinus somewhat modifies—or, arguably, clarifies—Origen's hermeneutic terminology in key places, as we shall see.

Surveying the world around him, Origen perceives that the Christian message has spread and prevailed as no previous philosophy or system of laws has done. This development proves for him that the Scriptures were in fact divinely inspired. Christ's coming retrospectively confirms and explicates the Old Testament prophecies that were made concerning him; the prophecies have been fulfilled, the veil of Moses has been removed (2 Cor 3:15), and Origen implies that we now have the possibility of progressing beyond the beginning stages of understanding (Prin 4.1.7; SCh 268:284); we can learn to read spiritually as *socii* and *participes*, as sharers in divine wisdom (Prin 4.2.7; SCh 268:328).

On this theme, Rufinus amplifies Origen's prescriptions. They agree that laziness or arrogance, which is the mind-set of those who "wish to appear wise to themselves" or who "think that they already know, before they have learned" (Prin 4.2.1–2; SCh 268:294, 304), will prevent one from learning anything. One must approach the text reverently, *religiose et pie*, as befits divine rather than merely human studies, which are preferably done, Rufinus adds, under the guidance of a master; then, perhaps, *Deo revelante*, the student will learn what it is suitable for him to learn.

---

[8] Parenthetical references are to the SCh text, accompanied by Rufinus's Latin translation, Origène, *Traité des principes*, ed. H. Crouzel and M. Simonetti, vol. 3, SCh 268 (Paris: Éditions du Cerf, 1980); and to the English translation by G.W. Butterworth, Origen, *On First Principles* (Gloucester, MA: Peter Smith, 1973), occasionally emended where necessary.

According to Origen, the style of writing found in the Scriptures—the artistry of the Holy Spirit, a "divine elevation" (Prin 4.1.6; SCh 268:282) which owes nothing to human rhetorical devices—should alert us to the presence of meanings to be sought beneath or beyond the verbal surface. Even a middling intelligence—so he claims—should perceive that the tales of battles, weddings, procreations, and *omnis illa narratio*, are really "forms and figures of hidden, sacred things" (Prin 4.2.2; SCh 268:302–3), and even when one does not understand a hidden meaning, one should sense intuitively that *something* is indeed hidden there *(intellegitur tamen quia latet quid)* (Prin 4.2.3; SCh 268:306).

On the contrary, Jews, heretics, and even faithful but simpleminded readers have been led into error, Origen finds, by attempting to understand the scriptural figures "sensibly," that is, physically *(aisthetos;* Rufinus significantly glosses this term: *secundum litteram . . . sensibiliter ac uisibiliter*, Prin 4.2.1; SCh 268:294). Thus, the Jews have denied the divinity of Christ because they attempted to "keep closely to the text [*lexei*] of the prophecies concerning him," and so they argued that Jesus did not "sensibly" proclaim release to the captives (Isa 61:1) or build a real material city of God (Ezek 48:15); they found no real wolf, that is, no "four-footed animal," dwelling with a lamb nor any actual leopard lying down with a kid (Prin 4.2.1; SCh 268:294; Isa 11:6).

Avoiding such errors based on physical misreadings, Origen proposes to demonstrate the right way of understanding the Scripture *(recta via intellegentiae,* Prin 4.2.2; SCh 268:300). The complex intent of the Holy Spirit, he perceives, is to open the deeper mysteries of the Scripture to the spiritually qualified and also to provide for the needs of "simpler" readers, while excluding altogether those who would trample sacred mysteries underfoot. Accordingly, he finds a pedagogical, progressive structuring of meaning in the Scripture, offering "edification" on each of three levels. His construction parallels the Platonic composition of the human being as body, soul, and spirit:

> One must therefore portray the meaning of the sacred writings in a threefold way upon one's own soul; that is, so that the simple man may be edified by what we may call the flesh of the scripture, this name being given to the obvious interpretation

[Rufinus glosses here: *communem et historialem intellectum*, "the common and historical interpretation"]; while those who have begun to make a little progress and are able to perceive something more than that may be edified by the soul of scripture; and those who are perfect and like the men of whom the apostle says: "We speak wisdom among the perfect" . . . these may be edified by that spiritual law, which has "a shadow of the good things to come."[9]

For the simplest readers, then, the Scriptures offer narratives and precepts to be taken at face value. The second level has to do with moral application associated with the epistles of Saint Paul, and the third with the prophetic or anagogical vision of the world to come.

Origen observes that the Holy Spirit occasionally inserts into Scripture impossible narratives or incongruous prescriptions; in such passages, a "body" of meaning is not at all to be found (Prin 4.2.5; SCh 268:316), and meaningful reading can take place only on the second and third levels, those of the "soul" and the "spirit." This passage has given rise to much commentary. Origen seems here to come into conflict with an axiomatic inerrancy principle, namely that the Scripture, divinely inspired, cannot contain errors, self-contradictions, or anything contrary to scientific or historical truth. Modern critics, however, have diagnosed the problem as merely one of terminology. J. Daniélou,[10] Henri de Lubac,[11] and H. Crouzel[12] essentially agree in finding that what Origen calls the "body" (*soma*) or "flesh" (*sarx*) of the text corresponds to our concept of its *proper* meaning. For example, in Isaiah's prophecy

---

[9] Origen, *On First Principles*, 4.2.4: SCh 268:310–12; Butterworth, 275–6. Rufinus's text reads: *Tripliciter ergo describere oportet in anima sua unumquemque diuinarum intellegentiam litterarum: id est, ut simpliciores quique aedificentur ab ipso, ut ita dixerim, corpore scripturarum (sic enim appellamus communem istum et historialem intellectum); si qui uero aliquantum iam proficere coeperunt et possunt amplius aliquid intueri, ab ipsa scripturae anima aedificentur; qui uero perfecti sunt et similes his, de quibus apostolus dicit: Sapientiam autem loquimur inter perfectos. . . . Hi tales ab ipsa spiritali lege, quae umbram habet futurorum bonorum, tamquam ab spiritu aedificentur.*

[10] J. Daniélou, *Origène* (Paris: 1948), 182, quoted by J. Christopher King, *Origen on the Song of Songs as the Spirit of Scripture: The Bridegroom's Perfect Marriage-Song* (Oxford: Oxford University Press, 2005), 52.

[11] De Lubac, *Histoire et Esprit*, 113–14.

[12] H. Crouzel, *Origène* (Paris: 1985), 92–93, cited by King, 53.

cited above in which a wolf would dwell with a lamb, the wolf and the lamb are *properly* understood to be four-footed animals; the *literal*, or *intended*, meaning of the prophecy is expressed *figuratively* by the wolf and the lamb and is a prediction of peace and reconciliation. Origen offers many other clear examples. On Genesis 1–3, he writes, "Who is so silly as to believe that God, after the manner of a farmer, 'planted a paradise eastward in Eden' . . . ? And when God is said to 'walk in paradise in the cool of the day' and Adam to hide himself behind a tree, I do not think anyone will doubt that all of this, expressed in a narrative that seems to have happened, but did not happen bodily [*somatikos*], indicates in a figurative manner certain mysteries" (Prin 4.3.1; SCh 268:343–44).[13]

Modern translators of Origen, however, have often rendered his "bodily" sense as "literal meaning." J. Christopher King sharply criticizes H. Crouzel (and implicitly also Butterworth's English version) on this ground and concludes:

> The conflation of 'letter' and 'body'—as represented in Crouzel's *'sens littéral ou corporel'*—displays a tendency to substitute a merely hermeneutical problem (how to generate appropriate and intended meanings from a text) for Origen's fundamentally epistemological one (how to generate in the mind forms of understanding appropriate to all of the text's virtualities). This conflation is especially observable in the persistent use of the term 'literal sense' to designate both the 'letter' (> 'literal') and the 'body' or bodily *aisthêsis* (> 'sense') of Origen's hermeneutic. In fact, however, the phrase 'literal sense' is altogether foreign to Origen's Greek usage.[14]

It needs to be noted that the problem King identifies does not originate with the modern translators, but with Rufinus, who consistently glosses Origen's "somatic" level of meaning in terms of *historia* or *littera*. Two examples have been noted already above. Likewise, when Origen asserts that certain Scriptures have no "bodily" sense (*somatikon*), Rufinus interpolates a gloss: *hoc quod diximus corpus, id est consequentia historialis intellegentiae* (Prin 4.2.5; SCh 268:316: "what we have called the body, that is the logical sequence of the historical understanding"); again, in the same paragraph, Rufinus

---

[13] Trans. Butterworth, 288, cf. SCh 268:345.
[14] King, *Origen on the Song of Songs*, 53–54.

renders *somatikon* as *corporalem intellegentiam quae est historiae* ("the bodily understanding which is of the history"); further on, Origen's description of the spiritual meaning as wrapped in an "outer covering," which is the "bodily meaning," is rendered by Rufinus as *scripturae sanctae corpus . . . hoc ipsum quod diximus litterae indumentum* (Prin 4.2.8; SCh 268:334: "the body of holy Scripture . . . that which we have called the covering of the letter").

Already, in *On First Principles* and in other writings, Origen's trichotomy of body, soul, and spirit tends to resolve into two levels of interpretation. The first of these—"body" or "letter" or "history"—he identifies narrowly with the proper meanings of words, as we noted above; the second—the "spiritual" level—is reached in his analyses not only by mystical allegory but also by simple, figurative locutions, which Augustine and Thomas Aquinas (finally) will assign to the "literal" reading.

Origen continues: wherever historical facts could be adapted to spiritual understanding, the Holy Spirit wove them together into a single discourse (Prin 4.2.9; SCh 268:336). But in other places he finds that the Spirit intentionally inserted "stumbling blocks, as it were, and hindrances and impossibilities [Rufinus translates the Greek *skandala kai proskommata kai adynata* into Latin as *offendicula quaedam uel intercapedines . . . inpossibilia quaedam et inconvenientia*], in order that we may not be completely drawn away by the sheer attractiveness of the language, and so either reject the true doctrines absolutely on the ground that we learn from the scriptures nothing worthy of God, or else by never moving away from the letter fail to learn anything of the more divine element."[15] Rufinus adds a clarification: the interruptions of the historical sense were inserted to "present a barrier to the reader and lead him to refuse to proceed along the pathway of ordinary understanding [*intellegentiae huius uulgaris iter*]; and so, by shutting us out and debarring us from that, [the interruption] might recall us to the beginning of another way, and might thereby bring us, through the entrance of a narrow footpath, to a higher and loftier road and lay open the immense breadth of the divine wisdom."[16]

---

[15] Origen, *On First Principles*, 4.2.9; SCh 268:336; trans. Butterworth, 285.

[16] Origen, *On First Principles*, 4.2.9; SCh 268:336; trans. Butterworth, 285–86. Rufinus's rendering: *Procuravit diuina sapientia offendicula quaedam uel intercapedines*

In Origen's analysis, apparent scriptural incongruities are only partially situated in the text itself; they are also partially in the reader's role. In one respect, Origen conceives that the Scripture explains itself through the mechanism of typology; that is, the relationship between figures and prophecies in the Old Testament and their fulfillment in the New Testament is taken to reside inherently in the objective text. But much depends also upon the reader's authentic piety and intellectual abilities. Where these qualities are lacking, the Scripture will be found untrue and meaningless.

The reverent, intelligent reader, on the contrary, approaches the text with faith in divine providence, believing that understanding will be granted in proportion to one's spiritual qualifications. There is always the possibility of progression in wisdom as an ascent from bodily concerns to those of the soul and the spirit; Origen's tripartite structure of the Scripture thus holds a mirror to the composition of the reader's own being and potential. An instance of incomprehension, or a perception of an apparent untruth or contradiction, becomes for this reader a step toward higher, deeper participation in a mystery. Rufinus's translation contributes a significant metaphor of reading as a journey (*iter*), pathway (*transitus*), or passage (*callis*). One should approach the scriptural text with the expectation of being able to proceed through it smoothly, without stumbling, following a *consequentia historiae* or a *continuatus intellegentiae cursus*, which is an attitude of mind that necessarily precedes the experience of encountering a "stumbling block" and prepares one to recognize the incomprehension as a meaningful signal and, indeed, as a privileged invitation.

In this manner, Origen's description (as transmitted by Rufinus) of the scriptural text is intertwined with a theory of reader-response. Neither Origen nor Rufinus enters, however, into the readers' psychological processes other than to discriminate severely between those who possess the requisite intelligence, industry, and reverence for biblical study and those who do not. The horizon in *On First*

---

intellegentiae fieri historialis, inpossibilia quaedam et inconuenientia per medium inserendo; ut interruptio ipsa narrationis uelut obicibus quibusdam legenti resistat obiectis, quibus intellegentiae huius uulgaris iter ac transitum neget et exclusos nos ac recusos reuocet ad alterius initium uiae, ut ita celsioris cuiusdam et eminentioris tramitis per angusti callis ingressum inmensam diuinae scientiae latitudinem pandat.

Principles is the sacred text itself, objectively conceived as a unified totality, and the interpreter's conscious purpose is to understand its composition on its own terms.

Saint Augustine

Augustine's classic textbook on hermeneutics, *De doctrina christiana* (begun in 396 and completed in 427), was preceded by several exploratory treatises, including *De magistro* (389)[17] and *De catechizandis rudibus* (ca. 400)[18] in which we find elements of a theory of linguistics.[19] In *De magistro* he anticipates the modern notion of *l'abitraire du signe*. Words are signs; as such, they cannot convey to us the substance of the things to which they refer. Unless the thing is known beforehand, the word that refers to it can have no meaning. "We learn the meaning of the word, that is, the signification which is hidden in the sound, when the thing itself which it signifies has been cognized; [we do not] perceive the thing through such signification."[20] Words do not even convey without distortion the knowledge or understanding of the speaker. They may well bring to mind what we know already or what we may accept on faith; they direct us to consult the "guardian truth" that resides within the mind: Christ the inner teacher.

Does Augustine allow even the possibility of reading an unfamiliar text? One might observe that his model of the reading process resembles the stage in which a child may pretend to read pages pre-

[17] Augustine, *De magistro*, in *Aurelii Augustini Opera* 2.2, ed. W. M. Green, CCSL 29 (Turnhout: Brepols, 1970), 157–203. Translated by Whitney J. Oates in *Basic Writings of St. Augustine* (New York, NY: Random House, 1948), 1:361–95.

[18] Augustine, *De catechizandis rudibus*, in *Aureli Augustini Opera* 13.2, ed. I B. Bauer, CCSL 46 (Turnhout: Brepols, 1969), 115–78; *Aureli Augustini Hipponensis episcopi De catechizandis rudibus liber unus*, trans. and intro. Joseph Patrick Christopher, Catholic University of America, Patristic Studies vol. 8 (Washington, D.C.: The Catholic University of America, 1926).

[19] *De utilitate credendi* (391) and *De spiritu et littera* (412) pursue closely related themes in response to Manichaean and Pelagian teachings, respectively. For a recent commentary, see Brian Stock, *Augustine the Reader: Meditation, Self-Knowledge, and the Ethics of Interpretation* (Cambridge, MA, and London, England: 1996). Part 1:1–121 provides an analytic summary of the *Confessions*; part 2:124–206 is devoted to the other treatises.

viously memorized. This same model governs much of the reading which took place in the early monastic institution, as we shall see.

The sense of the inadequacy of words, as described in *De magistro*, also informs Augustine's treatise on catechetics, *De catechizandis rudibus*. He writes, "Intuition floods the mind, as it were, in a sudden flash of light [*quasi rapida coruscatione perfundit animum*] while the expression of it in speech is a slow, drawn out, and far different process."[21] In the process of speech, he continues, the original intellectual apprehension hides itself in the recesses of the mind, where it it is imprinted on the memory, and "from these we construct those audible symbols which are called language." But the words that come out do not even resemble the memory imprints, much less the original spark of understanding.

A further estrangement intervenes between the teacher's words and the pupil's understanding. By focusing on the latter's experience, however, Augustine finds a remedy. Teaching becomes an exercise of charity. Here, as in *De doctrina christiana*, charity is posed as the goal of all instruction. The sacred history that the catechist teaches is nothing other than the prefiguration of the coming of Christ, love in person. Christ himself sets the example of teaching in that he "emptied himself, taking the form of a servant . . . he humbled himself and became obedient unto death, even death on a cross" (Phil 2:7-8). The teacher performs a discursive self-emptying as he expresses his understanding in "broken and mutilated words" (Cat rud 10; Christopher, 48: *decurtata et mutilata verba*). The result Augustine foresees is a true completeness of communication that overcomes the theoretical impossibility described in *De magistro*: "When people are affected by us as we speak, and we by them as they learn, we dwell in each other [*habitemus in invicem*] and thus both they, as it were, speak in us what they hear, while we, after a fashion, learn in them what we teach."[22]

De doctrina christiana situates the activity of reading the Scriptures within this charitable intersubjective exchange.[23] Augustine

---

[20] Augustine, *De magistro*, 10.34; CCSL 29:193; Oates, 1:388.

[21] Augustine, *De catechizandis rudibus*, 2; Christopher, 16–17.

[22] Augustine, *De catechizandis rudibus*, 12; Christopher, 54–55.

[23] Augustine, *De doctrina christiana*, CCSL 32 (Turnhout: Brepols, 1972). Translated by D. W. Robertson as *On Christian Doctrine* (Upper Saddle River: Prentice

concedes at the outset that certain people can bypass texts entirely and receive direct illumination from God. But for most people, the path of spiritual development leads through reading, and they will need human teaching to guide their interpretation. "Those things which can be learned from men should be learned without pride. And let anyone teaching another communicate what he has received without pride or envy. . . . For charity itself, which holds men together in a knot of unity, would not have a means of infusing souls and almost mixing them together if men could learn nothing from men."[24]

The kind of teaching that Augustine has to offer is precisely not the subservience from which Paul would have us freed. Careful distinction is made between the act of reading to others and the act of teaching reading; likewise, Augustine distinguishes between interpreting passages of Scripture and advising in general how they are to be understood: "Just as a man who knows how to read will not need another reader from whom he may hear what is written when he finds a book, he who receives the precepts we wish to teach will not need another to reveal those things which need explaining when he finds any obscurity in books."[25] The discipline of interpretation—hermeneutics—should ideally free the mind from obedience to schoolmasters and from all other forms of intellectual subjugation.

Accordingly, Augustine's treatise anticipates various categories of problems and seeks to remove impediments to understanding that might threaten to reinstate servitude. Chief among these is the estrangement between signs and what they signify, which he had described in *De magistro*. Approaching the problem first on the level of words, he prescribes as a "sovereign remedy" the knowledge of languages, Hebrew and Greek as well as Latin. One

---

Hall, 1958); occasionally emended for clarity as needed. Parenthetical references are to this edition and this translation.

[24] Augustine, *De doctrina christiana*, prologue 5–6; CCSL 32:3–4; Robertson, 5–6. *Immo uero et quod per hominem discendum est, sine superbia discat, et per quem docetur alius, sine superbia et sine invidia tradat, quod accepit. . . . Deinde ipsa caritas, quae sibi homines invicem nodo unitatis adstringit, non haberet aditum refundendorum et quasi miscendorum sibimet animorum, si homines per homines nihil discerent.*

[25] Augustine, *De doctrina christiana*, prooemium, 9; CCSL 32:5; Robertson, 7.

should refer translations to the originals if possible. Faulty texts and mistranslations are to be emended (Doct chr 2.21; CCSL 32:46–47). To resolve a given obscurity, it helps to compare and collate translations; something of value may be found in each (Doct chr 2.17; CCSL 32:42–43). And where the interpretation seems to obscure the sense, it will be better to find a word-for-word rendering, even one "too closely bound up in the words" (Doct chr 2.19; CCSL 32:44; *qui se verbis nimis obstrinxerunt*), however unidiomatic or even incorrect in Latin it might be, in order to perceive the correct meaning. Latin grammar is a "law" to which the spiritually weak will continue to cling, but for Augustine, it is one made to be broken.[26] Whatever impedes clear, conceptual understanding is to be swept away. In many examples, Augustine finds that the better Latin wording (*magis latinum*) will be less clear (*minus apertum*). In such cases he unhesitatingly chooses colloquial discourse, including barbarisms: for example, rather than tolerate an ambiguous nominative form such as *os* (which could be from *oris*, "mouth," or *ossis*, "bone"), he will prefer to read Psalm 138:15 as *Non est absconditum a te ossum meum* ("My bone is not hidden from thee"; Doct chr 3.7; CCSL 32:81).[27]

Once elementary linguistic difficulties have been cleared, the reader faces deeper perplexities. What is the purpose of scriptural obscurities? Rather than contending with each difficult passage, Augustine would have us first read all of the canonical Scriptures and memorize as much as possible. "Know these books even if

---

[26] For other statements by the Latin fathers denigrating classical grammar, see Pierre Riché, *Education and Culture in the Barbarian West: Sixth through Eighth Centuries*, trans. John J. Contreni (Columbia, SC: University of South Carolina Press, 1976), 1553, n. 99. Thus, Gregory also declares, *indignum vehementer existimo, ut verba caelestis oraculi restringam sub regulis Donati* (*Moralia in Iob*, dedicatory letter "Ad Leandrum" 5). In n. 5 of the SCh edition of *Morales sur Job: Livres 1 et 2*, ed. Robert Gillet, trans. André de Gaudemaris, SCh 32 (Paris: Editions du Cerf, 1952), 122, Robert Gillet gives patristic references and cites also the survival of this topic in writings by Jean-Jacques Rousseau.

[27] Other examples: "Whether one says 'among men' by saying *inter homines* or by saying *inter hominibus* does not affect the person considering things rather than signs. . . . Whether *ignoscere* [to forgive] is spoken with a long or short third syllable makes little difference to a man asking God to forgive his sins" (Augustine, *De doctrina christiana*, 2.13.19; CCSL 32:45; Robertson, 46).

they are not understood" (Doct chr 2.14; CCSL 32:41); then, having acquired a general "familiarity with the language of the Holy Scriptures," it will become possible to approach the more difficult passages via those which are easier to understand (Doct chr 2.14, CCSL 32:81; 3.37, CCSL 32:99). Rarely will we find ambiguities on the literal level of meaning, Augustine maintains, which cannot be resolved "either by examining the context which reveals the author's intention, or by comparing translations, or by consulting a text in an earlier language" (Doct chr 3.8; CCSL 32:82).[28]

Augustine continues to be concerned with the question of figurative language. Here he refers directly to Paul: "'For the letter kills, but the Spirit gives life' (2 Cor 3:6). That is, when that which is said figuratively is taken as though it were literal, it is understood carnally. . . . There is a miserable servitude of the spirit in this habit of taking signs for things, so that one is not able to raise the eye of the mind above things that are corporal and created to drink in eternal light."[29] Augustine proposes that if one uses divinely instituted signs, knowing and venerating what they ultimately refer to, one is indeed spiritual and free; and even if a reader does not know what a given sign refers to, as long as he recognizes that it is merely a sign, he is not in servitude (Doct chr 3.13; CCSL 32:85). Some things are to be taken literally, some figuratively, some both ways, and a figure may well signify different things in different places. Augustine would take differences in historical circumstances and changes in community standards into account (e.g., with regard to the polygamy of the patriarchs). In the last analysis, all interpretations are to be referred to the rule of charity: "Whoever thinks that he understands the divine Scriptures

---

[28] This passage should be compared to Augustine's statement in *De Genesi ad litteram* 1.21 (PL 34:262): where a passage of Scripture offers a number of possible interpretations, we should choose first the meaning intended by the writer; where that is unclear, we should examine the context; and where that is unavailable, we should choose the reading that concords with orthodox faith: *Id potissimum deligamus, quod certum apparuerit eum sensisse quem legimus; si autem hoc latet, id certe quod circumstantia Scripturae non impedit, et cum sana fide concordat: si autem et Scripturae circumstantia pertractari ac discuti non potest, saltem id solum quod fides sana praescribit.*

[29] Augustine, *De doctrina christiana* 3.5.9; CCSL 32:83; Robertson 84.

or any part of them so that it does not build the double love of God and of our neighbor does not understand it at all." However, even if one misunderstands a scriptural author's intended meaning, as long as one refers it to the building up of charity, one is "not deceived."[30]

Nothing could be further from Augustine's hermeneutics than textual "fundamentalism," as we now call it.[31] Far from being fettered to a sacred wording, he is prepared to consult different translations and compose his own Latin version as needed. Where a difficulty arises, he invites contributions from as many sides as possible—philology, textual criticism, history, science, dialectics, the arts—bringing all legitimate categories of knowledge to bear on the point in question. His approach is more flexible, more open than that of Origen. Having set charity as the ultimate goal of inquiry, he allows the reader to choose any number of pathways toward that goal, and "if [the reader] is deceived in an interpretation which builds up charity . . . he is deceived in the same way as a man who leaves a road by mistake but passes through a field to the same place toward which the road itself leads."[32] It is better to take shortcuts than to delay along the way, "for the Lord himself, although he saw fit to become our road, did not wish to hold us on it, but wished that we pass on, lest we cling in infirmity to temporal things."[33]

Augustine's instructions are aimed at elite readers, especially those who will be called to preach and teach in their turn. He presumes not only literacy on their part but also acquaintanceship with other languages, access to a variety of texts, general understanding of Christian teachings, and a high degree of spiritual and

---

[30] Augustine, *De doctrina christiana* 1.40; CCSL 32:29; Robertson, 30.

[31] Mary Carruthers, *The Book of Memory: A Study of Memory in Medieval Culture* (Cambridge, UK: Cambridge University Press, 1990), 11, comments, "Fundamentalism regards a work of literature as essentially not requiring interpretation. It emphasizes its literal form as independent of circumstance, audience, author—of all those factors that are summed up in rhetorical analyses by the word 'occasion'. . . . True fundamentalism understands words not as signs or clues but takes them as things in themselves."

[32] Augustine, *De doctrina christiana*, 1.41; CCSL 32:30; Robertson, 31.

[33] Augustine, *De doctrina christiana*, 1.38; CCSL 32:28; Robertson, 30.

intellectual maturity. His concept of spiritual freedom scarcely differs from the modern ideal of freedom of inquiry, appropriate to a humanistic, scholarly enterprise. Charity, for Augustine, is as much a scientific principle—a criterion for interpretation—as it is a possibility for actual human interaction. Yet there are notes in *De doctrina* that echo the lived experiences of friendship and discipleship recounted in the *Confessions*. The sharing of ideas, he finds, is the "means of infusing souls and almost mixing them together" (Doct chr, prologue 6, quoted above on p. 52). He is skeptical, as we have seen, about the ability of words to convey what they signify. Just as in reading or listening one mainly *recognizes* what was intuitively known beforehand, so also the interpretation of Scripture leads to charity as its foreordained conclusion. Yet he remains paradoxically confident that thoughts may indeed be communicated—incarnated—in human language, mysteriously without suffering any deterioration or change, "as the Word of God was made flesh without change so that he might dwell among us" (Doct chr 1.12; CCSL 32:13).[34]

These idealistic impressions of human intercourse link the exercise of interpretation to the way of life that the monastery will be designed to provide. Augustine was indeed "incurably coenobitic," as Timothy Fry observes.[35] We recall his advice that one should first read all of the canonical books *even without understanding them (yet)*, memorizing them if possible, as monks do. Understanding would come later, in its own time. Rather than struggling with obscurities, he would have us focus first on the more open passages, those that clearly state teachings of the faith or precepts for living—practical spirituality. Only then, once one has become generally familiar with the "language of divine Scriptures" and has learned to discriminate literal from figurative writing, should

---

[34] Brian Stock, *Augustine the Reader*, 190–206, discusses *De doctrina*, emphasizing themes prevalent in the *Confessions*. "The reading process mediates between the doctrines about love in the texts and the comparable sentiment in our minds. . . . Love operates vertically, descending from the text to the reader, and horizontally, as readers relate to audiences. Christianity emerges as a textual community built around shared principles of interpretation" (196).

[35] *Rule of Saint Benedict 1980*, ed. Fry, 61.

one venture into more difficult interpretative terrain (Doct chr 2.14; CCSL 32:41). These instructions anticipate the techniques of ruminative *meditatio* taught by monastic writers, to whom we shall shortly turn.

Saint Gregory the Great

In the writings of Gregory the Great, the interpretation of the objective scriptural text is balanced by a lively appreciation of the reader's role and activity. A favorite Gregorian metaphor conveys his concept of exegesis: A man who surveys a forest from above cannot see how deep are the valleys or how extensive are the plains concealed within it; but if he begins to walk through it, he quickly realizes that there is much that he had not previously seen, and nightfall may well catch him on the way.[36] Gregory walks deep into the scriptural forest and reports in detail his findings in thirty-five books of *Moralia* (moral expositions) on the book of Job, twenty-two homilies on Ezekiel, forty homilies on the gospels, and expositions of the Song of Songs and the first book of Kings (not to mention the *Dialogues* or the treatise on *Pastoral Rule*). Almost all of Gregory's works are in fact readings cast in the form of line-by-line commentaries on Scripture.

Gregory was born into a patrician Roman family and became the chief civil magistrate of the city before joining a monastery, which he founded around the age of thirty-five. That retreat, which he would always recall with nostalgia, lasted only a few years; thereafter, from 579 to 585 he functioned as a papal agent in Constantinople, and in 590 he was elected pope, the first of his name and the first monk to assume that office. During his pontificate, he was preoccupied with maintaining stability in a time of great disorder marked by the Lombard invasions in northern Italy. He negotiated treaties, dealt with civil authorities, struggled to eliminate corruption within the church, and initiated a successful missionary expedition to England, led by Augustine of Canterbury.

Gregory's profile, one that will fit also a very few outstanding figures in later church history, is that of the contemplative called to

---

[36] Gregory the Great, *In librum primum regum*, prologue 2; CCSL 144:50.

intense administrative and political activity. He was beset by poor health all his life. His writings oriented the culture of the entire period between the patristic age and the beginnings of Scholasticism in the thirteenth century. "Everyone in fact had read him and lived by him," writes Jean Leclercq, who cites borrowings by Isidore of Seville, Bede, Anselm, Bernard of Clairvaux, and many others.[37] His presence is still vibrant in the writings of Teresa of Avila and John of the Cross. In the early modern age, his reputation came under attack, notably by Adolf Harnack in his *History of Dogma*.[38] Scholars of the late twentieth century, however, have vindicated him as a founder, after Cassian and Benedict, of medieval spirituality, and as such he has become the subject of a lively renewal of study in recent decades.[39]

The *Moralia in Job* was originally presented as conferences to monks who accompanied him to Constantinople in 579. Set down in notes, it was revised and expanded by the author, and the transcription of the text was completed during the early years of his papacy. The *Homilies on Ezekiel* similarly originated in oral delivery, as they were presented in rapid succession to a presumably mixed audience of monks and clergy in 593–594, and set down at that time by *notarii*. Eight years later, Gregory reviewed the texts and authorized their copying and distribution. My discussion in the following pages will dwell on these two major works, particularly on the *Homilies on Ezekiel* in which his reflections on the read-

---

[37] Leclercq, *Love of Learning,* 32.

[38] Adolf Harnack, *History of Dogma,* 7 vols. (New York: Dover, 1961; from the third German edition of 1900), 5:262, cited by Bernard McGinn, *The Growth of Mysticism,* vol. 2 of *The Presence of God: A History of Western Christian Mysticism* (New York, NY: Crossroad, 1999), 434, n. 28: "Gregory has nowhere uttered an original thought; he has rather at all points preserved, while emasculating, the traditional system of doctrine, reduced the spiritual to the level of coarsely material intelligence . . . and associated it with popular religion of the second rank."

[39] The best general study of Gregory is that of Claude Dagens, *Saint Grégoire le grand: Culture et expérience chrétiennes* (Paris: Études Augustiniennes, 1977). Dagens reflects the climate of opinion created by Jean Leclercq, *Love of Learning,* 31–44, and Henri de Lubac, *Exégèse médiévale,* 1.1:187–93; 1.2:537–48, 653–56; and 2.1:53–77. More recent, but less useful in my opinion, is Carole Straw, *Gregory the Great: Perfection in Imperfection* (Berkeley: University of California Press, 1988).

ing and interpretation of the Scriptures are found in their most concentrated, explicit form.[40] The *Moralia* and the *Homilies* offer performances of reading— renderings, demonstrations, representations—originally directed to live audiences. He has these audiences in mind from beginning to end of the reading process, and they remain imaginatively present to him long after the oral delivery of his sermon, throughout the revision and distribution of the written text. He reflects often on the interaction between the scholarly and the human dimensions of his project and on the constantly changing balance between its contemplative and active phases. These statements are found especially in prefaces; for example, they can be found in the dedicatory letter to Bishop Leander of Seville ("Ad Leandrum"), which accompanies the *Moralia*, and in the opening paragraphs of the *Homilies*. Modern scholars have abstracted these statements from their original contexts and assembled them into what might be called Gregory's theory of reading.[41] This kind of summary is necessary and valuable, but Gregory is not principally a theologian,

---

John Moorhead, *Gregory the Great* (London and New York: Routledge, 2005), presents an anthology of translated excerpts from Gregory's writings. Gregory's theology is summarized in the introduction to the SCh edition of the *Moralia in Iob*: *Morales sur Job: Livres 1 et 2*, introduction and notes by Robert Gillet, trans. André de Gaudemaris, SCh 32, (Paris: Éditions du Cerf, 1952). For a good compilation of Gregory's statements on the reading process, see Patrick Catry, "Lire l'écriture selon saint Grégoire le grand," *Collectanea Cisterciensia* 34 (1972), 177–201.

[40] The authoritative texts are those of the CCSL, Marcus Adriaen, ed. *Moralia in Iob*, 3 vols., CCSL 143, 143A, and 143B (Turnhout: Brepols, 1979, 1979, and 1985); and *Homiliae in Hiezechihelem prophetam*, CCSL 142 (Turnhout: Brepols, 1971). There are no modern published English translations available for either text, as far as I know; the translations given here are my own. The partial SCh edition of the *Moralia*, with facing French translations, includes books 1–2 (SCh 32, cited above, n. 39); books 11–14 and books 15–16, ed. A. Bocognano, SCh 212 and 221 (Paris: Éditions du Cerf, 1974 and 1975); books 18–19, SCh 476 (Paris: Éditions du Cerf, 2003); and books 30–32, SCh 525 (Paris: Éditions du Cerf, 2009). The two recent volumes offer the text as edited by Adriaen, with French translations by the *moniales* of Wisques. The complete text and French translation of the *Homilies on Ezekiel* are presented in *Homélies sur Ézéchiel*, ed. and trans. Charles Morel, 2 vols., SCh 327 and 360 (Paris: Éditions du Cerf, 1986 and 1990).

[41] Patrick Catry's study, "Lire l'écriture selon saint Grégoire le grand," is especially useful. See also Claude Dagens, "Culture biblique et vie spirituelle," 55–81.

and after one has gained an overview of his ideas, one will still feel the need to quote him abundantly and at length in order to reenter the immediacy of his writing.

Scripture, for Gregory, is the Word of God: *scriptura*, more often *eloquium*, singular or plural, usually qualified as *divinum* or *sacrum: divinum eloquium, sacra eloquia, divina locutio.*[42] Metaphorically, Scripture is a letter or letters written by the Creator to his creatures, dictated by the Holy Spirit to the prophets, evangelists, and apostles who simply held the pen (Mo, preface 2; SCh 32:124–25). Our role is to read attentively. "The emperor of heaven . . . has written you letters concerning your life," he writes to a doctor named Theodore, "but still you neglect to read them ardently! Study them, I beg you, and meditate daily on the words of your Creator."[43] The letters were written to us personally, for the Writer had us (and still has us) in mind. We have to read or listen to them, hearing the voice of the writer that is present to us, as a master's face is constantly present to obedient servants who are anxious to read his expressions and do his will.

Scripture is much more than a text, in modern understanding. It is a "lamp" guiding the life of the reader; it is a "created light" which shines for us only if it is lit by the "uncreated light," the spirit of life which enlightens our reading (Hiez 1.7.17; SCh 327:258). It is a mirror which is offered to the "eyes of the mind," in which we see our "internal face" in its ugliness or beauty (Mo 2.1.1; SCh 32:179; cf. Cassian, Conf 10.11.6; SCh 54:92). It is a "measuring reed" by which we gauge how far we have progressed spiritually, or how far behind we are falling (Hiez 2.1.14; SCh 360:78). The Scripture itself progresses, following the development of the reader. *Sacra lectio* is an interaction, fully reciprocal in nature. The reader reads the Scripture and, ultimately, he or she is also read by it.

To describe this mutuality, Gregory develops an allegory of reading from the first chapter of Ezekiel. His attention is drawn to the image of the wheel (Ezek 1:15); the teachings of Scripture are found now lower, now higher, communicating on the literal level

---

[42] Concerning these terms see Catry, 177–78.
[43] Ep 5.46, cited by Dagens, 59.

to beginners and spiritually to the more adept. As the mind moves from the literal to the allegorical plane, the wheel turns, raising the mind with it (Hiez 1.6.2, 7; SCh 327:198, 204). Ezekiel describes four creatures (*animalia*), each with four faces, which Gregory identifies as the four evangelists. Each creature is accompanied by its wheel: "And when the living creatures went, the wheels went beside them; and when the living creatures rose from the earth, the wheels rose. Wherever the spirit would go, they went, and the wheels rose, following him; for the spirit of life was in the wheels" (Ezek 1:19-20). Gregory explains:

> Eleuantur uero a terra animalia cum sancti uiri se in contemplatione suspendunt. Et quia unusquisque Sanctorum quanto ipse in Scriptura sacra profecerit, tanto haec eadem Scriptura sacra proficit apud ipsum, recte dicitur: Cum ambularent animalia, ambulabant pariter et rotae; et cum elevarentur animalia de terra, elevabantur simul et rotae, quia diuina eloquia cum legente crescunt, nam tanto illa quisque altius intellegit, quanto in eis altius intendit. . . . Fitque ut Scripturae sacrae uerba esse caelestia sentias, si accensus per contemplationis gratiam temetipsum ad caelestia suspendas. Et mira atque ineffabilis sacri eloquii uirtus agnoscitur, cum superno amore legentis animus penetratur.

> ———————

> The creatures are lifted from earth when holy men are suspended in contemplation. The more a saint progresses in Scripture, the more the same Scripture progresses in him. . . . Divine eloquence grows with the reader, for one understands it the more deeply as one's intention searches more deeply within it. . . . What happens is that you feel the words of holy Scripture to be heavenly, if you yourself, enkindled through the grace of contemplation, are lifted up to heavenly things. When the reader's intellectual soul is pierced by supernal love, the wonderful and ineffable power of the sacred text is truly acknowledged.[44]

Scripture follows the reader as he searches out its meaning on the level appropriate to his spiritual development and progresses to

---

[44] Gregory the Great, *Homélies sur Ézéchiel*, 1.7.8; SCh 327:244. For comment on this passage see de Lubac, *Exégèse médiévale* 1.2:655–66, and McGinn, *Growth of Mysticism*, 40.

higher, deeper understandings. The reader changes, and the Scripture itself changes in the process. "Wherever the Spirit went, as the Spirit went, the wheels were raised, following him" (Ezek 1:20):

> Quo enim spiritus legentis tendit, illuc et diuina eloquia leuantur, quia si in eis altum quid uidendo et sentiendo quaesieris, haec eadem sacra eloquia tecum crescunt, tecum in altiora ascendunt. Bene autem de eisdem rotis dicitur: Sequentes eum. Legentis enim spiritus, si quid in eis scire morale aut historicum quaerit, sensus hunc moralis historiae sequitur. Si quid typicum, mox figurata locutio agnoscitur. Si quid contemplatiuum, statim rotae quasi pennas accipiunt et in aere suspenduntur, quia in uerbis sacri eloquii intelligentia caelestis aperitur.

> Wherever the spirit of the reader tends, there also divine eloquence is raised, for if you seek to see and feel something high [*altum quid uidendo et sentiendo*], the same sacred eloquence grows with you, and rises with you. So it is rightly said of the wheels that they "follow him," for if the spirit of the reader seeks moral or historical knowledge, the moral meaning of the history follows him; if he seeks a typical meaning, a figure of speech is presently recognized; and if he seeks a contemplative meaning, all at once the wheels seem to take on wings and are suspended in air, for in the words of sacred eloquence a heavenly understanding opens.[45]

The reader finds what he seeks in Scripture, that is to say, he finds what he is moved and inspired to seek by the Holy Spirit, who lights the page. In one and the same sentence of Scripture, a given reader will find what he needs on the historical level, another will seek a typological sense, and another will encounter a contemplative meaning. As the "Spirit of life touches the soul of the reader,"—as he is stirred to righteous anger, moved to patience, inspired to preach, or called to repent—different texts and/or levels of interpretation will come to mind (Hiez 1.7.11–14; SCh 327:250–54). The wheels move, stay, or are raised (Ezek 1:21): "the sacred reading will be found to match the state of the seeking reader" (*sacra lectio talis inuenitur, qualis et fit ipse, a quo quaeritur*). Gregory writes, "Are you progressing in active life? Scripture moves with you. Have you reached a state of constancy? It stays

---

[45] Gregory the great, *Homélies sur Ézéchiel*, 1.7.9; SCh 327:246.

with you. Have you risen by the grace of God to the contemplative life? It flies with you" (Hiez 1.7.16; SCh 327:256).

Gregory's conception of the reciprocity between the reader and the scriptural text reflects his monastic formation, and it anticipates modern reading-cognition theory. Concerned as he is with the reader's progress, Gregory emphasizes everywhere the patient, loving pedagogy of the Spirit, who nurtures and nourishes a diverse readership including *parvuli* (spiritual infants), *magni* (those who are greater and stronger in understanding), and others in all stages in between. Scripture contains both difficult, obscure texts and those which are transparent to interpretation; "It is neither so closed as to intimidate, nor so open as to suffer cheapening . . . the more it is meditated, the more it inspires love, for it brings help to the soul of the reader with humble words, while raising him with their sublime meanings, and as it were growing as the readers grow: it is recognized as familiar by simple minds, while the learned find it always new" (Mo 20.1.1; CCSL 143A:1003).

Gregory invokes a traditional, alimentary metaphor to describe the levels of Scripture as food (*cibus*) and drink (*potus*). The more difficult passages must be chewed—ruminated, expounded, interpreted—before they can be swallowed; the easier ones can be imbibed directly as liquid (Hiez 1.10.3; SCh 327:382–84).[46] Like Ezekiel (Ezek 3:1), we are commanded to "eat this book," that is, eat it and drink it. "We open our mouths as we prepare our intelligence to receive the understanding of the sacred word" (*quando sensum ad intelligentiam sacri uerbi praeparamus*; Hiez 1.10.5; SCh 327:386). That reception would be beyond our powers, however, if the Spirit did not feed us, measuring out to us what we are capable of receiving each day, so that today we understand what we were unable to grasp the day before.

The "digestion" of Scripture, the full absorption and retention of understanding, takes place, of course, in the actions of daily life. Gregory develops the metaphor in terms of filling the "belly" and the "entrails" of the heart (*in cordis uisceribus*); many readers, he maintains, remain famished after reading or hearing the word

---

[46] Implicitly, Gregory evokes here the Biblical metaphor of "milk" versus "solid food" in 1 Cor 3:1-2 and Heb 5:12-14.

when they fail to put divine precepts into practice. They may have tasted, but they are not satisfied if they continue to value earthly riches and fame; they have sipped but not reached drunkenness, that is, the true change of heart which is conversion (Hiez 1.10.7; SCh 327: 388–90). Heretics, on the other hand, are described as having, as we say, eyes too big for their stomachs: *Plus secreta Dei student perscrutari quam capiunt* ("They try to investigate more of the secrets of God than they can grasp"; Mo 20.8.18; CCSL 143A:1016). Rather than retaining ("digesting") what they do understand and applying it to virtuous conduct, heretics seek only to show themselves as erudite or eloquent. Searching out matters that are beyond them, they consume more of the "honey" of spiritual intelligence than they can keep down—Gregory refers to Proverbs 25:16—with the result that they vomit the excess and lose whatever they had previously understood as well.

The alimentary imagery—developed at length and not without humor—leads him to a central concept which he will often restate elsewhere (e.g., Hiez 1.9.30, SCh 327: 372; 2.5.4–5, SCh 360:230–34): truly religious minds receive in depth what they are capable of understanding and put that much into living practice; they then feel and show reverence (*venerari*) concerning what they do not (yet) understand, awaiting that in patience, "for often the humility of the chosen ones opens the intelligence, even concerning things that had seemed impossible to understand" (Mo 20.8.19; CCSL 143A:1017: *Plerumque humilitas ea etiam electorum sensibus aperit, quae ad intelligendum impossibilia esse uidebantur*).

Gregory's emphasis on living practice points us toward the finality of reading and interpretation: "God speaks to us through all of sacred Scripture for one sole purpose, which is to draw us to the love of himself and of our neighbor."[47] For Gregory as for Augustine,

---

[47] Gregory the Great, *Homélies sur Ézéchiel*, 1.10.14; SCh 327:398: *Nam si in uerbis Dominicis uirtutem requirens, ipse aliter quam is per quem prolata sunt senserit, etiamsi sub intellectu alio aedificationem caritatis requirat, Domini sunt uerba quae narrat, quia ad hoc solum Deus per totam nobis sacram Scripturam loquitur, ut nos ad suum et proximi amorem trahat* ("For [a commentator] seeking virtue in the words of the Lord may understand them differently than did the one who first pronounced them, yet if through a different interpretation he seeks to build up charity, then his words are those of the Lord, for in all of Holy Scripture God speaks to us

the goal is charity; as long as the text is interpreted in that sense, even if it is understood in a manner different from that intended by the human writer, one is hearing the word of God. Correctness of interpretation matters less to Gregory than does the realization of charity on any level available—literal, allegorical, or any other.

It follows that truly charitable reading cannot remain a merely solitary exercise. Its purpose is fulfilled when it is shared and experienced with others. Augustine's view of teaching as a "way of infusing souls and mixing them together" (Doct chr, prologue 6; CCSL 32:6) is brought to life by Gregory in the act of preaching. As he delivers his homily, passing on his interpretation of Scripture, his own reading is fully absorbed—"digested"—and applied actively to the love of his neighbors and to the labor of drawing them to the love of God. As he expounds the Scripture to them, he constantly adjusts his thought to their progress, imitating the nurturing pedagogy of the Spirit that he had discovered in his own reading.

Gregory addresses a diverse congregation, including *parvuli* and *magni*, in a Latin style which is direct and forceful. Like all of the Latin fathers, he eschews classical rhetoric; unlike them, he does in fact write simply, imitating the manner of the Scriptures: "for it is proper that the offspring resemble its mother."[48] In place of verbal ornamentation, he offers a richness of metaphors aptly placed, drawn from Scripture and from tradition, delivered with frank enthusiasm. *O quam mira est profunditas eloquiorum Dei!* Scripture is like a forest, as we recall; to study it is to venture into cool thickets of obscurity, where one may find shelter from the heat of the world (Hiez 1.5.1; SCh 327:170), but where one may easily lose one's way (*In librum i regum*, prologue 2). Scripture is like the sea: we cross it on a boat made of the wood of the cross (Hiez 1.6.13; SCh 327:214). It is a river where lambs can walk and elephants can swim.[49] It is the scroll presented to Ezekiel (Ezek 2:9),

---

with just one purpose, which is to draw us to the love of himself and of our neighbor"). Cf. Augustine, *De doctrina christiana* 1.40–41, discussed above, p. 55.

[48] Gregory the Great, *Moralia in Iob*, dedicatory letter "Ad Leandrum" 5; SCh 32:122: *ut quasi edita soboles speciem suae matris imitetur.*

[49] Gregory the Great, *Moralia in Iob*, dedicatory letter "Ad Leandrum" 4; SCh 32:120: *Quasi quidem quippe est fluvius, ut ita dixerim, planus et altus, in quo et agnus ambulet et elephas natet.*

which is written on both sides; as it is unrolled—expounded—we see the historical or literal meaning on the outside and the the spiritual, allegorical meaning on the inside (Hiez 1.9.29–30; SCh 327: 368–72). The jars at the wedding of Cana were first filled with water, that is, the historical sense of the reading; then the water was turned into the wine, just as history is turned by the mystery of allegory into spiritual understanding (Hiez 1.6.7; SCh 327:204). The exposition of the Scripture is like grinding pepper with a mortar and pestle: the more it is ground, the stronger is its power (Mo 29.8.19, CCSL 143B:1447; cf. Mo Praef. 6; CCSL 32:128, and Mo Praef. 1.36.54; CCSL 32:176). And elsewhere: "Should I not compare a word of Scripture to a stone in which fire is hidden? It feels cold in the hand, but as soon as it is struck by iron, it sends out sparks. . . . Thus, when the text is struck by the attentive mind, inspired by God, it produces the fire of hidden meanings and sets the soul ablaze" (Hiez 2.10.1; SCh 360:482).

The images come effortlessly, it seems. Yet beneath them one senses a constant exercise of discretion on Gregory's part. The preacher, he maintains, must not attempt to broker sublimities that may be beyond his listeners' grasp; he should not be more concerned with displaying himself than with attending to their needs (Mo 20.2.4; CCSL 143A:1004). He will strive to "read" his audience as acutely as he does his text. He must use care not only in the use of rhetoric but also on the level of conceptualization: "In teaching the Scriptures, we must present not only the great mysteries that intoxicate us but also the tiny, subtle things that are perceived by taste." [50] He weighs carefully what he has to say, how much he has to say, to whom he is speaking, and under what circumstances (Hiez 1.11.12–17; SCh 327:464–468). That alertness fosters restraint, but it also prompts him to depart from the original plan of a sermon and to risk tangential free-associations as the occasion may demand. In an oft-quoted passage, he compares scriptural commentary to a river:

---

[50] *Moralia in Iob*, 20.2.4; CCSL 143A:1004: [*in*] *doctrina sacri eloquii, non solum exhibenda sunt magna et arcana quae debriant, sed etiam parua et subtilia quae quasi per gustum notitiam praestant.*

Fluvius quippe dum per alveum defluit, si valles concavas ex latere contingit, in eas protinus sui impetus cursum divertit, cumque illas sufficienter impleverit, repente sese in alveum refundit. Sic nimirum, sic divini verbi esse tractator debet, ut, cum de qualibet re disserit, si fortasse iuxta positam occasionem congruae aedificationis invenerit, quasi ad vicinam vallem linguae undas intorqueat et, cum subiunctae instructionis campum sufficienter infuderit, ad sermonis propositi alveum recurrat.

As a river flows along its course, if it encounters valleys on either side, into these it pours itself, and when they have been filled, then it returns swiftly to its original channel. Thus indeed, thus the commentator on the divine word should be, for if he happens to find an occasion for edification, he turns the flow of his discourse as though into that neighboring valley, and when he has sufficiently flooded that plain, then he returns to the course of his sermon. (Mo, dedicatory letter "Ad Leandrum" 2; SCh 32:117)

The exposition which results from this principle is digressive and seemingly unsystematic. Beryl Smalley comments, "To us it is a most annoying system . . . [one that] precludes any attempt at coherence or logical arrangement."[51] More recently, Carole Straw finds that "Gregory is elusive. Artless and honest, he is nevertheless a mysteriously subtle personality not easily confined to conventional categories."[52]

The latter, more sympathetic assessment still misses the mark, I believe. Gregory's is a calculated spontaneity, anything but artless. His references to his own writings confirm that he has reread his text and imposed editorial control. His thought process—somewhat cramped in the earlier *Moralia* by the order of exegesis—becomes progressively more fluid and more digressive, rather than less so, as his mastery of the form develops. What he expresses and imitates with his free-associative technique is indeed the freedom of the Spirit that "blows where it wills" (John 3:8), as he is fond of quoting.

---

[51] Beryl Smalley, *The Study of the Bible in the Middle Ages* (Notre Dame, IN: University of Notre Dame Press, 1964), 34.

[52] Carole Straw, *Gregory the Great*, 7.

As he responds to his audience's needs, the auditors contribute to his own understanding of the text. In the situation of preaching, as he acknowledges, the reading of the Scriptures is an enterprise of responsive collaboration:

> Scio enim quia plerumque multa in sacra eloquio, quae solus intellegere non potui, coram fratribus meis positus intellexi. Ex quo intellectu et hoc quoque intellegere studui, ut scirem ex quorum mihi merito intellectus daretur. Patet enim quia hoc mihi pro illis datur quibus mihi praesentibus datur. Ex qua re, largiente Deo, agitur ut et sensus crescat et elatio decrescat, dum propter uos disco quod inter uos doceo, quia—uerum fateor—plerumque uobiscum audio quod dico.
>
> _____
>
> I know that many passages in Sacred Scripture which I was unable to understand alone became clear to me in the presence of my brothers. I have tried then to learn on behalf of whom that understanding was given to me; clearly, it was given to me for the sake of those in whose presence it was given. The result is a growth of understanding and a lessening of pride, since it is because of you that I learn what I teach to you, and I must even confess that often I hear with you [for the first time] what I say. (Hiez 2.2.1; SCh 360:93)

The gift of insight is actually given not to him, but through him, to his auditors, for their sake and because of their merits. As they grow in charity and understanding, he grows by the gift of the Spirit; as they are moved to the desire for God, his understanding is likewise lifted (Hiez 1.10.40–41; SCh 327:434–36). Conversely, when he falls silent, the fault is theirs as well as his (Hiez 1.12.17; SCh 327:514). And when he has to reprove them, the blame must fall on himself first: *Dicam, dicam ut uerbi Dei gladius etiam per memetipsum ad configendum cor proximi transeat. Dicam, dicam, ut etiam contra me sermo Dei sonet per me* (Hiez 1.11.5; SCh 327:454: "I will speak, I will speak, so that the sword of the word of God passes through me to transfix the heart of my neighbor. I will speak, I will speak, so that even against myself the word of God will be sounded by me").

More than condescension to his congregation, the activity of preaching entails for Gregory an effort to join emotionally in their experience. Commenting on Ezekiel, he sees the prophet sitting among the captive people who hear the compassion in what he has to say: "for iron is joined to iron when it is first liquefied, so that it can adhere from both sides to itself" (Hiez 1.11.2; SCh 327:448: *Sic ferrum cum ferro iungitur, liquatur prius, ut postmodum uicissim a semetipso teneatur*).

Gregory's intellectual understanding is joined to that of his listeners through the medium of the scriptural text. As he brings his interpretation to them for their benefit and correction, he moves outward "into the field"; as he devotes himself to the love of his neighbor, his perception "widens" and his reading of the text is "raised." But he must then return "home" and retreat into self-examination and compunction as he applies the same reading to himself, testing his own state of mind against it (Hiez 1.12.10; SCh 327:502). By practicing what he preaches, by applying the text both ways, he acquires a power of speech that goes beyond school rhetoric; he "reads" within himself, what he "writes" in his sermon:

> Ad praedicandum namque plus conscientia sancti amoris ae-dificat, quam exercitatio sermonis, quia amando caelestia intra semetipsum praedicator legit quomodo persuadeat ut despici debeant terrena. Qui enim uitam suam interius pensat, et exem-plo suo foris admonendo alios aedificat, quasi in corde linguae calamum tingit, in eo quod manu uerbi proximis exterius scribit.

> In preaching, the interior awareness of holy love edifies more effectively than skill in speech. For it is in the love of heavenly things within himself that the preacher reads the manner in which he will persuade others to let go of earthly ones. One who examines carefully his own internal life, and by his own example admonishes others, dips, as it were, the pen in his own heart when he writes externally, in words, to his neighbors. (Hiez 1.10.13; SCh 327:396)

The preaching situation, which Gregory envisages as fully recipro-cal, enacts charity as the finality of interpretation, following the Augustinian rule.

Which in fact came first, preaching or reading? Perhaps it was in his own meditations that Gregory first experienced the reciprocity between reader and text that he describes in the al-legory of Ezekiel's wheels. He may then have sought to replicate that interaction as he faced his audience, as he learned from them and they from him, by the grace of the Spirit. Alternatively, we might suppose that the process actually worked in the other direction, and that it was in the act of preaching that he learned to read in the first place. Teachers commonly report that their own learning is completed only when they face the class. However, it is clear that the experience of preaching informed Gregory's final revisions of his sermon-transcripts, and that it is his evolved understanding of his reading that is contained in the texts that have come down to us.

What we now perceive in his works is a progress from reading to preaching to writing and to reading again, a cycle impelling forward movement in the manner of a wheel. There are mirror reflections to be noted at each stage. Gregory's description of preaching reflects his reading process and vice versa. Preaching, in the last analysis, is simply reading the Scripture aloud: reading and "reading," that is, interpreting; reading aloud to other readers. Proceeding from preaching to writing, Gregory anticipates that the cycle will continue with future readers and auditors to whose presence he continues to respond.

Gregory was a monk, a prelate, a statesman, a mystic, a reformer, a preacher, and teacher; he was not a scholar in the manner of Origen or Jerome or a systematic theologian like Augustine, but he was a universal figure in his own right, very much on a par with his patristic predecessors. He speaks, however, to a more diverse, less elite audience than they did. His formation proceeded through the monastic institution; his characterizations of readers at various intellectual levels emerge seemingly from practical experience as well as academic theory. His emphasis on spiritual pedagogy and his conceptions of the reading process also follow the trajectory of the monastic tradition, as we shall see in the next chapter.

In Gregory's *Moralia* and the *Homilies on Ezekiel*, exegesis truly becomes the *acte complet* envisioned by de Lubac: an analysis/ meditation that arises from line-by-line reading, guided by no a priori hermeneutic or overview, and develops into theological and mystical affirmations that freely flow in often unforeseeable directions. Gregory maintains a listening attitude in the initial reading, in the memorization/meditation process, and in the further stages of preaching and writing. By linking reading with preaching, he effectively extends the ancient formula of "When you pray, you speak to God; when you read, God speaks to you" to include speaking back to God through the same text by which he speaks to us. Preaching begins, of course, with the reading aloud of Scripture, followed by the shared experience of interpretation in the sermon. The essence of that activity resides, for Gregory, in the dialogue with a congregation. Where two or three are present and drawn together in charity around the text, he is convinced that the Holy Spirit is there among them, listening and speaking to them.

Gregory's synthesis stood as definitive through the following centuries, rightly called the "Gregorian Middle Ages." In the twelfth century, as we shall see, the reconsideration of reading developed by Hugh of Saint-Victor, Bernard of Clairvaux, and their contemporaries does not so much challenge Gregory's formulations as adapt them to the climate of spiritual and intellectual renewal. Still later, Gregorian echoes are heard in vernacular mystical writings from authors as diverse as Julian of Norwich and John of the Cross. In recent years, scholars following Jean Leclercq have found in Gregory the cornerstone of medieval monastic theology. I look forward to a similar rediscovery among modern students of literature of Gregory as a writer.

Chapter Three

Reading and Meditation

We turn now to look at reading from the point of view of the reader who occupies the center of this inquiry. We need to enter into actual reading experiences as explicitly described, prescribed, and remembered, rather than as implied by treatises on hermeneutics or by commentaries on texts. What did the reading process consist of? What outcomes were sought? What obstacles, material or psychological, were to be overcome? Turning back several centuries before Gregory the Great, I propose to review the transition from the classical concepts of reading to those introduced by Christianity, particularly by the monastic movement.[1] I will focus selectively on several leading themes: the sense of intellectual and spiritual freedom discovered in the reading process, the internalization and personal appropriation of texts as taught by early monastic authorities, and the flow of reading into meditation and mystical contemplation.

Classical Education

In antiquity, reading was taught as part of the program of literary education designed to train patricians for public service.

---

[1] This cultural transition has received abundant scrutiny in the modern era, beginning with the classic studies by Henri Marrou, *Saint Augustin et la fin de la culture antique* (Paris: De Boccard, 1937; 2nd ed. 1949); and *Histoire de l'éducation dans l'antiquité* (Paris: Seuil, 1948), translated by George Lamb as *A History of Education in Antiquity* (Madison WI: University of Wisconsin Press, 1982). On education in the early Middle Ages, see Pierre Riché, *Éducation et culture dans l'occident barbare, VIe–VIIIe siècles* (Paris: Seuil, 1962), translated by J. J. Contreni as *Education and Culture in the Barbarian West, Sixth through Eighth Centuries* (Columbia, SC: University of South Carolina Press, 1976); and *Écoles et enseignement dans le haut Moyen Âge, fin du Ve siècle–milieu du XIe siècle* (Paris: Picard, 1989). On Saint Augustine, see Stock, *Augustine the Reader*.

Ideally, the objective was to form the orator as a person who could (re)unite literary erudition, skill in oral presentation, and virtuous character—faculties constitutive of an ideal adult "manhood" (*humanitas*). But throughout this period, commentators including Plato, Cicero, and Quintilian perceived that in the competitive social and political arena, rhetorical skill might not always be accompanied by virtue. Literary education, Quintilian and others proposed, would aim to restore integrity.[2] Reading would provide resources for use in speaking: vocabulary, grammar, style, taste (the sense of appropriateness), knowledge of history, and knowledge of legal and political precedents, including an encyclopedic command of examples to cite in argumentation. Beyond training in skills, reading would contribute to character formation by providing models of behavior to imitate or to shun and by inculcating private and public moral values.

The teaching of reading and the general concept of the reading experience had passed from the Greeks to the Romans, apparently all but unchanged.[3] Marrou describes the classical pedagogy as a rigorous rote-learning process, proceeding in a prescribed sequence from the simplest elements to the more difficult constructions, with progress reinforced by beatings at every stage. "Its method was based on a purely rational a priori analysis of the thing to be learnt, in complete indifference to any of the learner's—i.e. the child's—psychological problems."[4] First came the alphabet, learned as a list of letters to be recited or sung in order. Then the child was taught syllables, still in a set order: beta-alpha-ba; beta-ei-be; beta-eta-be. . . .[5] Next came monosyllabic words, then words of two or more syllables. At this stage, rather than working with words in everyday usage, the child would be given lists that included rare medical terms, exotic proper names, and exercises in pronunciation based on gibberish "tongue-twisters" (or "gags" or

---

[2] Quintilian envisions a reunification of rhetoric and philosophy in the preface to his *Institutio oratoria*, ed. and trans. H. E. Butler, 4 vols., Loeb Classical Library (London: Heineman, 1920–22), 10–11.

[3] Marrou, *History*, 265–91.

[4] Marrou, *History*, 150.

[5] Marrou, *History*, 151.

"bridles").[6] Only after such preparation was the child allowed to read short continuous passages in which reading comprehension could be aided by context.

By the first century CE, a definite liberalization of the pedagogy became visible, informed by a growing interest in learning psychology. The *Institutio oratoria* of Quintilian (especially books 1 and 10) offers an authoritative summary of educational theory at this time and an assessment of the place of reading within it.

Quintilian is convinced that the aptitude for learning is as natural to the human being as flight is to birds (Inst 1.1.1; Butler 1:19). Accordingly, his teaching methods seek to elicit the child's spontaneous responses and to reinforce the child with praise and rewards rather than with punishment. Above all, Quintilian wants to avoid creating an aversion to literary learning in the child, which might well persist into adult years (Inst 1.1.20; Butler 1:28). At what age should a child be taught to read? Since little children are capable of moral training, they should also be capable of literary education, he reasons, and at that stage the child's memory is especially retentive. Quintilian recommends play-learning with ivory letters and suggests creating competitive games among groups of children, with prizes awarded to the winners.

In teaching the alphabet, Quintilian stresses that rote-learning the names of the letters in alphabetical order must be supplemented, as soon as possible, with attention to their written shapes. For this reason, he notes that the best teachers reverse or scramble the order of the letters so that the children will learn to recognize letters by their shape rather than by their place in the familiar sequence (Inst 1.1.25; Butler 1:32). The learning of the syllables, however, must proceed in the traditional manner and order, with much repetition, in order to train correct spelling. Quintilian generally approves of the traditional use of isolated difficult words and outlandish phrases.[7] He would in fact begin literacy instruction with Greek, rather than Latin, which the child would already ac-

---

[6] Marrou, *History*, 151–54.

[7] Quintilian anticipates indeed the "great debate" in reading education, still unresolved according to Smith, *Understanding Reading*, 221, 316–23, between advocates of "phonics" and those of "whole language."

quire from daily conversation (Inst 1.1.13; Butler 1:26). Systematic Latin study would, however, immediately follow in tandem with Greek in order to inculcate a culture of the native language free of foreign idioms and affected intonations. But care must be taken at this stage to avoid teaching common words and familiar speech; the beginning reader should rather study sayings of famous men or lines of poetry, texts that would form moral character as well as develop linguistic skills.

Writing—the actual, physical labor of forming letters with stylus or pen—is seen as an important exercise, even though dictation to a scribe may have been the usual practice among the aristocracy. A template may be used to train the child's hand until the correct outlines are learned. Writing, like speaking, is a productive rather than a receptive faculty (according to modern terminology) and so is especially valued by Quintilian, "for by this means alone can a true and deeply rooted proficiency be obtained" (Inst 1.1.28; Butler 1:34). Writing slows down the thought process and thus provides a good corrective to precocity, which is always distrusted and discouraged in traditional pedagogy. Reading out loud could serve a similar purpose, especially because of the real difficulties posed by the lack of punctuation and word-separation in the ancient written texts.[8] Quintilian would have the child read slowly for a long while until practice brings speed unaccompanied by stumbling or error.

Memorization remains an essential feature of education at all stages, from the first approach to the alphabet through the most sophisticated adult enterprises. Quintilian cites memory as "the surest indication" of the young child's native ability (Inst 1.3.1; Butler 1:54). He significantly associates memorization with free, critical rereading and anticipates the concept of meditative "digestion" developed by Christian writers such as Gregory the Great:

---

[8] Marrou alludes to this important problem (*History*, passim), studied in detail by Paul Saenger, "Silent Reading: Its Impact on Late Medieval Script and Society," *Viator* 13 (1980), 366–414, and *Space Between Words: The Origins of Silent Reading* (Stanford, CA: Stanford University Press, 1997). See also Malcolm B. Parkes, *Pause and Effect: An Introduction to the History of Punctuation in the West* (Berkeley, CA: University of California Press, 1993).

Lectio libera est, nec actionis impetu transcurrit; sed repetere saepius licet, sive dubites sive memoriae penitus adfigere velis. Repetamus autem et retractemus, et ut cibos mansos ac prope liquefactos demittimus, quo facilius digerantur, ita lectio non cruda, sed multa iteratione mollita et velut confecta, memoriae imitationique tradatur.

Reading is free, and does not hurry past us with the speed [of oral delivery]; we can reread a passage if we are in doubt about it or wish to fix it in memory. We must return to what we have read and reconsider it with care, and just as we soften foods and almost liquefy them in order to digest them more easily, so our reading, not in a raw state but as it were chewed over and reduced to pulp but much repetition, should be committed to memory and imitation. (Inst 10.1.19; Butler 4:13)

Quintilian's system thus balances encouragement of the child's natural verbal impulses and abilities with a judicious use of defamiliarization. It is a truly humanistic program designed to free the learner from dependence on rote-repetition while providing a solid cultural foundation and a disciplined, confident practice of the language on an elevated level of discourse. This formation, concerned with character development as well as verbal skills, would ideally enable the patrician to make a valuable contribution to society by acting as a free, responsible individual in the political sphere.

The Conversion of Reading

When the Christian church fathers turned away from Cicero, Vergil, and Ovid, they explicitly rejected the content of the literature and its moral and aesthetic values. They retained, however, whether consciously or not, classical concepts of the reading act and techniques for teaching literacy. Jerome's educational program, detailed in letters to Roman women, adopts a number of Quintilian's specific recommendations.[9] In Letter 107 written to Laeta

---

[9] The complete edition of Jerome's letters, with facing French translations, is by Jérôme Labourt, 8 vols. (Paris: Les Belles Lettres, 1949–63). I refer also to the text and English translation by F. A. Wright, *Select Letters*, Loeb Classical Library (Cambridge,

concerning her daughter Paula, he advises: let the child be given wooden letters to play with; she should learn their names in order by rote in a song, but the alphabetical order should also frequently be changed so that she might learn to recognize the letters by sight as well as by sound; and as she begins to trace letters with a stylus on wax tablets, let her hand be guided by another hand or by a template (Letter 107.4; Wright: 344–46). Reading, as both Jerome and Quintilian conceive it, involves the auditory, visual, and tactile senses, as well as intellectual faculties. Literacy is associated with correct Latin pronunciation. It is important, Quintilian insists, that the child's nurse speak correctly—ideally, she herself should be a philosopher—for it is she whom the youngster will imitate, "and we are by nature most tenacious of childish impressions, just as the flavor first absorbed by vessels when new persists, and the color imparted by dyes to the primitive whiteness of wool is indelible. Further it is the worst impressions that are the most durable. For, while what is good readily deteriorates, you will never turn vice into virtue" (Inst 1.1.5; Butler 20–21). Jerome concurs: The native Latin tongue should not be distorted by rusticity or by foreign accents or by fashionable affectations (Letter 107.9; Wright 358; cf. Letter 22.29; Wright 124). Therefore, from the very beginning, let the child be taught to speak by a learned man, "for the very letters sound differently from the mouth of a learned man and of a rustic. And so you must take care not to let women's silly coaxing accustom your daughter to cut her words short" (Letter 107.4; Wright 348: *ne ineptis blanditiis feminarum dimidiata dicere filiam verba consuescas*). Underlying Jerome's characteristic satirical vehemence, we perceive fundamentally humanistic values: a concern for clarity coupled with contempt for obscurantism, an impatience to release the child from mechanical repetition, and to have the child accede to intellectual and spiritual freedom.

The sheer violence of the Christian effort to unlearn pagan literary culture confirms the classical view, expressed by Quintilian, concerning the difficulty of correcting bad habits and attitudes

---

MA: Harvard University Press, 1933). For a summary of Jerome's correspondence with women pupils, see Studzinski, *Reading to Live*, 66–74.

acquired in early childhood. One recalls immediately Jerome's dream, described in Letter 22 to Eustochium:"*Ciceronianus es, non Christianus,*" the judge declares, and orders him to be whipped, thus replicating and reversing the pedagogy by which he had initially learned to read (Letter 22.30;Wright. 126–28). Augustine's complex, ambivalent account of his education, recounted in book 1.13–20 of the *Confessions*,[10] conveys a comparable experience in which the effortless acquisition of his native Latin speech was painfully supplanted by systematic instruction in the alphabet and even more brutally by the process of learning Greek (*Confessions* 1.13–14). As an adult, he abjures the spontaneous delight he had taken in the poetry of book 4 of the *Aeneid*, and he concedes that in the last analysis,"your law, O God, permits the free flow of curiosity to be stemmed by force . . . your law prescribes bitter medicine to retrieve us from the noxious pleasures which cause us to desert you" (*Confessions* 1.14).[11] He then reaffirms the value of the elementary instruction, painful as it was, which now allows him to read and write what he himself wants, and to dedicate his verbal skills to God, freed at last from the direction of a pagan schoolmaster (*Confessions* 1.13).

In the struggle to reorient their literary culture toward Christian readings and values, Augustine and Jerome both seek to acquire an intellectual freedom based on disciplined mastery of the elements, rather than on spontaneous inclination or unquestioned servitude to conventional taste. Christian humanism would lead in turn to spiritual freedom in the Pauline sense. Jerome engages his adult pupils in Socratic dialogues driven by intellectual curiosity as well as by piety: Marcella never met him, he writes, without asking questions and suggesting counterarguments to the answers he gave (Letter 127.7;Wright 452); Fabiola's insistent inquiries on the book of Numbers eventually compelled him to write treatises on her behalf (Letter 77.7;Wright 326–28).

---

[10] Augustine, *Confessions*, ed. James J. O'Donnell, vol 1: *Introduction and Text* (Oxford: Clarendon Press, 1992), 10–15. Saint Augustine, *Confessions*, trans. R. S. Pine-Coffin (Harmondsworth, Middlesex, UK: Penguin Books, 1961), 33–41.

[11] For a thorough commentary on this account in the *Confessions*, see Stock, *Augustine the Reader*, chap. 1.

Retained, however, from the ancient authorities is a respect for deep-rootedness in education—Quintilian values the exercise of writing, as noted above, for this reason—and a corresponding distrust of shallow precocity.¹² Memorization thus remains an essential part of Jerome's program, even at the advanced level. The student should learn Greek and Hebrew and commit whole books of the Bible to the "storehouse of memory" (Letter 107.12; Wright 364: *cellarium memoriae*). The pedagogy previously based on Vergil is now applied to the Scriptures. With constant reading and meditation, the mind becomes a "library of Christ" (Letter 60.10; Wright 286: *bibliotheca Christi*). To the widow Furia, Jerome writes, "Assign yourself a fixed number of verses from Holy Scripture as a *pensum*, to offer to the Lord, and do not lie down to rest until you have filled your heart's basket with this precious yarn" (Letter 54.11; Wright 248). Instead of jewels and silks, she will develop a love of books, in which she will be less impressed with gilt decoration than with "correctness and accurate punctuation" (Letter 107.12; Wright 364: *emendata et erudita distinctio*).

Reading and prayer will continue to occupy the center of the student's vocation. "Read often and learn all you can," Jerome writes to Eustochium. "Let sleep steal upon you with a book in your hand, and let the sacred page catch your drooping head" (Letter 22.17; Wright 87). He continues, "Let the seclusion of

---

¹² In *Institutio oratoria* 1.3.4 (Butler 1:57), Quintilian develops the topic of shallow growth, familiar in the Christian parable of the sower: *Illud ingeniorum velut praecox genus non temere umquam pervenit ad frugem. Hi sunt, qui parva facile faciunt et audacia provecti, quidquid illud possunt, statim ostendunt. Possunt autem id demum, quod in proximo est; verba continuant, haec vultu interrito, nulla tardati verecundia proferunt. Non multum praestant sed cito. Non subest vera vis nec penitus immissis radicibus nititur; ut, quae summo solo sparsa sunt semina, celerius se effundunt, et imitatae spicas herbulae inanibus aristis ante messem flavescunt.* ("Precocious intellects rarely produce sound fruit. By precocious I mean those who perform small tasks with ease, and thus emboldened, proceed to display whatever they can; but their accomplishments are only of the most obvious kind: they string words together and trot them out, undeterred by any sense of modesty. They offer not much but quickly. They have no real power and what they have is but of shallow growth: it is as when we cast seed on the surface of the soil; it springs up too rapidly, the blade imitates the loaded ear, and yellows before the harvest time, but bears no grain.")

your own chamber [*cubiculi tui secreta*] ever guard you; ever let the Bridegroom sport with you within." And here he cites Cyprian's aphorism, *Oras: loqueris ad sponsum; legis: ille tibi loquitur* ("When you pray, you are speaking to your Spouse; when you read, he is speaking to you").[13] She should rise from the dinner table still hungry, able to read, pray, and sing the Psalms; she should keep vigils and become like a "grasshopper of the night," a "sparrow in solitude" (Letter 22.18; Wright 88). *Sic dies transeat, sic nox inveniat laborantem. Orationi lectio, lectioni succedat oratio* ("So let the day pass, and so let the night find her still laboring. Let reading follow prayer and prayer follow reading" [Letter 107.9; Wright, 360–61]).

By Jerome's time, it has become clear that attitudes toward reading have undergone noteworthy changes, as the classical techniques and practices have been adapted to Christian culture. Reading had been valued as one means among others employed in the training of the orator. From the study of literature, one accumulated cultural riches to be stored in the *cellarium* of memory, which would become an arsenal of weapons to use in argumentation in the political service of the state. In Jerome's usage, however, that *cellarium* evokes far different connotations derived from the Song of Songs: *Introduxit me rex in cellaria sua* (Song 1.3: "The king has led me into his storerooms"). The storehouse of memory has become a locus of contemplation where the Bridegroom sports with the Bride; it is a place that exists physically in the seclusion of Eustochium's chamber (Letter 22.25; Wright 108: *cubiculi tui secreta*).

It is the *process*, the experience of reading, that interests Jerome far more than any practical result or product. His lyrical descriptions conceive reading as an essentially private activity, inseparable from the prayer into which it flows. His aristocratic pupils attain a high level of intellectual and spiritual maturity; they have the freedom of access that the written textual medium affords, they are free to reread and reflect, and they apply critical judgment to their studies. But they also have plentiful recourse to rote-learning, repetition, and recitation, "childlike" procedures

---

[13] Jerome, Letter 22.25; Wright 108; cf. Cyprian of Carthage, *Epistulae* 1.15; PL 4:221: *Sit tibi vel oratio assidua vel lectio: nunc cum Deo loquere, nunc Deus tecum* ("You should apply yourself to prayer or to reading: at times you speak with God, at times he speaks with you").

that have acquired new value in religious textual usages that may bypass rational comprehension altogether. "Assiduity" is more important here than intelligence, as Cyprian had insisted: *Sit tibi vel oratio assidua vel lectio.*[14]

Jerome's letters offer strikingly vivid descriptions of the reading practice that we have come to refer to as *lectio divina.* He outlines an individualistic, essentially eremitic vocation, freely chosen—in defiance, if necessary, of familial pressures—and carried out in the midst of Roman society. But from the turn of the fifth century onward, and especially following the sack of Rome in 410, meditative reading became primarily associated with the monastic community, the coenobium, which alone could provide protected security; freedom from distractions; and the necessary, supportive interaction between collective and private worship. Following his departure from Rome, Jerome founded two monasteries in Bethlehem, one for men (ca. 390), of which he became the abbot, and the other for women, administered by Paula until her death in 404, and thereafter by Eustochium.[15]

Cassian's *Conferences*

During this same period, John Cassian (ca. 360–ca. 430) made a series of visits to the Egyptian desert in the company of a friend named Germanus.[16] Cassian recorded their conversations with notable Egyptian ascetics in the form of two treatises, the *Institutes*

---

[14] Origen places the same emphasis on assiduity in his Letter 4, to Gregory Thaumaturgos, cited in "Lectio divina," DS 9:473; translated by Michael Slusser in *Fathers of the Church* 98:192, quoted by Studzinski, *Reading to Live,* 29: "You, therefore, my true son, devote yourself first and foremost to reading the holy Scriptures; but devote yourself. For when we read holy things we need much attentiveness, lest we say or think something hasty about them. . . . And when you devote yourself to the divine reading, uprightly and with a faith fixed firmly on God seek the meaning of the divine words which is hidden from most people."

[15] Concerning Jerome's lifelong struggle to realize the monastic ideal, see J. N. D. Kelly, *Jerome: His Life, Writings, and Controversies* (New York: Harper and Row, 1975), chapters 6 and 12–13.

[16] For a study of Cassian's life and writings, see Columba Stewart, *Cassian the Monk* (New York and Oxford: Oxford University Press, 1998).

and the *Conferences*. These writings summarize the accumulated experience of Egyptian spirituality, "both in the coenobium and in the desert," from which Cassian derives a program of instruction for all who would enter the monastic profession. Particularly in the *Conferences*, Cassian discusses the reading of the Scriptures as a spiritual discipline inseparable from the way of life which surrounds it.[17]

Monasticism is a "profession," Cassian insists, analogous as such to farming or business. Monasticism proposes an ultimate goal (*telos*), which is the attainment of the kingdom of heaven; to achieve that, the monk must seek an intermediate goal (*scopos*), which is purity of heart. Like a target which focuses the aim of an archer, the *scopos* orients all of the monk's actions and thoughts. For its sake virtues are cultivated: discernment, humility, abnegation of self-will; for its sake also the monk undertakes fasts, vigils, labors, and most particularly reading and prayer. These activities are not valued for themselves. Echoing perhaps Augustine's distinction between things to be used and those to be enjoyed, Cassian defines ascetic practices, among which is reading, as tools for use, subordinated always to the purpose they serve.

Handling the tools expertly is a matter of professionalism acquired through training and assiduous practice. One begins with rudiments, as children first learn the alphabet by tracing letters from wax patterns (Conf 10.10.1; SCh 54:85; cf. Jerome's Letter 107), and then learn to form syllables, words, and sentences, before moving on to rhetoric and philosophy (Conf 10.8.2; SCh 54:82–83). Spirituality begins with the cultivation of virtues and repression of vices; this category of discipline is labeled with the Greek term *praktikē* (Conf 14.2–6; SCh 54:184–87). From there the monk may ascend to the level of the *theoretikē*, that of spiritual knowledge (Conf 14.8–9; SCh 189–92). This heading is subdivided into historical interpretation, tropology, allegory, and anagogy—a fourfold system of scriptural exegesis, one of the earliest on re-

---

[17] All English quotations of the *Conferences* are from Ramsey, silently emended where necessary.

cord.[18] But the theoretical level is not reached by a merely intellectual inquiry: "Whoever wishes to attain to the *theoretikē* must first pursue practical knowledge with all his strength and power. For the *praktikē* can be possessed without the theoretical, but the theoretical can never be seized without the practical" (Conf 14.2.1; SCh 54:184; Ramsey 505).

In the earlier stages of spiritual progress, reading serves to fortify the mind against the distracting "thoughts" which continually invade it.[19] It is the nature of the mind to be always preoccupied—like a millstone kept spinning by the rush of water—but it is in the power of the supervisor of the mill to decide what to grind. By constant reading, memorization, and recitation of the Scriptures, the mind maintains its orientation toward the purity which is its goal.

That state of focused spiritual awareness continually slips away from us, Cassian finds. Each time we try to recover it, there is a delay of searching, and "before any spiritual vision is brought forth, our heart's attentiveness, already conceived, vanishes" (Conf 10.8.5; SCh 54:83–84). To maintain the grasp, "Abba Isaac" in the tenth Conference prescribes continual repetition, day and night, of the formula from Psalm 69:1 (70:1): "O God, make speed to save me; O Lord, make haste to help me." The verse serves as a shield against attack; it expresses watchfulness, consciousness of one's own fragility, an absolute dependence on God, and—most importantly—the

---

[18] Cassian illustrates the concepts first with reference to the fourth chapter of Galatians, and second in an interpretation of Jerusalem; that is, the city of the Jews according to history; allegorically, it is the church of Christ; anagogically, it is the heavenly city of God; and finally, tropologically, it is the human soul (Conf 14.8.4; SCh 54:189; Ramsey, 510). He then offers other examples of allegory, anagogy, tropology, and historical exposition, citing different scriptural texts for each. Modern readers have noted that his ordering of these terms seems to fluctuate. "What we have here is more than a hesitation on the part of the author or an uncertainty on the part of the reader. There is real ambiguity here," de Lubac comments (*Exégèse médiévale:* 1.1:192; Sebanc 1:137). "It is obvious," writes Stewart, "that his heart is not in demonstrating how to apply the fourfold system" (*Cassian the Monk*, 94).

[19] Cassian's concern with thoughts (*logismos*) reflects the unacknowledged influence of Evagrius. See Simon Tugwell, *Ways of Imperfection: An Exploration of Christian Spirituality* (Springfield, IL: Templegate, 1985), 25–36.

assurance of God's presence, implied in the call to him as one's protector (Conf 10.10.3; SCh 54:86). The verse does perfectly express Cassian's root concept of purity. It enacts the rejection of the overrich "abundance" of thoughts, reaching rather toward spiritual and intellectual "poverty," that of the first gospel beatitude (Conf 10.11.1; SCh 54:90–91; see Matt 5:3).

Memorization of readings and constant review must continue until whole books of Scripture are retained. Cassian values repetition—emblematized by the child tracing and retracing the wax patterns of the letters—first, because the mind must in any case be occupied and so shielded from distraction, and secondly, more profoundly, because what is sought is retention—the taking possession of knowledge, securely grasped, stored in the depths of the personality.[20] Conceptual understanding is secondary. That comes later, mysteriously, over time, after the labor of memorization has been completed. Especially, Cassian suggests, at night, when we are free from the day's business, "free from every seductive deed or sight, silently meditating . . . at rest and as it were immersed in the stupor of sleep, there will be revealed an understanding of hidden meanings that we did not grasp even slightly when we were awake" (Conf 14.10.4; SCh 54:196–97; Ramsey 515). True understanding of Scripture cannot come, in any case, from hearing explanations offered by another person or even from meditation on a text which remains external. One cannot hold on to anything spiritual that comes to one "prefabricated," so to speak, or by chance. One learns truly—that is, permanently—only by one's own efforts (Conf 14.13.3; SCh 54:200). Ideally, with *studium* and *industria*, through repetitive memorization and meditation, the text eventually shapes the mind in its own image (Conf 14.10.2; SCh 54:196).

For Cassian—and later for Gregory the Great, as we have seen—the converse is also true: "As our mind is increasingly renewed by this study, the face of Scripture will also begin to be renewed, and the beauty of a more sacred understanding will somehow grow with the person making progress" (Conf 14.11.1; SCh 54:196; Ramsey, 515: *Crescente autem per hoc studium in-*

---

[20] Modern foreign language pedagogy contains a similar concept, that of "over-learning," e.g., in repetitive drills, in order to gain confidence in speaking.

nouatione mentis nostrae etiam scripturarum facies incipiet innouari, et sacratioris intellegentiae pulchritudo quodammodo cum proficiente proficient). Is he suggesting that the Scripture itself changes as the person changes? Of course, the objective text on the page would presumably remain unchanged; what is renewed is the "face of Scripture": the perception by the reader of the "beauty of a more sacred understanding." Looking beyond the objective text, Cassian conceives the Scripture as a living word, capable of responding to the experience of the reader in an intimate dialogue.

As this process continues and deepens, Cassian anticipates that the pious mind will return to even the most familiar verses not with boredom but with pleasure, as to well-aged, sweet wines stored in deep recesses of the mind, which brings them bubbling up "like an unceasing fountain out of the springs of experience and the watercourses of virtue, they will pour forth continual streams as though from the abyss of your heart" (Conf 14.13.5; SCh 54:201; Ramsey 518: *ut uina quaedam suaue olentia et laetificantia cor hominis, cum sensuum canitie et patientiae fuerint uetustate decocta, cum magna sui fragrantia de uase tui pectoris proferentur, et tamquam perennis fons de experientiae uenis et inriguis uirtutum meatibus redundabunt fluentaque continua uelut de quadam abysso tui cordis effundent).* Cassian now quotes Proverbs 5:15: "Drink water from your own cistern." When the texts have been perfectly and completely internalized, they become one's own. The psalms in particular are read then as though they were directed to one personally (*ad suam personam aestimet eos fuisse directos*); they become the expressions of one's own experience. Through a daily fulfillment (*quotidie geri*) one becomes not only a reader but their true and final author:

> Omnes quoque psalmorum adfectus in se recipiens ita incipiet decantare, ut eos non tamquam a propheta conpositos, sed uelut a se editos, quasi orationem propriam profunda cordis compunctione depromat uel certe ad suam personam aestimet eos fuisse directos, eorumque sententias non tunc tantummodo per prophetam aut in propheta fuisse conpletas, sed in se cotidie geri implerique cognoscat. Tunc enim scripturae diuinae nobis clarius perpatescunt, et quodammodo earum uenae medullaeque panduntur, quando experientia nostra earum non tantum percipit, sed etiam praeuenit notionem, sensusque uerborum

non per expositionem nobis, sed per documenta reserantur. Eundem namque recipientes cordis affectum, quo quisque decantatus uel conscriptus est psalmus, uelut autores ejus facti, praecedemus magis intellectum ipsius quam sequemur; id est ut prius dictorum uirtutem quam notitiam colligentes, quid in nobis gestum sit, uel cotidianis geratur incursibus superueniente eorum meditatione quodammodo recordemur. . . . Omnes namque hos adfectus in Psalmis inuenimus expressos, ut ea quae incurrerint, uelut in speculo purissimo peruidentes, efficacius agnoscamus et ita magistris adfectibus eruditi non ut audita, sed tamquam perspecta palpemus, nec tamquam memoriae commendata, sed uelut ipsi rerum naturae insita de interno cordis parturiamus adfectu, ut eorum sensus non textu lectionis, sed experientia praecedente penetremus.

Taking into himself then all the dispositions [*affectus*] of the psalms, he will begin to repeat them and to treat them in his profound compunction of heart not as if they were composed by the prophet but as if they were his own utterances and his own prayer; and will certainly take them as aimed at himself, and will recognize that the words were not only fulfilled formerly by or in the person of the prophet, but that they are fulfilled and carried out daily in his own case. For divine Scripture is clearer and its inmost organs, so to speak, are revealed to us when our experience not only perceives but anticipates its thought, and the meanings of the words are disclosed to us not by exegesis but by proof [*non per expositione sed per documenta*]. When we have the same disposition in our heart with which each psalm was sung or written down, then we shall become like its author, grasping its significance beforehand rather than afterward. That is, we first take in the power of what is said, rather than the knowledge. . . . For we find all of [our] dispositions expressed in the psalms, so that we may see whatever occurs as in a very clear mirror and recognize it more effectively. Having been instructed in this way, with our dispositions for our teachers, we shall feel things in our grasp rather than hearing them, and from the inner disposition of the heart we shall bring forth not what has been committed to memory but what is implanted in the very nature of things. Thus we shall penetrate its meaning not through the written text but with experience leading the way. (Conf.10.11.4–6; SCh 54:92–93; Ramsey 384–85)

Cassian's vocabulary must be interpreted with care and in context. He develops terms for subjectivity: *experientia*, "experience, lived understanding," and—especially difficult for the translator—*affectus*, "disposition, feeling." An *affectus* is "received" by the heart; it is the way we are psychologically "affected" or "moved" by something, positively or negatively. *Affectus* leads the will to act. Knowledge (*notio*, *notitia*) and understanding (*intellectus*) are conceived in the mind, but what we "take in" from experience is something deeper: it is the power (*virtus*) of that knowledge, felt even before we receive it intellectually (Conf 10.11.5: *prius dictorum virtutem quam notitiam colligentes*). Cassian engages us in a reciprocal, specular dialogue with the text, in which understanding comes about as one recognizes one's own (previous) experience in its mirror. But this perception is clearer than before, for the mirror is not at all dark but indeed most pure. That dialogue leads beyond subjectivity, beyond the rediscovery of memorized texts, to a perception of what is "implanted in the very nature of things." And finally, at the deepest level of mystical reading, Cassian describes a state of absolutely uncorrupted "fiery" prayer, which is not expressed in images or words or phrases:

> Non solum nullius imaginis occupatur intuitu, sed etiam nulla uocis, nulla uerborum prosecutione distinguitur, ignita uero mentis intentione per ineffabilem cordis excessum inexplebili spiritus alacritate profertur, quamque mens extra omnes sensus ac uisibiles effecta materies, gemitibus inenarrabilibus atque suspiriis profundit ad deum.

> [That incorruptible prayer] is not only not laid hold of by the sight of some image, but it cannot be grasped by any word or phrase. Rather, once the mind's attentiveness has been set ablaze, it is called forth in an unspeakable ecstasy of heart and with an insatiable gladness of spirit, and the mind, having transcended all feelings and visible matter, pours it out to God with unutterable groans and sighs. (Conf 10.11.6; SCh 54:93; Ramsey 385)

The mystical communion with the Scriptures can only be reached, Cassian reiterates, through the purification of the mind. Conceptual comprehension and facility with words do not add up to understanding and do not qualify one to teach. John, a young monk (presumably Cassian himself), is warned that his love of reading could well come to nothing if it were driven only by pride. He should not venture to speak up or raise questions during a conference unless absolutely necessary: "No one should presume to teach in words what he has not previously done in deed" (Conf 14.9.4; SCh 54:194). What erudite Jews, heretics, and other "unclean" people achieve is a *pseudonumon*, a "knowledge in name only." Not even assiduity in memorization of the Scriptures will serve, for there one becomes subject to a purely textual distractibility when a passage on which one attempts to reflect reminds one of another passage, "and so the mind is constantly whirling from psalm to psalm, leaping from a gospel text to a reading from the Apostle . . . having become a mere toucher and taster of spiritual meanings and not a begetter and possessor of them" (Conf 10.13.1; SCh 54:94; Ramsey 385–86). The purified mind, on the contrary, becomes capable of stability, of permanent retention of texts and meanings. "The biblical text dissolves into direct apprehension of its spiritual meaning, and finally even that meaning yields to the realities it signifies."[21] There is a reciprocity between the reader and the text by which both are ultimately constituted, created, (re) shaped. What Cassian calls theoretical knowledge—contemplation—is what they together realize and perform.

Reading in the Monastery

In Cassian's *Conferences*, we find many fundamental themes that will underpin the medieval development of *lectio divina*: the emphasis, first of all, on repetition and memorization of scriptural texts; the faith that these verbal learning activities would promote an ethical internalization; the sense of a dynamic, reciprocal interaction between reader and writing, one which could affect not only the reader but also the Scripture itself; the call to the reader to rewrite, to re-author as it were, the Scripture in lived application; and finally, the transcendent overflow of reading into mystical prayer. These concepts recur in the works of Gregory the Great, and they continue to resonate throughout the continuity

---

[21] Stewart, *Cassian the Monk*, 113.

of writing that links Gregory to Bernard of Clairvaux and other twelfth-century masters.

We need now to look at their implementation, which took place mainly in the monastery, from the fifth century onward. Who were the monastic readers? What was the level or mode of their literacy? What techniques of reading did they employ? At what times and in what places? How were texts made available to them, and in what material form? These are practical questions, whose answers would lead us, to some degree, into the immediacy of the reading experience theorized by Cassian and by the writers who followed him.

The monastic rules provide glimpses of reading activity in an institutional context. The earliest that has survived is the Rule of Pachomius (d. ca. 346) in Egypt, translated by Jerome (404).[22] The *Asceticon* of Basil in Cappadocia dates from a few years later, from just before Basil's death in 379.[23] Augustine composed rules for men and women (ca. 397).[24] More than thirty rules are attested before the end of the seventh century.[25] Of these, the most influential was, of course, the Rule of Saint Benedict, composed ca. 530. These documents have been repeatedly scanned by religious scholars seeking to clarify the antecedents of modern monastic practice[26] and also by historians of education on the secular, academic

[22] Jerome, *Translatio regulae sancti Pachomii*, PL 23:61–86.

[23] For English translations, see W. K. L. Clarke, *The Ascetical Works of St. Basil* (London: SPCK, 1925), cited in *Rule of Saint Benedict 1980*, ed. Fry, xxiii, 30–34; Anna M. Silvas, *The Asketikon of St. Basil the Great* (Oxford: Oxford UP, 2005).

[24] George Lawless, ed., *Augustine of Hippo and his Monastic Rule* (Oxford: Clarendon Press, 1987).

[25] Adalbert de Vogüé, "*Sub regula vel abbate*: A study of the Theological Significance of the Ancient Monastic Rules," in *Rule and Life: An Interdisciplinary Symposium*, ed. M. Basil Pennington, CS 12 (Kalamazoo, MI: Cistercian Publications, 1971), 21–64.

[26] Leclercq, *Love of Learning*, summarizes in chapter 1 the role of culture and education in the Benedictine monastery. See also more recent writings by Adalbert de Vogüé, "*Sub regula vel abate*," and *The Rule of Saint Benedict: A Doctrinal and Spiritual Commentary*, trans. John Baptist Hasbrouck, CS 54 (Kalamazoo, MI: Cistercian Publications, 1983). See also Benedetto Calati, "La 'lectio divina' nella tradizione monastica benedittina," *Benedictina* 28 (1981), 407–38.

side.[27] As we look more closely at reading practices, recent studies of literacy and paleography will also need to be taken into account.[28] My hope in surveying this material is to integrate in some measure these normally separated points of view.

The opening paragraph in Benedict's Prologue addresses the monk as a member of a militia "armed with the strong and noble weapons of obedience" (RB Prol. 3). The coenobitic monk is called to "serve under a rule and an abbot" (RB 1.2: *militans sub regula uel abate*). Another institutional concept, however, suggests itself toward the end of the Prologue: the monastery will be "a school for the Lord's service" (RB Prol. 45: *dominici schola servitii*). This phrase, often quoted, has prompted various interpretations.[29] Benedict's principal concern, doubtless, is training for the "battle of holy obedience" (RB Prol. 39: *sanctae . . . oboedientiae militanda*)[30] rather than humanistic Christian education. But subsequent chapters of the Rule convey the view of reading as an essential stage in that battle or that service. As Jean Leclercq asserts, "the Rule of St. Benedict supposes learned monks. . . . One of the principal occupations of the monk is the *lectio divina*, which includes meditation: *meditare aut legere*. Consequently one must, in a monastery, possess books, know how to write them and read them, and therefore, if it be necessary, learn how to read."[31]

---

[27] Pierre Riché summarizes monastic education, with copious citations from the rules, in chapter 4 of *Education and Culture in the Barbarian West*, 100–122. See also Mary Carruthers, *The Book of Memory: A Study of Memory in Medieval Culture* (Cambridge, UK: Cambridge University Press, 1990), especially chapter 5, "Memory and the Ethics of Reading," 156–88.

[28] Brian Stock's cultural studies in *The Implications of Literacy: Written Language and Models of Interpretation in the Eleventh and Twelfth Centuries* (Princeton, NJ: Princeton University Press, 1983), and *Listening for the Text: On the Uses of the Past* (Baltimore, MD: Johns Hopkins University Press, 1990), have been complemented by the paleographical researches of Paul Saenger, especially "Silent Reading" and *Space Between Words*; see also Michael T. Clanchy, *From Memory to Written Record: England 1066–1307* (Oxford, UK and Cambridge, MA: Blackwell, 2nd ed. 1993).

[29] For discussion and references, see Pierre Riché, *Education and Culture in the Barbarian West*, 110.

[30] On the translation of this phrase, see Timothy Fry's note to RB Prol. 39 (*RB 1980*, 164).

[31] Leclercq, *Love of Learning*, 15–17.

Omnes litteras discant.[32] The rules agree that all monks and nuns must learn to read. The Rule of Pachomius, in Jerome's translation, states that no one should be admitted to the monastery who had not been taught letters, and that instruction would be completed if necessary within the walls. As a minimum, every monk should know the psalms and the New Testament.[33] Likewise, according to the Rule of Ferreolus (sixth century), "No one who would claim the name of monk may be allowed to be ignorant of letters. Let him hold all of the psalms in his memory, and let him not use any excuse to prevent him from being occupied with that study."[34] The point of the exercise is stressed even before we pass through the gate: it is not actually the ability to read in the abstract which is required; the monk will be encouraged not to consult a variety of texts but rather to study Scripture intensively and commit sizeable portions of it to memory.

The Rule of the Master allots three hours a day to reading, instruction, and memorization drills. In winter, from Prime to Terce, boys and illiterate adults are to learn their letters while other monks study the Psalms: "during these three hours they are to read and listen to one another, and take turns teaching letters

[32] Caesarius of Arles, *Regula ad virgines* 17 (PL 67:1109). Cf. Aurelian, *Regula ad monachos* 32 (PL 68:391) and *Regula ad virgines* 26 (PL 68:402); Ferreolus, *Regula* 11 (PL 66: 963–64).

[33] *Regula sancti Pachomii*, trans. Jerome, 139–40 (PL 23:78): *Et si litteras ignoraverit, hora prima, et tertia, et sexta vadet ad eum qui docere potest, et qui ei fuerit delegatus, et stabit ante illum, et discet studiosissime, cum omni gratiarum actione. Postea vero scribentur ei elementa, syllabae, verba, ac nomina; et etiam nolens legere compelletur, et omnino nullus erit in monasterio, qui non discat litteras, et de Scripturis aliquid teneat: qui minimum usque ad novum Testamentum et Psalterium* ("And if he is ignorant of letters, at the first, third, and sixth hours, he will go to the person appointed to teach him, and stand before him, and learn most studiously, giving thanks. Thereafter the basic elements will be written out for him, syllables, words, and and names; and even if he is unwilling, he will be required to read. And there will be no one in the monastery who does not learn letters; and let him learn something of the Scriptures, at a minimum the New Testament and the Psalms").

[34] Ferreolus, *Regula* 11 (PL 66:963): *Omnis qui nomen vult monachi vindicare, litteras ei ignorare non liceat. Quin etiam psalmos totos memoriter teneat: neque se quacumque excusatione defendat, quominus sancto hoc studio capiatur.*

and the psalms to those who do not know them" (RM 50.15).[35]
During summer afternoons, "some monks are to read, others listen, others learn and teach letters, others study psalms which they
have transcribed. When they have mastered and memorized them
perfectly, let their deans take them to the abbot to recite by heart
the psalm or canticle or lesson of any kind" (RM 50.63–65). This
picture corresponds closely to that of the "textual community"
drawn by Brian Stock in his observation of eleventh-century
heresies: "These textual communities were not entirely composed
of literates. The minimal requirement was just one literate, the
interpres, who understood a set of texts and was able to pass on
his message. . . . Individuals belonging to textual communities
existed in a halfway house between literacy and non-literacy."[36]
Mutatis mutandis, in both early and later religious communities,
"literacy" and "non-literacy" (or "orality") will be found in similarly nuanced states and transitional behaviors.

Reading normally alternates with manual labor in the monastic daily schedule. The Rule of Saint Benedict (RB 48.3-4)
specifies that in the summertime, manual work takes place in
the early morning and reading during the heat of the day, "from
the fourth hour until the time of Sext." In winter the pattern is
reversed, with reading assigned to the morning and labor to later
hours (RB 48.10-11). We have seen that the Rule of the Master
follows a similar *horarium*, as do all the other sixth-century rules.[37]

---

[35] *The Rule of the Master*, trans. Luke Eberle, CS 6 (Kalamazoo, MI: Cistercian
Publications, 1977), chapter 50: "Daily Labor at Various Times According to the
Season," 208–12. Critical edition: *La règle du maître*, tome 2, Chapitres 11–95,
ed. and trans. Adalbert de Vogüé, SCh 106 (Paris: Éditions du Cerf, 1964). The
Latin text reads: *Ergo in his tribus horis inuicem et legant et audiant, uicibus litteras
et psalmos ignorantibus ostendant* (RM 50.15; SCh 106:224). . . . *Tunc ordinatione
praepositorum suorum sequestratae a se per loca diuersae decadae, alii legant, alii audiant,
alii litteras discant et doceant, alii psalmos, quos habent superpositos, meditentur. Nam cum
eos maturauerint et memoria perfecte tenuerint, adducti a praepositis suis ipsum psalmum
aut canticum seu quamuis lectionem memoriter abbati restituant* (RM 50.63–65; SCh
106:235–36).

[36] Brian Stock, *Listening for the Text*, 23.

[37] Adalbert de Vogüé, *The Rule of Saint Benedict: A Doctrinal and Spiritual Commentary*, 241-2, comments as follows: "Three quarters of the day are assigned

Reading also is mandated in all seasons during the rest period after the midday meal. It is specially emphasized during the forty days of Lent, when, according to Benedict, each monk is to receive a book from the library and read the whole of it straight through (RB 48.14-15).[38] Caesarius of Arles addresses a sermon to his monks on Lenten reading, exhorting them to study Scripture in their cells and labor at memorization, with no excuses accepted for failing to do so.[39]

Normally, reading was performed out loud and in groups. Accordingly, the Rule of the Master specifies that the various deaneries (groups of ten) be separated during the reading and instruction period in order to avoid "having the entire community crowded together and disturbing one another with their voices; let one of the ten in each place do the reading while the rest of the group listen" (RM 50.10). All the rules call for reading aloud at meal times. The monks are directed to listen attentively so that as the body is nourished by food, the spirit will likewise be nourished by the Word of God.[40] Even private, individual reading was done aloud, as an oft-quoted passage from Benedict's chapter 48 implies: *Post sextam autem surgentes a mensa pausent in lecta sua cum omni silentio, aut forte qui voluerit legere sibi sic legat, ut alium non*

---

to work, and one quarter to reading. But this last part is not considered last in importance, but rather the first: the best hours of the day are reserved to *lectio*. Moreover, although reading properly so-called occupies only a limited time, it is prolonged during the other occupations by the exercise of 'meditation.' . . . Thus the entire day rings with the divine Word. The part assigned to it seems secondary, but is in fact limitless."

[38] *In quibus diebus quadragesimae accipiant omnes singulos codices de bibliotheca, quos per ordinem ex integro legant* (RB 48.15). A. Mundó, "Bibliotheca, Bible et Lecture de carême d'après S. Benoit," *Revue Bénédictine* 60 (1950), 65–92, finds that what is meant by *bibliotheca* here is the nine sections of the Bible. Smaragdus's ninth-century commentary on the Rule of Saint Benedict clarifies, however: *De bibliotheca dicit, id est, de cellula ubi libri reconduntur. Nam quod Graece bibliotheca, Latine repositio librorum dicitur* (PL 102:886). See also Pierre Riché, *Education and Culture*, 119, n.133.

[39] Caesarius of Arles, Sermo 238, *Sancti Caesarii Arlatensis sermones*, CCSL 104:949–53.

[40] See, for example, Caesarius' *Regula ad monachos* 9 (PL 67:1100), and his *Regula ad virgines* 16 (PL 67:1109); see also Isidore of Seville, *Regula monachorum* 9.2 (PL 83:878).

inquietet (RB 48.5: "After Sext and their meal, [the brothers] may rest on their beds in complete silence; should a brother wish to read privately, let him do so, but without disturbing the others"). The same implication has been drawn from Augustine's observation in the *Confessions* (6.3) that his teacher, Ambrose, often read silently, either in order to avoid questioning from onlookers or simply in order to spare his voice; Augustine's comment suggests that Ambrose's behavior was exceptional and that reading aloud was in fact the more usual practice.[41]

It was, in fact, indispensable in the *first* reading of a text (*praelectio*), as a step toward understanding. Paul Saenger's studies of late antique manuscripts have shown that from the second century CE onward, the *interpuncta* that had been placed between words during the classical period disappeared, leaving the reader to contend with unseparated text (*scriptura continua*).

> The typical Roman book contained neither punctuation, distinction between upper- and lowercase letters, nor word separation. . . . The Romans developed no clear conception of the word as a unit of meaning. Instead, Roman grammarians considered the letter and syllable to be basic to reading. The Roman reader, reading aloud to others or softly to himself, approached the text syllable by syllable in order to recover the words and sentences conveying the meaning of the text.[42]

[41] This passage continues to be much discussed. Mary Carruthers, *The Book of Memory*, 170–1, recalls the seminal article by Josef Balogh, "'Voces paginarum': Beiträge zur Geschichte des lauten Lesens und Schreibens," *Philologus* 82 (1927): 84–109, 202–40, who refers in turn to Nietzsche. Carruthers comments, "In a scholarly tradition going back to the late nineteenth century, Augustine's response is characterized as one of 'surprise and wonder' at Ambrose's 'strange' habit. I do not find these traits in what Augustine says, however. Instead this seems to me a sympathetic portrait of a very busy man's efforts to make time for the kind of scholarly study that refreshes him" (171). For Carruthers, Ambrose's silence indicates that the reader has withdrawn into meditation. Brian Stock, *Augustine the Reader*, 61–2, adds that "Augustine was desperate to escape from himself. . . . Viewing the bishop, even at a distance, he saw something that he had apparently not seen before—the silent decoding of written signs as a means of withdrawing from the world and of focusing attention on one's inner life. . . . [S]ilent reading in [*Confessions*] 6.3 is an exemplum of self-reliance within a scheme of reliance on God."

[42] Paul Saenger, "Silent Reading," 370–71. For an overview of this history see the same scholar's *Space Between Words*. In his introduction and in chapters

The situation Saenger describes held true through the end of sixth century; it was only from the seventh century onward that "canonical word separation" was reintroduced by English and Irish scribes and became normal in Europe thereafter. In the era of Saint Benedict, a monk making his first approach to an unpunctuated text, formatted in *scriptura continua*, would undoubtedly have needed to vocalize in order to read.

Jerome, it is true, had sought to remedy this difficulty as early as the late fourth century. In his translation of the book of Isaiah, he "provides for the benefit of the reader" (*nos quoque utilitati legentium providentes*) a system of division *per cola et commata* that he had previously observed in copies of prose writings by Cicero and Demosthenes, in which each line of text represents a phrase or a sentence.[43] The result is not unlike the text layout given to the major prophets in printed Bibles today. Cassiodorus expresses admiration for Jerome's technique (*Institutiones* 1, preface, and 15.12) but testifies that many of the manuscripts available to his community were not so divided. Accordingly, he calls for scribes to reread and correct these and directs them to introduce small points to set off sections of text. In this connection, he comments eloquently on the difficulties and the beauties of correct oral reading:

> But in order to add visible embellishment to all these things, place marks of punctuation [*posituras*], which the Greeks call *theses*, that is, small, round points [*puncta brevissima pariter et rotunda*] . . . in every section of the text, because they make the discourse bright and clear when, as is explained below, they shine from their appropriate places. What a thing it is to pass without stumbling [*inoffenso gradu*] through the most holy thoughts, to enter into an interior understanding of the most edifying precepts; to set properly the periods of the modulated voice, and to divide the composition into members in such a way that, with their parts so perceived, they become beautiful!
> . . . These punctuation marks or points are paths of meaning

---

2–3, Saenger describes various early word-spacing formats and punctuation marks used to break up the *scriptura continua*.

[43] Jerome announces the system in the preface to his translation (PL 28:771). For a photograph of a page laid out in this manner, see Saenger, *Space Between Words*, 16.

and lights of discourse, for the readers are taught by them as well as if they were being instructed by the most famous expositors. (*Institutiones* 15.12)[44]

It is an apparent paradox, which Saenger draws on neurophysiological research to explain, that unseparated text causes the reader to stumble, whereas punctuation and spacing allow him to understand and so proceed fluently (*inoffenso gradu*). Cassiodorus refers here to the difficulty of determining grammatical constructions, especially, of course, in texts of any theological complexity. With spacing and/or punctuation, however, the reader is enabled to phrase the passage correctly, and so may proceed into an inner experience of its meaning (*venasque praeceptorum saluberrimas subtiliter introire*). That leads, for Cassiodorus, to a perception of beauty, which will be rendered in oral performance.

Of course, reading aloud could strain the vocal cords, as in the case of Ambrose, according to Augustine. This may be one reason why Quintilian and other ancient authorities recommend reading softly rather than out loud, articulating with the tongue under one's breath.[45] According to Isidore of Seville, such quiet reading would promote understanding even better than does reading in full voice: "Quiet reading [*lectio tacita*] is more acceptable to the senses than reading aloud; the understanding is better instructed when the reading voice is quiet, and the tongue moves in silence. For reading out loud [*clare legendo*] tires the body and dulls the sharpness of the voice."[46]

From the available witnesses, at any rate, we gather that oral pronunciation, in full voice or softly, was normally necessary at the

---

[44] *Sed ut his omnibus addere videaris ornatum, posituras, quas Graeci thesis vocant, id est puncta brevissima pariter et rotunda . . . singulis quibusque pone capitibus, quoniam illustrem et planissimam faciunt orationem quando, sicut inferius exponitur, suis locis aptata resplendent. Quale est enim inoffenso gradu per sensus ire sanctissimos, venasque praeceptorum saluberrimas subtiliter introire; terminos suos modulatae voci competenter affigere, totamque dictionem sic per membra dividere ut suis partibus considerata pulchrescant! . . . Positurae seu puncta quasi quaedam viae sunt sensuum et lumina dictionum, quae sic lectores dociles faciunt tamquam si clarissimis expositoribus imbuantur* (*Cassiodori Senatoris Institutiones*, ed. R. A. B. Mynors [Oxford, UK: Clarendon Press, 1937], 48).

[45] *Institutio oratoria* 11.2.34; see Carruthers, *Book of Memory*, 74.

[46] Isidore of Seville, *Sententiae* 3.14.9, PL 83:689.

beginning of the reading process and throughout all of its subsequent phases. Augustine uses the verb *pronuntio* to mean "construe" or "inflect" (*De doctrina* 3.6; CCSL 32:79–80), as in cases where the reader must determine whether a phrase is meant as a statement or a question. "Pronunciation" is again needed in order to determine whether a Latin vowel is long or short (*De doctrina* 3.7; CCSL 32:81). Pronunciation, in all senses of the word, will continue to be necessary as the reader proceeds to the next phase, that of *meditatio*. The meaning of this important term has been much discussed. In classical usage, the verb *meditari* (or *meditare*) meant "consider, reflect," in the sense of preparing oneself to do something.[47] More specifically, Cicero uses it to mean "rehearse," as in the famous description of the orator, Demosthenes, who overcame stuttering by practicing a repetitive drill: *Perfecit meditando, ut nemo planius esse locutus putaretur* (*De oratore* 1.260). This technical meaning is taken over by the earliest monastic rules, where it means chiefly repetition, recitation, and memorization. *Meditatio* takes place in the memorization *process* while the text is being learned, alone or in groups, and also in psalmody and the recitation of previously memorized texts, while the monk is at work, away from the written page.[48] By extension, the term acquires the internalized, reflective dimensions conveyed by the modern concept of "meditation," as derived from the psalms.[49] Isidore of Seville and others thus remind us that one should "meditate in the heart what is sung in the mouth."[50] Even there, meditation is usually anchored

---

[47] Jean Leclercq, *Love of Learning*, 20.

[48] Concerning these two senses of the term, see Adalbert de Vogüé, "Les deux fonctions de la méditation dans les Règles monastiques anciennes," *Revue d'Histoire de la Spiritualité* 51 (1975): 3–16.

[49] For example: *In lege eius meditetur die ac nocte* (Ps 1:2: "And on his law he meditates day and night"); *Et erunt ut complaceant eloquia oris mei, et meditatio cordis mei in conspectu tuo semper* (Ps 18:15 [19:14]: "Let the words of my mouth and the meditation of my heart be acceptable in thy sight"); *Memor fui dierum antiquorum, meditatus sum in omnibus operibus tuis, in factis manuum tuarum meditabar* (Ps 142:5 [143:5]: "I remember the days of old, I meditate on all that thou hast done; I muse on what thy hands have wrought").

[50] *Regula monachorum* 6.2 (PL 83:876): "*Hoc meditetur corde quod psallitur ore;*" *Regula Tarna[n]tensis* 8.13 (PL 66:981): "*Ea plantentur in corde, quae proferuntur in voce;*" see also Adalbert de Vogüé, "Les deux fonctions," 7, nn. 22 and 23.

to a text and not allowed to wander freely. We will need to return to this idea. But much of early monastic spirituality is contained in the originally narrow range of meanings, which should not be prematurely overstepped.[51]

Strictly construed, *meditatio* is all but synonymous with reading, as in Benedict's phrase, *meditare aut legere* (RB 48.23). It is frequently described as "rumination"—the activity of chewing the cud, associated with clean animals (Lev 11:3, Deut 14:6).[52] Jean Leclercq vividly expounds this tradition, synthesizing various meanings of the metaphor (see above, pp. 7–8).

Coming and going from his cell to services or meals, or constantly while at work, the monk repeats verses, ceaselessly "turning them over in memory" (*volvens memoriter*).[53] "Monks at work should recite or sing [*meditari aut psallere debent*] in order to alleviate their labor with the delight of poems or of the word of God."[54]And

---

[51] All modern historians have noted the ancient meanings of *meditatio*, as opposed to "meditation," and yet the distinction is often blurred. Brian Stock, *After Augustine: The Meditative Reader and the Text* (Philadelphia, PA: University of Pennsylvania Press, 2001), 15, associates *meditatio* with silence, misunderstanding, I believe, the essentially oral nature of this activity: "In Augustine, and especially in Gregory the Great, meditative silence implied a nonperceptible presence . . . [and] the text of the Bible, in which the divine being was thought to reside, was silent until it was read, and silent again after the oral reading was finished and the meditation had begun. To proceed from *lectio* to *meditatio* was thus to ascend from the senses to the mind." Mary Carruthers, *The Book of Memory*, 171–3, similarly blurs the concept of *meditatio* with reference to Augustine and Ambrose.

[52] Caesarius of Arles, in his *Sermones*, frequently evokes this image; for example, in 99.3, he finishes the sermon thus: *Et ut haec . . . vestrae memoriae inhaerant, et ea velut munda animalia in ore cordis revolvere et spiritaliter ruminare possitis, breviter recapitulationem facimur . . .*; cf. 88.6, 114.6, 117.6, etc. In a work that is devoted to the poet Caedmon, Bede uses the same image in chapter 4.24 of his *History of the English Church and People*, rev. ed., trans. Leo Sherley-Price (London: Penguin Books, 1968), 252: "So Caedmon stored up in his memory all that he learned, and like one of the clean animals chewing the cud, turned it into such melodious verse that his delightful renderings turned his instructors into auditors."

[53] Rule of Pachomius, chapter 6, trans. Jerome; cf. 3, 13, 28, 50 (PL 23:65–72).

[54] Isidore of Seville, *Regula monachorum* 5.5 (PL 83:874): *Monachi operantes meditari aut psallere debent, ut carminis verbique Dei delectatione consolentur ipsum laborem.* A PL footnote cites Augustine, *De opere monachorum*, 17, as a source of this passage.

monks sent out into the fields to tend flocks are directed to recite the psalms, just as other monks do.[55]

> Let the ploughman with the plough handle in his hand sing Alleluia; the sweating reaper should entertain himself with psalms; and as the vintner trims the vine with his sickle, he should sing a Davidic song. Let these be your poems; these, as the people say, should be your love-songs; let these be the pipings of shepherds, these the instruments of cultivation. The things done by men of this world are of no concern to monks; let the meditation of their hearts [*meditatio cordis*] be directed to the fear of God.[56]

Meditation/memorization ensures that when readers return to the book, they will be able to "read" it more easily, as children learning to read today will do with texts they have previously memorized. I have referred above (p. 14) to Isidore of Seville's comment in this regard:

> Lectio memoriae auxilio eget. Quod si fuerit naturaliter tardior, frequenti tamen meditatione acuitur, ac legendi assiduitate colligitur. Saepe prolixa lectio longitudinis causa memoriam legentis obtergit. Quod si brevis sit, submotoque libro sententia retractetur in animo, tunc sine labore legitur, et ea quae lecta sunt recolendo a memoria minime excidunt.

> Reading needs the aid of memory, and even if memory is sluggish, it is sharpened by frequent meditation, and recovered by assiduous reading. Often a prolix reading will overwhelm the memory with its length, but if it is short, and if one reconsiders its meaning in the mind, with the book put aside, then it may be read without effort, and the things which one has read, once recollected in memory, will not be lost.[57]

---

[55] Ferreolus, *Regula ad monachos* 11 (PL 66:964): *Similiter etiam his qui pastores pecorum, ut est moris, de congregatione mittentur, curae erit vacare psalmis ut caeteri.*

[56] *Regula Tarna[n]tensis* 8 (PL 66:981): *Arator stivam tenens Alleluia cantet; sudans messor psalmis se avocet; et dum palmitem curvum tondet vinitor falce, aliquid Davidicum canat. Haec sint vestra carmina; haec, ut vulgo aiunt, amatoriae cantiones; haec pastorum sibilus; haec instrumenta culturae. De his, quae huius saeculi homines agunt, nihil curae sit monachis; sed meditatio cordis eorum in timore Domini sit intenta.*

[57] *Sententiae* 3.14.7–8 (PL 83:689).

In the meantime, *submoto libro* ("with the book put aside"), the discipline of *meditatio* releases the reader from servitude to the written page. There are Pauline implications to be considered here: while reciting or singing Scripture at work in the field, one is freed from obedience to the "custodian" (Gal 3.25)—the *littera*, the law, the text—and one then assumes an elementary form of spiritual freedom. Cassian had quoted the proverb, "Drink from your own cistern" (Prov 5:15), describing the internalization of Scripture, to be brought up like well-aged, sweet wine from the depths of the mind (Conf 14.13.5, see above, p. 85). Even with frequent repetition, Cassian alleges, holy thoughts will seem always new, having been rediscovered by the reader's own effort in the context of his own lived experience. The monk who has labored to memorize texts, whenever and however they were made available, and who has managed to decipher them, overcoming eyestrain, his own uncertain literacy, and sluggish concentration—Benedict, Caesarius, and other authorities cite these "excuses" as unacceptable, of course—has indeed learned them through his own effort. By reciting or singing these texts while at work, away from the book, he makes them his own.

Proceeding from Cassian's *Conferences* to the monastic documents of the sixth century, we devolve necessarily from an idealized spirituality into a world of practical applications. "Spiritual freedom," institutionalized in the coenobium, mobilized for service "under a rule and an abbot,"[58] becomes subject to increasingly minute supervision; where Augustine and Jerome had addressed an intellectually mature, fervent, and self-disciplined readership, Benedict finds it necessary to assign patrols during rest periods to ensure that recommended reading actually takes place (RB

---

[58] Concerning the implications of this phrase, see Adalbert de Vogüé, "Sub regula uel abate," 21–64. De Vogüé alludes to the potential theological problem residing in a monastic rule being taken as a "law," i.e., as a "return to the regime of the Old Covenant" (22). De Vogüé resolves the question by referring to the tradition of the gospels and the book of Acts, and by emphasizing the personal character of the abbot's authority. But for Simon Tugwell, *Ways of Imperfection*, 71–9, the emphasis on supervision and external constraints remains pervasive, especially in the Rule of the Master.

48.17).The textual community described in the Rule of the Master—the small-group instruction on summer afternoons (see p. 92 above)—ideally would have enacted an Augustinian orientation of studies to fraternal charity; in these groups we also find, however, a very heterogeneous population, including children and semi-literate adults less than well-equipped for higher religious experiences.[59] Did the constant recitation of Scripture lead to the ethical internalization that Cassian describes? Often enough, the documents warn against mechanical, thoughtless repetition, and hint at a daily struggle against boredom. Cassian had described a purely defensive use of scriptural recitation as a shield against invasive secular "thoughts"; sixth-century rules recommend this recitation as opposed to idle chatter (*fabulae, fabulare*) or even less than edifying work songs.[60]

To what extent did the emphasis on orality and memorization compensate for a scarcity of books, as well as for the difficulty in reading them? Benedict's provision of just one book from the *bibliotheca* (see note 38, p. 93 above), to be read by each monk throughout the Lenten period (RB 48.15), seems to evoke a very limited library, and this impression is supported by careful provisions in other rules for borrowing and returning codices to the appointed *sacrarius* (see, e.g., Isidore of Seville, *Regula monachorum* 8.1). Benedict does include among recommended readings "the Conferences of the Fathers, their Institutes and their Lives," and the Rule of Saint Basil (RB 73.5); Ferreolus alludes to the public reading of the passions of the martyrs (*Regula ad monachos* 18). But, in general, the goal of literacy was the memorization of Scripture. Seldom were reading possibilities envisaged beyond that canon. From the earliest times through the Middle Ages, it is not a breadth of reading knowledge that is sought—extension in breadth will always remain suspect—but an intensive reading that leads to application in action and internalization in depth.

The emphasis on orality and memorization in monastic rules responds in part to practical necessities and in part to deeper urgencies

---

[59] The authorities all acknowledge that illiterate people, following the example of Saint Anthony, can receive illumination directly from the Holy Spirit, but the writers invariably note that such cases are rare exceptions to the general rule.

[60] See *Regula Tarna[n]tensis* 9, and Isidore of Seville, *Regula monachorum* 5.5.

of spirituality. "Pronunciation," as we have noted, was indispensable in the initial deciphering of the written page and also in the process of committing texts to memory. Recitation of texts was performed not without the duress of supervision. Yet even in later centuries, among highly educated people in situations where material and social constraints had been eased, reading aloud continued to occupy a central place in the curriculum. Indications in the works of Bede (d. 735), the letters of Alcuin (d. 804), and the treatises of Smaragdus of Saint Mihiel (d. 824), among others, confirm the continuing emphasis on intensive *meditatio* as a vital necessity in religious life.[61] For John of Salisbury, M. T. Clanchy notes that "Latin letters were a cue for speech, not a substitute for it. . . . Like musical notation, medieval letter script was understood to represent sounds needing hearing."[62]

This observation applies generally to reading in a religious environment. Reading aloud transforms reading into prayer. Pronouncing the words under one's breath, one quite literally "tastes" them in the mouth (these tactile and gustatory dimensions of reading seem conspicuously absent from modern, secular reading experience). Sounding words "out loud" (*voce magna*, or *clare legendo*) engages the sense of hearing and opens the ethical implications of the listening attitude. By this means, the reader also discovers the emotional inflections contained in the meaning of the words and enacts the protagonist's role.[63] Having learned, then, the text "by heart,"—in all senses of that expression, as Leclercq urges (see above, p. 7)—the reader steps away from the page and takes personal possession of the text as a performer, as a (re)creator, and ultimately as an author in his own right. Released from servitude to writing, he assumes, ideally, his own spiritual freedom.

[61] For references, see "Lectio divina," Dict. Sp. 482; concerning the *libelli precum* of the Carolingian period, see Bernard McGinn, *The Presence of God: A History of Western Christian Mysticism*, vol. 2: *The Growth of Mysticism*, (New York, NY: Crossroad, 1999) 136.

[62] M. T. Clanchy, *From Memory to Written Record*, 284–85.

[63] Walter J. Ong comments that "In oral speech, a word must have one or another intonation or tone of voice—lively, excited, quiet, incensed, resigned, or whatever. It is impossible to speak a word orally without any intonation" (*Orality and Literacy: The Technologizing of the Word* [London and New York: Routledge, 1988], 101–2).

Inevitably, in daily monastic practice, as the utopia envisioned by Cassian became a material reality, losses of purity were incurred. As an emblem of imperfection, we glimpse the figure of the monk at work, repeating the phrases he has mechanically memorized without thought or feeling. That would be an intellectual failure as much as a moral one. Repeated injunctions to take the verses to heart do not entirely address the problem.[64] How can one rekindle fervor when the words had been drained of meaning? The authorities had entrusted intellectual understanding to time and faith and humility; understanding would come not from a voluntary, insistent questioning, but unconsciously, during sleep for example, as the Holy Spirit willed. It would seem, however, that the claims of the mind could not be indefinitely deferred. The meaning of the term *meditatio* was clearly destined to expand. The relationship between the processes of *lectio divina* and the interpretation of the scriptural text remained as yet an open question, one that would preoccupy the church fathers for many years to come.

---

[64] E.g., Isidore of Seville, *Regula monachorum* 6.2 (PL 83:876); *Regula Tarna[n] tensis* 8 (PL 66:981), quoted above in n. 55.

Chapter Four

Reading into Writing

The long centuries between the death of Gregory the Great in 604 and the birth of Bernard of Clairvaux in 1090 are a period of relative stasis. As an innovator in theology, John Scottus Eriugena stands almost alone, and after his death circa 877, there ensues a "dramatic pause in the history of Bible studies," lasting about a century and a quarter.[1] After the year 1000, the tempo quickens again, and at that moment we perceive that something of importance has occurred in the interim. A contribution has been made; foundations have been placed on which the work that follows will stand. Bernard McGinn comments, "Even to transmit a tradition over such an extended period of time is to play a role in forming it."[2] More lyrically, Jean Leclercq evokes these "earlier centuries, centuries so happy that no need to produce was felt; it was enough to be alive. . . . What the monks did for Christian culture must not be measured only by what they produced, but by what was produced by the non-monastic centuries which came after them and owe to them not only the transmission of the texts but, what is more important, a spiritual tradition and the life of the spirit itself."[3]

What exactly took place? The period following Gregory's death was a time of sorting and settling, when the discoveries of the Fathers were absorbed and, to use the Gregorian metaphor, fully "digested." From about the seventh century onward, commentaries on Scripture carry an increasing burden of secondary literature. Emphasis now shifts from original encounters with

---

[1] Smalley, *The Study of the Bible*, 44.

[2] Bernard McGinn, *The Growth of Mysticism*, 120.

[3] Leclercq, *Love of Learning*, 312.

the sacred text to the deferential conservation of intervening authorities. In the work of quoting, copying, and paraphrasing, the activity of reading flows into writing in an unbroken continuum. That development had been speculatively foreseen by Cassian and Gregory; in the texts that came after them, it becomes observable in actuality.

In this connection, Leclercq draws attention to the phenomenon of reminiscences: the approximate quotations, cited often without attribution to their original authors, which recur constantly throughout medieval religious writing. The element of approximation is important, he notes. Most often, it would appear that the writer is quoting from memory—drawing water from his own well, in Cassian's metaphor. He assumes these quotations as his own: "Reminiscences are not quotations, elements of phrases borrowed from another. They are the words of the person using them; they belong to him. Perhaps he is not even conscious of owing them to a source."[4] *Dicta mea dicta sunt patrum* ("My sayings are the sayings of the Fathers"), wrote John of Fécamp, in a phrase that Leclercq often quotes. It means that that the later writer, appropriating the "words of the Fathers" as his own, subordinates his individual identity to theirs, and also perhaps theirs to his. He may then freely transform quotations and amalgamate them as needed.

Where one text quotes or refers to another, we have a record of reading-reception. Medieval writers assimilate their readings with great freedom and in many different ways. They select the text they quote, abstracting and omitting as necessary. They recompose the quoted text, altering the original order or logical sequence of ideas. They add interpretive commentary before or after a quotation, or interpolate phraseology at any point in the middle. By such means they recontextualize the text, subordinating it to their immediate needs, bringing it into association with other quoted texts and with their own ideas. Quotation marks do not exist. The border between quoted and quoting text remains generally fluid, as does the distinction between quotation and paraphrase. Some writers do attribute quotations to their authors, especially when patristic sources are involved, where references to named authorities can

---

[4] Leclercq, *Love of Learning*, 94.

signal deference to orthodoxy. Citations of Scripture, however, are usually not footnoted, and that absence acknowledges the sacred character of the text, assumed to be familiar to the eventual reader with whom the writer shares the attitude of reverent, tacit recognition. Indeed, medieval writers often quote texts that quote other texts, performing a reading of a reading, as when a writer quotes Augustine or Gregory quoting a psalm. The Psalms are quoted constantly in all modes of reference. Their use involves a particular psychology whereby the writer adopts the psalmist's voice, his first-person singular or plural, as his own; literary transfers of identity take place among the various individual participants in the reading, linked across distances in space and time, who face a God invoked in the second-person singular, the timeless, identical interlocutor addressed by all.

The medieval literary form that accommodates the process of reading-reception is that of the compilation, the *florilegium*. From the seventh century onward, there appear a number of anthologies, variously entitled *sententiae, excerpta, florilegia, deflorationes*[5]—collections of scriptural and patristic "sentences" or "excerpts" or "flowers" set under topical headings and assembled for various uses by individuals and communities. Many other literary genres are formed by compilation technique, which becomes an almost universal denominator of the writings of this period. The Carolingian "liturgical Renaissance" begins indeed with the sacramentaries, lectionaries, and other types of service anthologies imported from Rome which are copied and distributed at this time for use in the celebration of the Mass and of the monastic daily Office.[6] Adaptations of monastic liturgical books (*libelli precum*) are also composed for the use of individual laity. Benedict of Aniane's

---

[5] These poetic titles are virtually synonymous. Jean Leclercq (*Love of Learning,* 228–29) distinguishes between collections designed for use scholastic *disputationes* and those associated with monastic reading and meditation. The examples studied in this chapter belong to the latter category.

[6] For an introduction to the history of liturgy, see Frank C. Senn, *Christian Liturgy, Catholic and Evangelical* (Minneapolis, MN: Fortress, 1997). For systematic outlines of the Mass and the divine Office, and a glossary of terminology, see John Harper, *The Forms and Orders of Western Liturgy from the Tenth to the Eighteenth Century* (Oxford: Clarendon, 1991).

Concordia Regularum gives the text of the Rule of Saint Benedict chapter by chapter, listing for each one the varying stipulations on the given subject found in all the other significant available rules.[7] Smaragdus's commentary, more theoretical and spiritual in character, cites the Rule of Saint Benedict phrase by phrase, defining key words by etymology, adducing scriptural citations, and interweaving unattributed paragraphs from patristic sources.[8]

In the domain of biblical exegesis, Bede's commentaries on Genesis (CCSL 118A), Luke, and Mark (both in CCSL 120) are introduced in prefatory letters as anthologies of the Fathers, digested and simplified for the benefit of his English readers. Bede devised, in fact, a system of referential *sigla* consisting of the first two letters of each Father's name (Am = Ambrose, Gr = Gregory, etc.), placed in the margin to mark the beginning and end of a quoted passage. He adds much of his own thought to theirs—more than his modest prefaces imply—whenever the "Author of lights" has "opened" his understanding. But he expresses an anxiety to maintain the separation, "lest I be said to steal the sayings of my elders and to compose them as my own," and he earnestly requests that any future copyists of his commentary should not forget to append his bibliographical marks.[9] Later generations do not share Bede's scruples. John of Fécamp's *Confessio theologica* (dated before 1018) is presented by its author as a patristic anthology (*defloratiuncula*) and includes extended, unattributed patristic and liturgical quotations in the context of a personal and original meditation. I shall return to this important work in some detail.

Chapters on Reading

The structural concept of the compilation, recognizable in many different forms, continues to underlie literary production through the early medieval period and beyond. It was principally in anthologies and digests composed by Isidore of Seville,

---

[7] Benedict of Aniane, *Concordia regularum*, PL 103.

[8] See n. 14 below.

[9] Bede, *In Lucae evangelium expositio*, prologus, CCSL 120:7. For an introduction to Bede's writings see George Hardin Brown, *Bede the Venerable* (Boston, MA: Twayne, 1987).

Smaragdus, and others that the spiritual teachings of Cassian and Gregory were transmitted to the "barbarian" generations that followed them.[10] These collections assemble readings under topical headings. Of particular interest are the chapters on reading and prayer, which convey the theory of *lectio divina* and extend the lengthening didactic tradition.

The *Sententiae* of Isidore of Seville (ca. 560–636), widely circulated and frequently copied, provides a point of departure. Here follows book 3, chapter 8, *De lectione* ("On reading").[11] Passages from it are copied verbatim and joined to additional material in five other early medieval works (and no doubt elsewhere as well). In the following pages, I propose briefly to survey this instance of transmission in order to note the treatment given to Isidore's text in each of the environments in which it is placed.

1. Orationibus mundamur, lectionibus instruimur; utrumque bonum, si liceat; si non liceat, melius est orare quam legere.

2. Qui vult cum Deo semper esse, frequenter debet orare, frequenter et legere. Nam cum oramus, cum Deo ipsi loquimur; cum vero legimus, Deus nobiscum loquitur.

3. Omnis profectus ex lectione et meditatione procedit. Quae enim nescimus, lectione discimus; quae autem didicimus, meditationibus conservamus.

4. Geminum confert donum lectio sanctarum Scripturarum: sive quia intellectum mentis erudit, seu quod a mundi vanitatibus abstractum hominem ad amorem Dei perducit. Excitati enim saepe illius sermone, subtrahimur a desiderio vitae mundanae; atque accensi in amorem sapientiae, tanto vana spes mortalitatis huius nobis vilescit, quanto amplius legendo spes aeterna claruerit.

5. Geminum est lectionis studium: primum, quomodo Scripturae intelligantur; secundum, qua utilitate vel dignitate dicantur. Erit enim antea quisque promptus ad intelligendum quae legit, sequenter idoneus ad proferendum quae didicit.

6. Lector strenuus potius ad implendum quae legit, quam ad sciendum erit promptissimus. Minor enim poena est nescire

---

[10] Jean Leclercq, *La Spiritualité du Moyen Âge. Histoire de la Spiritualité Chrétienne*, vol. 2 (Paris: Aubier, 1961), 88.

[11] Isidore of Seville, *Sententiae* 3.8, ed. Pierre Cazier, CCSL 111 (Turnhout: Brepols, 1998), 228–30.

quid appetas, quam ea quae noveris non implere. Sicut enim legendo scire concupiscimus, sic sciendo recta quae didicimus implere debemus.

7. Lex Dei et praemium habet, et poenam legentibus eam. Praemium in eis qui eam bene vivendo custodiunt; poenam vero qui eam male vivendo contemnunt.

8. Omnis qui a praeceptis Dei discedit opere, quotiens eadem Dei praecepta legere vel audire potuerit, corde suo reprehensus confunditur, quia id quod non agit memoratur, et teste conscientia interius accusatur. Unde et David propheta deprecatur dicens: "Tunc non confundar, dum respicio in omnia mandata tua" [Ps 118.6 (119.6)]. Graviter namque unusquisque confunditur quando mandata Dei vel legendo, vel audiendo respicit, quae vivendo contemnit. Corde enim reprehenditur, dum mandatorum meditatione docetur, quia non implevit opere quod divina didicit jussione.

---

1. By prayers we are purified, by readings we are instructed; it is good to have them both together, if possible; if not, it is better to pray than to read.

2. Whoever wishes to be always with God should pray frequently, and frequently read. For when we pray, we ourselves speak with God; when we read, God speaks with us.

3. All progress comes from reading and meditation. What we do not know, we learn from reading; what we have learned we conserve in meditations.

4. The reading of the Holy Scriptures confers a double gift: it informs the mind's understanding, and it removes the person from the world's vanities, while leading him to the love of God. Inspired by its discourse, we are drawn from the desire for earthly life; and once enkindled with the love of wisdom, the vain hope of this mortality seems unworthy, and the eternal hope all the more brightly shines in the reading.

5. The study of reading is concerned with two things: first, how the Scriptures may be understood; secondly, for what purpose or with what dignity they may be spoken. The reader will be eager at first to understand what he reads, and then it will be appropriate for him to pass on what he has learned.

6. The attentive reader will be more concerned with putting what he reads into practice than with acquiring knowledge. There is less of a fault in not knowing what you should seek

than in not applying what you do know. Just as we desire to gain knowledge from reading, so also, once we have gained the knowledge of correct doctrines, we must seek to practice them.

7. God's law has a reward and a penalty for those who read it. The reward is for readers who keep the law by living it; the penalty is paid by those who disrespect the law by living badly.

8. Whenever anyone departs from the precepts of God in his actions, each time he reads or hears them he will be confounded by the accusation in his heart. For he remembers then what he has not done, and stands accused by the witness of his own conscience. Accordingly David, the prophet, prayed in these words: "Then I shall not be put to shame, having my eyes fixed on all thy commandments" (Ps 118.6 [119.6]). But each person will be put to shame when he attends to the commandments of God by reading or hearing them, but disrespects them in living. In his heart he stands accused whenever he is taught by meditation on the commandments, because he does not apply in action what he has learned by divine injunction.

We recognize immediately a number of familiar monastic themes: the alternation of reading and prayer, with the former subordinated to the latter; the aphorism about reading as God's speech to us, comparable to our speech to him; the search for a balance between instruction and purification of the mind; the vision of spiritual progress from reading to understanding to meditation (that is, conservation in memory) to communication of what is learned to faithful application in action; and the final warning that without action, the knowledge gained from reading may serve only to condemn the reader. These concepts derive from Cassian, Augustine, Benedict, Gregory, and others, but Isidore does not footnote, and exact attributions are in most cases impossible to make. There are reminiscences and many approximate quotations of sources. Much of the wording may in fact be original to Isidore.

The literary genre of Isidore's *Sententiae*, that of lists of utterances organized under topical headings, is that of a *florilegium*, today sometimes called a "digest." From the fully extended discussions of ideas found in authoritative sources, the compiler extracts "flowers"—dried flowers, as they might seem—reductions of thought processes to the most compact form possible, for the purpose of preservation in memory. Isidore himself comments elsewhere, we recall (see p. 99 above), that prolixity burdens memory, and that short texts can be more easily retained and (re)read. The procedure of reduction facilitates retention, but sacrifices context and logical sequence. A list of utterances follows no necessary logical order of its own. We do discern groupings of associated ideas; in comparison to other compilers, Isidore is relatively systematic. Yet the sentences tend to float, disconnected from one another. A chapter in a *florilegium* usually does not attempt a sustained exposition, but offers rather a loose collection of items made conveniently available to a reader who can learn some or all of them in that form, and eventually, for his own purposes, recontextualize them (rehydrate them, as it were) in expositions of his own.

Isidore's chapter 8 is preceded by a long chapter on prayer and is followed by chapter 9, "On Assiduity in Reading"; then follow chapter 10, "On Doctrine without Grace"; chapter 11, "On Arrogant Readers"; chapter 12, "On Carnal Readers and Heretics"; chapter 13, "On Pagan Books"; and chapter 14, "On the Conference." These topics are in fact closely related to one another. Taken together, chapters 8–14 make a coherent statement on literary ethics and aesthetics. Here we encounter the traditional warnings against pride in knowledge, which is doomed to remain on the surface of the scriptural text; its deeper mysteries are opened, on the contrary, by the humility of the spiritual reader. Isidore praises the simplicity of the Scriptures, as opposed to the (spurious) intellectual complexity and ornate elegance of pagan literature: "The cosmetic of grammatical art is not to be imposed on simpler writings." He concludes with the concession that *meliores esse grammaticos quam haereticos* ("grammarians are better than heretics"), and that grammar can be of benefit to life when properly used (Sent 3.13.11). Implicitly, an aesthetic of rugged simplicity justifies Isidore's own enterprise of reduction and simplification.

Let us turn now to subsequent *florilegia*, in which Isidore is quoted and excerpted among other authorities. The *Liber scintillarum* (Book of Sparklets), assembled by Defensor of Ligugé in the seventh century, is addressed to an unspecified general reader.[12] In

---

[12] Defensor of Ligugé, *Liber scintillarum*, ed. Henri Rochais, CCSL 97 (Turnhout: Brepols, 1957).

his prologue, the compiler explains that wherever in his reading he found a sentence that "sparkled" (*sententiam reperiens fulgentem*) like a diamond or a gem, he picked it up. These items make up a collection, just as many drops make a fountain; as bright sparks fly from a fire, so one will find here gleaming *minutae sententiae*. Defensor suggests that the reader may spare himself the wearisome labor of reading many pages, since he will find in this one volume whatever he seeks. But lest any of the sentences be thought apocryphal, he has taken the precaution of attributing each to its original author.[13]

The book is comprised of eighty-one chapters on all manner of moral subjects: charity, patience, justice, envy, faith, hope, grace, curiosity, friendship, hatred, discipline, and others. The very last chapter is entitled "On Readings" (*De leccionibus*), and no contextual link is made between this chapter and those which precede it (Scint 79: "On Idle Words," and 80: "On the Brevity of This Life"). It begins, as all others do, with quotations from Scripture; then follow lists of sayings attributed to patristic authors in an inexact chronological order: Augustine, Jerome, Gregory, Isidore, Hilary, and Basil. Isidore has here the greatest number of citations, with twenty-three taken from his *Sententiae* and two from his *Synonyma animae peccatricis* (Synonyms of the Sinful Soul). From the material found in Isidore's chapters 3.8–14 of the *Sententiae*, Defensor retains roughly half. He keeps half of chapter 8 (quoted above, pp. 108–9), most of chapter 9, and about half of chapters 10–14. Defensor offers a digest of a digest: he occasionally synthesizes paragraphs, he omits sentences that might have seemed repetitive, and he preferentially retains the brief aphorisms with which Isidore often concludes his paragraphs. Defensor thus collects in the one chapter, "On Readings," material which Isidore distributes in seven chapters under different headings.

The comparison of Defensor's *Scintillarum* with Isidore's *Sententiae* brings out certain elements of the reading-reception process.

---

[13] Defensor of Ligugé, *Liber scintillarum*, prologus: *Veluti de igne procedunt scintille, ita hunc minutae sententiae pluresque libri inueniuntur fulgentes. Ad quarum inter hoc scintillarum uolumen, quod qui legere uult labore sibi amputat, ne per ceteras paginas iterandum lascescat; hic habentur quod repperiri desiderat. Sed ne opus, quasi sine auctore, putetur apocrifum, unicuique sententiae per sigula proprium scripsi auctorem.*

Defensor is more conservative than Isidore; his quotations are exact and carefully attributed. Even so, he moves beyond his sources through procedures of reduction, simplification, and synthesis. His preferential selection of specially "sparkling" nuggets produces an evaporation of logical context, which was still present in Isidore. The format of the list of sayings tends to reduce to uniformity the individual identities of the sources quoted; increasingly over time, readers grouped the "Fathers" together as a single, undifferentiated category of tradition. In these and other respects, Defensor mirrors the behavior of the reading mind struggling to absorb a large amount of material and to make it available for repetition and reflection once the book is put aside.

The *Diadema monachorum* (Crown of Monks) and the *Commentary on the Rule of Saint Benedict*, both completed by Smaragdus circa 816, mark further stages in the evolution of reading theory.[14] In the prologue to the *Diadema*, Smaragdus, abbot of Saint Mihiel in Lotharingia since 814, states that he has plucked "sweet-smelling flowers" (*bene olentes flosculos*) from the "meadow" of the "orthodox Fathers," and that he has collected these sayings into a little book for the benefit of his monks. The book is divided into one hundred chapters designed to be read aloud during evening chapter meetings, in parallel to the morning readings from the Rule of Saint Benedict. Smaragdus's collection covers a wide range of familiar moral topics with an emphasis on meaningful reflection. To the citations from Scripture and patristic sources he adds sayings and anecdotes of the Egyptian desert hermits, which he generally places at the end of each discussion.

---

[14] Smaragdus of Saint-Mihiel, *Diadema monachorum*, PL 102:593–690; Smaragdus of Saint-Mihiel, *The Crown of Monks*, trans. David Barry, CS 245 (Collegeville, MN: Cistercian, forthcoming); *Expositio in regulam S. Benedicti*, ed. A. Spannagel and P. Engelbert, Corpus Consuetudinum Monasticarum 8 (Siegburg, Germany: F. Schmitt, 1974); Smaragdus of Saint-Mihiel, *Commentary on the Rule of Saint Benedict*, trans. David Barry, CS 212 (Kalamazoo, MI: Cistercian Publications, 2007). For an introduction to Smaragdus's life and works, see Jean Leclercq, "Smaragdus," in *An Introduction to the Medieval Mystics of Europe: Fourteen Original Essays*, ed. Paul E. Szarmach (Albany: SUNY Press, 1984), 37–51; and the introductory essays by Terrence Kardong, Daniel LaCorte, and Jean Leclercq in *Commentary on the Rule of Saint Benedict*.

The chapter entitled "On Reading," the third in the *Diadema*, follows chapters on prayer and psalmody. The placement of these related topics together near the beginning of the book indicates the importance that Smaragdus gives to them. He begins with a passage copied from Isidore's *Sententiae*, corresponding to 3.8.1–4, 7, quoted above. The rest of the chapter consists of quotations from Gregory's *Moralia* and *Homilies on Ezekiel*—important passages indeed, often recalled by modern as well as by medieval authors, which I have referred to above.[15] Smaragdus's selection from these two authors and the fusion he effects between them produce a short treatise on reading and spiritual progress. Isidore's view that reading draws the mind from earthly vanities to the love of God is followed by Gregory's description of the same rising movement: "Holy Scripture calls the soul of the reader to the heavenly country, and transforms his heart, moving it from earthly desires to the embrace of eternal things."[16] Other Gregorian sentences—notably, that Scripture "grows" with the reader, reflecting the latter's state of soul; that it offers reassuring help to "little ones" *(parvuli)*, while testing stronger minds with subtleties and complexities; and that it is indeed to be "eaten" as life-giving nourishment—seem to amplify Isidore's comments concerning the progression from intellectual understanding to active application. The chapter "On Reading" concludes with a quotation from Gregory's *Homilies on Ezekiel* 1.7.8. Smaragdus removes, however, Gregory's allegorical interpretation of Ezekiel's wheels and animals (Ezek 1.19) and rephrases the text in order to retain only its moral message:

> At uero si animal ambulet, id est bene uiuendi ordines quaerat, et per gressum cordis inueniat quemadmodum gressum boni operis ponat, ambulant pariter et rotae, quia tantum in sacro eloquio prouectum inuenis, quantum apud illud ipse profeceris.

---

[15] *Moralia in Iob*, 20.1, and *Homiliae in Hiezechilelem*, 1.10.2, 1.7.16–17, and 1.7.8.

[16] Smaragdus, *Diadema monachorum*, 3; PL 102:597–98; cf. Gregory, *Moralia in Iob*, 20.1, CCSL 143A:1003.

And if the creature moves, that is, if he seeks ways of living well, and finds by a movement of his heart how he should advance in good work, so also the wheels move, for you find as much progress in sacred eloquence as you yourself have progressed. (Gregory, *Homilies on Ezekiel* 1.7.8; SCh 327:244)

———————

At vero si bene vivendi ordines [lector] quaerat, et per gressum cordis inveniat quemadmodum pedem boni operis ponat, tantum in sacro eloquio profectum invenit, quantum apud illum ipse profecerit.

———————

And if [the reader] seeks ways of living well, and finds by a movement of his heart how he should advance in good work, then he finds as much progress in sacred eloquence as he himself has progressed. (Smaragdus, *Diadema monachorum* 3; PL102:598)

The grammatical subject of the sentence in Gregory, *animal* (Ezekiel's "living creature"), is more directly understood to be the reader himself in Smaragdus; the result is that Gregory's exegesis is transformed into a simplified statement on seeking a correct way of life. Smaragdus offers a reading of Gregory through the prism, as it were, of Isidore. It is a synthesis which reduces the distinctiveness of both writers. Smaragdus brings Gregory's thinking down to the level of Isidore's relatively practical monitions and somewhat raises the complexity of the latter in exchange. Neither writer is cited by name in this chapter. There is no concern for preserving their respective historical identities; Smaragdus has transmitted their writings and transformed them in the process, appropriating them to himself and even more so to his own readers, the assembled monks who will eventually apply them to their own spiritual life.

In his *Commentary on the Rule of Saint Benedict*, Smaragdus quotes the same passage from Isidore but adds significant wording to join the topic of reading more closely to that of prayer.[17] The headings for his discussion are taken from two lines from the fourth

———————

[17] Smaragdus, *Expositio in regulam S. Benedicti*, 2.4.55–56; Corpus Consuetudinum Monasticarum 8:134–36; Barry, CS 212, 227–29. This passage is the basis for Jean Leclercq's searching 1984 essay, "Smaragdus," (see n. 14 above). It is also quoted by Magrassi, *Praying the Bible*, 20.

chapter of the Rule, "The Tools for Good Works": *Lectiones sanctas libenter audire, orationi frequenter incumbere* (RB 4.55-56: "Listen willingly to holy reading, and devote yourself often to prayer"). Smaragdus's paragraph begins with enthusiasm:

> "Lectiones sanctas libenter audire." Lectionis enim sacrae cognitio cultoribus suis sensus acumen ministrat, intellectum multiplicat, torporem excutit, otium amovet, vitam componit, mores corrigit, salubrem gemitum facit et lacrymas compunctio corde producit; loquendi tribuit facundiam et aeterna laborantibus promittit praemia; spiritales divitias auget, vaniloquium vanitatesque compescit, et desiderium Christi patriaeque coelestis accendit, quae semper orationi socia semperque orationi debet esse connexa.

> "Listen willingly to holy readings." The knowledge of sacred reading provides those who cultivate it with keenness of perception, increases their understanding, shakes off sluggishness, does away with idleness, shapes their life, corrects their behavior, causes wholesome groaning, and produces tears from a heart pierced by compunction; it bestows eloquence in speaking and promises eternal rewards to those who toil; it increases spiritual riches, curbs vain speech and vanities, and enkindles the desire for Christ and our heavenly homeland. It is always associated with prayer, and must always be joined to prayer.

The passage from Isidore then follows (Sent 3.8.1–4, quoted above), into which Smaragdus makes a meaningful interpolation, given here in brackets: *Quae enim nescimus, lectione discimus; quae enim didicerimus meditationibus conservamus [et ut conservata a nobis impleantur, oratione adipiscimur]. Geminum enim confert donum sanctarum lectio scripturarum* ("What we do not know, we learn by reading, and what we have learned, we conserve by meditation, [and we obtain by prayer that what we have conserved may be fulfilled]. The reading of the sacred Scriptures confers a double gift").[18]

In these passages, Smaragdus's own thought comes into view. Reading, he asserts, enkindles among other things the desire for

---

[18] Smaragdus, *Expositio in regulam S. Benedicti*, 2.4.56; Corpus Consuetudinum Monasticarum 8:136; Barry, CS 212:227.

Christ and for heaven, which must necessarily accompany prayer. That is to say, reading fosters what is elsewhere called *intentio*: the focus, we might say, of intellectual and emotional faculties upon the goal; the presence of mind and heart to God, without which prayer is meaningless.[19] Reading, conserved by *meditatio*, prompts fully "intentional" prayer, and by prayer one obtains fulfillment or implementation of what has been conserved in life and action.

To conclude this section, Smaragdus adds a note taken from Isidore (Sent 3.9.1; cf. Prov 4.8) on the value of assiduity in acquiring a true, deep familiarity with Scripture. Under the next heading, Smaragdus further explores the relationship of reading to prayer:

> "Orationi frequenter incumbere." Incumbere dicit, instare, vel incubare. Et congrue nos post lectionis auditionem orationi jussit frequenter incumbere. Non enim a lectione dissentit oratio, nec ab oratione aliena est lectio. Aliquoties autem proferunt unum, aliquoties vero diversum. Sed quia oratio dicitur oris ratio, neutra illarum orationis nomine caret, utroque rationabiliter cautae, utroque vero rationabiliter sunt dictatae.

> "Devote yourself often to prayer." *Incumbere* ["to lean toward, incline to, devote to"] means *instare* ["to approach, urge, press upon, be intent on"] or *incubare* ["to lie upon, brood over"]. And so appropriately the Rule commands us, after the hearing of the reading, to devote ourselves often to reading. For prayer is not opposed to reading, nor is reading foreign to prayer. Sometimes they express the same thing, sometimes different things. But since *oratio* means *oris ratio* ["the reason of the mouth"][20] neither of them is deprived of the name of prayer; both are decreed in keeping with reason, both in fact are dictated in keeping with reason.[21]

Sounding intently the meanings of the words he uses, Smaragdus brings reading, prayer, and action—understanding, spirituality, and

---

[19] Smaragdus, *Diadema monachorum*, 1 (PL 102: 594). For further exposition of the important term *intentio*, see Jean Leclercq, "Smaragdus," 40.

[20] Isidore of Seville, *Etym.* 1.5.3 (PL 81:82)

[21] Smaragdus, *Expositio*, 2.4.56; Corpus Consuetudinum Monasticarum 8:136; Barry, CS212:228. I have emended Barry's English translation to follow more closely the Latin wording.

will—into an intricate interdependency. The central term is indeed *oratio*, prayer, for which reading provides the foundation. By *oratio* Smaragdus means "not so much a particular exercise as such, but rather a permanent disposition," according to Jean Leclercq, who also emphasizes that Smaragdus is not referring here to the group expression of the collective, but rather to something personal, individual, and spontaneous in nature.[22] This is an important question of interpretation to which I shall return shortly.

Two other compilations will serve to complete this survey. The treatise, *De virtutibus et vitiis* ("On virtues and vices") by Alcuin (735–804), contains a fifth chapter entitled *De lectionis studio* ("On the exercise of reading"). Alcuin begins with Gregorian evocations—reminiscences rather than exact quotations—and proceeds into the familiar text from Isidore:

> Sanctarum lectio Scripturarum divinae est cognitio beatudinis. In his enim quasi in quodam speculo homo seipsum considerare potest, qualis sit, vel quo tendat. Lectio assidua purificat animam, timorem incutit gehennae, ad gaudia superna cor instigat legentis. "Qui vult cum Deo semper esse, frequenter debet orare, frequenter et legere."[23]

> ———————

> The reading of the Holy Scriptures is a [fore-] knowledge of divine blessedness. In these texts, as in a mirror, a person can consider himself, how he is and in what direction he is tending. Assiduous reading purifies the soul, instills the fear of hell, and incites the heart of the reader to supernal joys. "He who wishes to be always with God must pray frequently and read."

The rest of this short chapter similarly mingles reminiscences and quotations, along with a citation from Psalm 118:103 (119:103). Here, as in Smaragdus's *Diadema*, the patristic sources have been

———————

[22] Jean Leclercq, "Smaragdus," 40. There are indications, however, that Smaragdus is referring to collective as well as individual prayers, expressed in verbal formulae and accompanied by ritual prostration; see A. de Vogüé, "*Orationi frequenter incumbere*: Une invitation à la prière continuelle," *Revue d'Ascétique et Mystique* 44 (1968): 3–9.

[23] Alcuin, *De virtutibus et vitiis* 5 (PL 101:616). The quotation is from Isidore of Seville, *Sentential* 3.8.2 (PL 83:679).

absorbed and seamlessly joined together without concern for their original identities or respective, distinctive ideas, in order to create a statement on reading as spiritual understanding applied to action.

Our final instance, noted for the record, is a sermon entitled *De studio sapientiae, lectione et meditatione legis Dei* ("On the pursuit of wisdom, reading, and meditation of God's law"), long attributed to Saint Augustine but visibly derived from Alcuin. Here we find the complete text of the latter's chapter on reading (unattributed), along with other material from the same treatise.[24] The process of evolution and transmission continues: a succession can be traced from Isidore to Alcuin to pseudo-Augustine . . . to Migne's Patrology, the last great compilation in the medieval tradition.

The chapters just surveyed convey a broad agreement on certain principles of reading theory. They all stress that intellectual understanding is only the first step in the process; deeper mysteries of Scripture are discovered not by the intelligence (*intelligentiae ingenium*, associated with *desidia* [idleness]) but by humble assiduity in the exercise of reading (*lectionis studium*) and, above all, by application to action. The objective is not knowledge but purification of the mind. The pursuit of knowledge for its own sake is associated with pride and with the quest for personal fame. Worldly ambition would block the progress of spiritual understanding and condemn the prideful reader to remain *outside* the scriptural text, excluded from its interior meaning.

The ethical system transmitted by Isidore and his epigones appreciably reduces and stiffens the patristic heritage. Whereas Augustine and Gregory the Great had foreseen a development of intellectual and spiritual faculties in tandem, the later writers categorically separate the two. Gregory's *parvuli* are beginners on both levels; his *magni* are readers who are intelligent, educated (*docti*), *and* spiritually proficient. When, however, Gregory is quoted in association with Isidore—for example, by Smaragdus in the *Diadema*, as noted above—subtleties are lost, and the result is a simple equation of intelligence with laziness and knowledge with pride, all of which are to be excluded from spirituality. With the exception of

---

[24] This sermon is numbered 302 and is printed in the appendix among *Sermones suppositi* (PL 39:2323–24).

Smaragdus in the *Commentary on the Rule*, the compilers are not concerned with nuances of interpretation, nor even primarily with contemplation, but rather, most insistently, with active application. They are aware that the literature of the Fathers is vast and in need of cataloguing. They address their own future readers—for example, in the *Diadema*, the monks gathered before their abbot in an evening assembly—who will have little access to the original sources and who may lack the intellectual resources needed to understand them in depth. A certain "dumbing down" process, *si liceat*, is justified by the anticipation of their practical needs.

The construction of compilations, and the techniques of synthesis we have observed do reflect the theory of reading that these chapters convey. The rearrangement of patristic literature under topical headings, rather than under the names of the authors, is already a step toward application and a step away from scholarship. In the world of practice, the past scarcely matters. The compilers conserve with great piety the patristic tradition while paradoxically forgetting the original contexts in which the ideas of the Fathers developed. Little or no need is felt to (re)connect the items selected. The interpretation of the materials conserved remains tacit, deferred perhaps indefinitely, and awaited as a possible outcome of experience that will occur when and if the Holy Spirit intervenes.

Liturgy and Private Prayer

In theory, Cassian and other early authorities orient their discussions of reading and *meditatio* to an individual reader. But by necessity or by design, most of the reading that was done in the monastery—the environment most conducive to reading—was done out loud and in groups. In the afternoon classes described in the Rule of the Master and in the mealtime readings and conferences (*collationes*) described in other rules, we glimpse an increasing regulation of reading, which is subject to group interaction and assigned to given times and places within the daily routine. It would seem, however, that on these occasions, a certain freedom of group discussion was encouraged. The sermons of Gregory the Great model the process of reading-interpretation that can take place in the dialogue between the reader acting as preacher and the (actual or virtual) congregation. Isidore specifies that "It is better to listen to a conference than to read"; the conference fosters docility, he continues, and in the questions that may be put forward by listeners, hesitations in interpretation are quickly resolved and hidden truths are confirmed (provided, he adds, that the discussion does not degenerate into contentious debate and displays of cleverness).[25]

During the early medieval period, *meditatio*, properly speaking the act of prayerful reading, becomes increasingly absorbed into corporate worship. The choice of pericopes—that is, readings from Scripture accompanying the Mass—had in early centuries been coordinated with the liturgical calendar; this system, confirmed and further articulated in later lectionaries, has survived to the present day. Cassian's recommendations concerning the reading of the Psalms become institutionalized, in the Rule of Saint Benedict, in the form of a cycle of recitations covering all one hundred fifty psalms each week. This practice forms the core of the monastic daily Office. For each hour, the Rule specifies the introduction and the psalms that are to be chanted, together with refrains, responsories, and concluding prayers. In the centuries following Benedict, the ancillary material continues to expand to the point where, in the Cluniac monasteries of the tenth and eleventh centuries, *laus perennis* becomes a literal reality in liturgy, occupying all twenty-four hours of each day. Chanted prayers surrounding each psalm encode and ritualize reading-response, orienting it toward Christian and specifically Christological interpretations;[26] the collect which follows further serves to relate individual reception of the text to the sense of group worship.[27]

What is the place of reading in relation to liturgy, and what is its function within the celebration? How can the balance be set between private devotion and participation in the community? These are related questions that have been debated throughout

---

[25] Isidore of Seville, *Sententiae* 3.14 (CCSL 111:239).

[26] Jean Leclercq, *La spiritualité du moyen âge*, 85.

[27] On "Psalter collects" see *The Prayers and Meditations of St. Anselm*, trans. Benedicta Ward, (Harmondsworth, Middlesex, UK: Penguin Books, 1973), 36-37 and n. 3.

the history of the church and which came again into focus in the course of the twentieth-century liturgical movement. In the discussions preceding Vatican II, some commentators perceived a conflict between liturgy and contemplation, as between a purely extrinsic worship and a personal spirituality achieved necessarily outside the public celebration.[28] That opposition reflects a modern, post-romantic sensibility, in that it pits the individual against society; it is a construct that Catholic scholars have ultimately rejected in the search for a deeper understanding that is more in harmony with that of the Middle Ages.

Expressing this more traditional view, Louis Bouyer characterizes the liturgy as a "school for meditation": there is an inseparable connection formed between responsorial chant, personal prayer, and the group prayer of the collect.[29] He proceeds to describe three phases. First, chant is a reading (or rather a recitative) performed as a celebration; it is the instinctive response of the human heart to the initiative of God, who anticipates human prayers, speaking to us in the words that he teaches us to use in speaking to him: *Une contemplation qui ne peut rester détachée de ce qu'elle contemple* ("A contemplation that cannot remain detached from that which it contemplates"). It tends toward silent prayer, the second phase: a deepening solitary reflection—*meditatio*, in a word. The process is concluded logically and necessarily by the collect, the third phase, which acknowledges the human community surrounding the individual at prayer.

Modern Catholic authorities have asserted the primacy of the liturgical celebration. As Mariano Magrassi emphasizes, "the Word is living when the speaker is present and it is actually coming from his mouth. Only the presence of Christ prevents the Word from becoming a purely historical document. The church can claim this presence because it is identified with Christ. . . . 'It is he himself who speaks when the holy Scriptures are read in

---

[28] This view is argued by Jacques and Raïssa Maritain, *Liturgy and Contemplation* (New York: P. J. Kennedy, 1960). See Magrassi, 2 and n. 3.

[29] Louis Bouyer, *Introduction à la vie spirituelle: Précis de théologie ascétique et mystique* (Paris: Desclée, 1960), 41–47.

church'."[30] Private reading may then be construed as preparation for corporate worship, and it is related to the confession of sins and other personal exercises serving to focus *intentio*, that is to say, the presence of the individual to God. Alternatively, private reading would follow the celebration as a natural continuation, in which the pedagogy derived from hearing the Word in the liturgical context—in the arrangement of chants and scriptural readings deployed in the ceremony—continues to inform study and rereading. Modern teachers of *lectio divina* also encourage *lectio continua* in private Bible study in order to supplement and correct the fragmented selection of the pericope system.

The various modes of reading, solitary and in concert, may be situated along a spectrum of "ecclesiality" ranging from private study at one end to the celebration of the Mass at the other.[31] The monastic daily Office occupies a middle position; it is a prayer assembly, arguably a "devotion act within a whole spiritual discipline designed to lead the monk toward the goal of 'spiritual freedom,'" rather than "an action of the whole people of God engaged in their public work."[32]

Returning, however, to the early medieval sources, one must divest the word "devotion" of its association with later prayer practices, and one must also be prepared to question the distinction between private prayer and public liturgy, appropriate though that may be to modern lay spirituality. The term *oratio* in Smaragdus's usage retains a certain flexibility. In the *Diadema* and in the *Commentary on the Rule*, which were just discussed, this word can denote communal as well as private prayer, and his references to reading imply that this activity may take place in public, mostly as audition, in fact.[33] What is of importance to this commentator

---

[30] Magrassi, *Praying the Bible*, 3; the quotation is from Vatican II's *Sacrosanctum Concilium* (Constitution on the Sacred Liturgy), 7.

[31] Pierre-Marie Gy, "Sacraments and Liturgy in Western Christianity," in Bernard McGinn and John Meyendorff, eds., *Christian Spirituality: Origins to the Twelfth Century* (New York: Crossroad, 1985), 371–72.

[32] Frank Senn, *Christian Liturgy*, 171 and 212.

[33] The paragraph on reading in the Smaragdus's *Commentary on the Rule* is set under the phrase, *Lectiones sanctas libenter audire*, and the next paragraph further specifies, *post lectionis auditionem orationi jussit frequenter incumbere* (Corpus Consuedinum

is not the contrast between public and private but rather the participation of mind and heart—*intentio mentis, intentio cordis*; the "light of the heart," *lumen cordis*—that the person praying brings to either or both.

On the question of solitary versus group worship, Peter Damian (1007–1072) summarizes medieval monastic views in a short treatise on the phrase *Dominus vobiscum*.[34] Should a hermit praying in solitude use the phraseology of dialogue with a present congregation, as though exchanging blessings with stones and furniture? Peter replies categorically that the members of the church make up one body connected by the bond of charity; all of its members are one, and each one constitutes the whole. On the analogy of the physical human body, Peter notes that eyes, feet, hands, and other members have their particular functions, but it is the whole body that feels or performs through each; likewise, through the sacrament of its intimate unity, the whole church is present in any one person who is linked to it by faith and fellowship. Not otherwise did commentators on the Song of Songs, beginning with Origen, understand the figure of the Bride as personifying both the whole church and the individual soul. The unity of the church, according to Peter, admits neither the isolation of the one person nor divisions among the many. It follows that the merely physical distances which may separate the people of the church do not attenuate their true spiritual presence to each other.[35]

Accordingly, Peter notes that the Scripture alternates between singular and plural verbs, as is observed throughout the psalms: for example, in Ps 85:1 (86:1): *Inclina, Domine, aurem tuam et exaudi me, quoniam inops et pauper sum ego* ("Incline thy ear, O Lord, and

---

Monasticarum 8:134–35). In the same connection, a note in the *Diadema* refers to the public dialogue between celebrant and congregation: *Quando autem stamus ad adorationem, vigilare et incumbere ad preces tot corde debemus . . . ideo et sacerdos fratrum praeparat mentes dicendo: Sursum corda* (PL 102:595).

[34] PL 145:231–52.

[35] *Etiam si per corporalem situm partibus videatur dividi, unitatis tamen intimae sacramentum nullatenus a sua valet integritate corrumpi* (PL 145:235). "The priest should acknowledge the spiritual presence of others, and not hesitate to greet them, even when he is alone" (*Obtutus itaque fidei salutationis eius verba intendit, et accipit quod adesse cominus per spiritualem praesentiam cernit* [PL 145:246]).

answer me, for I am poor and needy"); and in Ps 80:2 [81:1]: *Exsultate Deo adiutori nostro* ("Sing aloud to God our strength"). As Peter insists, the solitude of one person who recites them does not conflict with the plural voice, nor does the singular voice deny the presence of a multitude. The many who participate in a Mass are one in spirit, and they become one through affective and intellectual participation, *intenta mentium devotione*; likewise, as a member of the church, truly joined to it, the individual person may pronounce when alone the words which are spoken together by the congregation, and so not inappropriately exert the function of the whole (*unversitatis officium*).

Carolingian *Libelli Precum*

Peter Damian's argument tends to abolish the objective distinction between private and public worship. Concerning the alternation of singular and plural verbs in the psalms and in other scripturally-based prayers, he summarizes the early medieval understanding that the voice of a Biblical *persona* such as that of the "prophet" David may be assumed by a person or people at prayer and delegated from one person to another. On that basis, it becomes possible to write prayers for another's use. From the ninth century onward, *libelli precum* (little prayer books) begin to appear, composed for the use of prominent individual laypersons.[36] Several were attributed to Alcuin and supposedly presented to Charlemagne himself. These books adapt the monastic daily Office, providing short prayers for specified moments of daily life and longer prayers drawn from patristic texts on various themes (penitence, thanksgiving, creed, etc.), along with litanies, hymns, and other materials. As gatherings of texts within texts, the prayer books are comparable to the *florilegia* surveyed above. But unlike the collections of sentences assembled by Isidore or Defensor, these liturgical compilations offer exercises in *lectio divina* which translate reading directly into prayer.

Spontaneous private prayer, as the ancient authorities had warned, must be fortified against distractions. Left to its own devices,

---

[36] André Wilmart, ed., *Precum libelli quattuor aevi karolini: Nunc primum publici iuris facti cum aliorum indicibus. Prior pars* (Rome: Ephemerides Liturgicae, 1940). See also *De psalmorum usu*, attributed to Alcuin, PL 101:465–508; the *Officia*

the mind falls prey to various categories of "thoughts," which are analyzed by Evagrius: material worries, plans, temptations, and so forth.[37] As a shield against invasion, Cassian prescribes the formula from the psalms, "Be pleased, O God, to deliver me! O Lord, make haste to help me" (Ps 69:1 [70:1]).[38] The same concern prompts a stipulation in the Rule of Saint Benedict: "Prayer should be short and pure [i.e., unmixed] unless it is prolonged under the inspiration of divine grace" (RB 20.4). The later commentators further stipulate that prayer should be short, pure, and frequent.[39] It was thought to be difficult for monks under the best of circumstances, and no doubt impossible for active lay people, to sustain the purity of prayer for more than an instant, unless the mind were occupied by consecrated wording and more mysteriously supported by the power the scriptural texts convey.

In response to this need, the monastic daily Office has focused at all times upon the Psalter. The prayer books present extracts, including as a minimum the seven penitential psalms. In the psalms, properly read and spiritually understood, it is assured that one will find answers to every personal need and circumstance:

> In the psalms you will find, if you study them with an intent mind [*intenta mente*], and reach a spiritual understanding of

---

per ferias, also attributed to Alcuin, PL 101:509–612; and the *Breviarium psalterii* by Prudence of Troyes, PL 40:1135–38. The complex textual history of these compilations is studied by Radu Constantinescu, "Alcuin et les 'Libelli Precum' de l'époque carolingienne," *Revue d'Histoire de la Spiritualité* 50 (1974), 17–56. For general comments, see Jean Leclercq and Jean-Paul Bonnes, *Un maître de la vie spirituelle au XIe siècle: Jean de Fécamp* (Paris: Librairie Philosophique J. Vrin, 1946), 60–62, and Ward, *Prayers and Meditations*, 35–38.

[37] For a summary of Evagrius's system, see Tugwell, *Ways of Imperfection*, 25–36.

[38] Cassian, *Conferences*, 10.10.

[39] On this theme, Hildemar's Commentary (also attributed to Paul the Deacon) is cited by Jean Leclercq, *La Spiritualité du Moyen Âge*, 105; see Smaragdus's *Commentary*, 3.20; Corpus Consuetudinum Monasticarum 8:210–11. Isidore of Seville comments, *Pura est oratio quam in suo tempore saeculi non interueniunt curae. . . . Tunc ergo ueraciter oramus, quando aliunde non cogitamus. Sed ualde pauci sunt qui tales orationes habeant. Et licet in quibusdam sint, difficile tamen ut semper sint* (*Sententiae* 3.7.8, CCSL 111:222).

them, the incarnation of the Word of God, his passion, resurrection and ascension. In the psalms you will find an intimate prayer, if you study them with an intent mind, such as you could not in any way conceive by yourself. In the psalms you will find an intimate confession of your sins, and a complete prayer for divine mercy; in the psalms also you will find intimate thanksgiving for all things which have happened to you.[40]

Once again, it is stressed that the necessary accompaniment of reading, as of prayer, is *intentio*. To achieve and orient that focus of mind and heart, the compilers of prayer books present each psalm within the traditional three-part structure of liturgical meditation. For example, let us look at the first penitential psalm (Ps 6 [6]) as it is presented in the prayer books from Troyes and Tours published by Wilmart.[41] The first part is the psalm text itself, which would be chanted responsorially in a church service; in the prayer books it is cited by the first line, *Domine ne in furore tuo arguas me* ("O Lord, rebuke me not in thy anger"), and followed by the *kyrie* and the *pater noster*. The second part consists of a personal prayer. Voiced in the first-person singular, the prayer echoes one or two verses from the psalm just read and evokes other associated psalms, reinforcing a Christian interpretation pertaining to the individual:

> Domine convertere et eripe animam meam, salvum me fac propter misericordiam tuam [Ps 6:5 (6:4)]. Respice et exaudi me domine deus meus; inlumina oculos meos. Ne umquam obdormiam in mortem; nequando dicat inimicus meus: Praevalui adversus eum [Ps 12:4-5 (13:3-4)]. Ab occultis meis munda me domine, et ab alienis parce servo tuo [Ps 18:13-14 (19:12-13)].

---

[40] Preface to *De psalmorum usu liber*, attributed to Alcuin (PL 101:465): *In psalmis itaque invenies, si intenta mente perscruteris, et ad spiritualem intellectum perveneris, Domini Verbi incarnationem, passionemque, et resurrectionem, atque ascensionem. In psalmis invenies tam intimam orationem, si intenta mente perscruteris, quantum non potes per teipsum ullatenus excogitare. In psalmis invenies intimam confessionem peccatorum tuorum, et integram deprecationem divinae atque Domininicae misericordiae. In psalmis quoque invenies omnium rerum, quae tibi accidunt, intimam gratiarum actionem.*

[41] *Libellus trecensis* and *Libellus turonensis*, authors unkown, in A. Wilmart, *Precum libelli*, 27 and 76.

Turn, O Lord, save my life; deliver me for the sake of thy
steadfast love [Ps. 6:5 (6:4)]. Consider and answer me, O Lord
my God; lighten my eyes lest I sleep the sleep of death; lest my
enemy say, "I have prevailed over him" [Ps 12:4-5 (13:3-4)].
Cleanse me of my hidden faults, O Lord, and from strange sins
deliver your servant [Ps 18:13-14 (19:12-13)].

The third, final phase of the psalm meditation is the collect, which is
in the first-person plural, expressing the aspiration of the community:

Exauditor omnium deus exaudi nostrorum fletuum supplicum
vocem [Ps 6:9 (6:8)], et tribue infirmitatibus nostris perpetuam
sospitatem, ut dum dignanter gemitum nostri laboris [Ps 6:7
(6:6)] suscipis, tua nos semper misericordia consoleris.

God, you who hear all prayers, hear the sound of our suppliant
weeping [Ps 6:9 (6:8)], and grant to our weakness perpetual
safety, so that as you deign to accept the moans of our weari-
ness [Ps 6:7 (6:6)], you may always console us with your mercy.

The collect again echoes phrases from the psalms, as though to
answer the previous prayer, or rather to underscore the sense that
the wording of the psalms contains both the prayer and the answer.
In the course of what is actually a dialogue between singular and
plural voices, the Scripture is realized, experienced in intimacy, and
then shared with a community, whose felt spiritual presence—*intenta devotio mentium*, in Peter Damian's phrase—is the manifesta-
tion that God is also present and has heard the person whom he
has inspired to turn to him.

Surrounding the central core that is the Psalter extract, the prayer
books provide supporting materials of various types. One necessary
inclusion, prerequisite to any lay spirituality, is a detailed penitential
inventory organized in overlapping categories: sins of commission
and omission, both known and unknown; sins in word, in deed, in
thought, and in the will; sins with each of the five senses; sins with
each part of the body, as listed from the feet to the top of the head;
sins of theft, fornication, murder, false witness, harmful scheming,
consent to wickedness, sacrilege, idle words, impure desires, and so on.
The confessional prayers attempt to cover all eventualities, including
potential sins as well as those actually committed or contemplated.

Another type of text, one derived from the monastic pattern, provides short prayers for the hours and/or for each moment in the daily routine: on rising from bed, on washing oneself, on getting dressed, on going out, and so on.[42] Others are given by theme: prayers for wisdom, for protection against unclean thoughts, on behalf of those on journeys, and prayers addressed to the Cross, the Trinity, and others. The discourse associated with these various texts is one of humility, expressed in a radically simplified grammar. Familiar patterns include the repetition of initial formulae, such as *Domine Iesu adoro te*, or *miserere mei*, or *gratias tibi ago*, through these conventions; responsive repetitions, as in the litany of the saints (*Sancta Maria, ora pro nobis*; *Sancte Petre, ora pro nobis*, etc.); lists, as in confessional prayers; and series of parallel phrases: *Te adoro. Te laudo. Te glorifico. Te benedico*, etc. These prayers are ancillary or preparatory in character. They serve to focus the *intentio*, that is to say, the effective presence of mind and heart that one brings to the liturgy of the Psalter.

Of particular interest to the study of reading are the patristic texts, fragments, and conflations which are found throughout the prayer books. Some prayers carry traditional attributions to authors, such as Jerome, Ambrose, Isidore, and Augustine. Elsewhere, patchworks of recognizable passages appear, unattributed, freely recomposed, and adapted to liturgical and spiritual needs. Invocations from Augustine's *Confessions* and *Soliloquies* are frequently conflated in this manner, defying modern attempts to disassemble and label the constituent pieces. A prayer given in the book of Tours[43] for the hour of Prime reads in part as follows:

> Domine deus omnipotens qui de nihilo mundum istum creasti. Deus a quo omne bonum sumimus. Deus sapientia in quo et a quo et per quem omnia. Deus vera et summa vita. Deus beatitudo cuius nos fides excitat, spes erigit, caritas iungit. Deus supra quem nihil. Extra quem nihil. Sine quo nihil. Deus sub quo totum. In quo totum. Cum quo totum. Deus qui facis magna et inscrutabilia et mirabilia, quorum non est numerus. Deus qui nos ad imaginem et similitudinem tuam fecisti. Deus

[42] See *Libellus coloniensis*, in Wilmart, *Precum libelli*, 25–26.
[43] Wilmart, *Precum libellli*, 71. The translation of this passage is my own.

qui nos exaudibiles facis et prestes ut pulsantibus aperiatur, te invoco, te adoro. . . . O Domine quia ego servus tuus. Ego servus tuus et filius ancillae tuae. Disrumpe vincula mea ut tibi sacrificare possim absoluta libertate sacrificium laudis.[44] Accipe quaeso illud de manu linguae meae quam formasti et excitasti ut confiteatur nomini tuo, super me quoque perfundantur ossa mea dilectione tua, et dicant: Domine quis similis tibi?[45] Dicant et responde.[46] Et dic animae meae: Salus tua ego sum. Sed dic ut audiam. Ecce aures cordis mei ante te domine. Aperi eas. Et dic animae meae: Salus tua ego sum. Curram post hanc vocem et adprehendam. Noli abscondere a me faciem tuam, ut videam eam. Angusta est domus animae meae quo venies ad illam. Dilatetur abs te. Ruinosa est, refice eam. Habet quae offendant oculos tuos, fateor et scio, sed quis mundabit eam? Aut cui praeter te clamabo, Ab occultis meis munda me domine. Et ab alienis parce servo tuo.[47] O aeterna veritas, et vera caritas, et cara aeternitas.[48]

Lord, God all powerful, who created this world from nothing, God from whom we take all that is good; God, wisdom, in whom, by whom, and through whom are all things; God the true and highest life; God, blessedness, whose faith excites us, whose hope uplifts us, and whose charity joins us together; God above whom is nothing, outside whom is nothing, without whom is nothing; God beneath whom is everything, in whom is everything, with whom is everything; God who performs great and inscrutable and marvelous things without number; God, you who made us in your image and likeness; God who makes us worthy to be heard, and who opens the door to those who knock: you do I invoke, you I adore. . . . O Lord, I am

---

[44] Augustine, Conf 9.1.1, ed. O'Donnell, 231: *O domine, ego seruus tuus, ego seruus tuus et filius ancillae tuae. Dirupisti uincula mea; tibi sacrificabo hostiam laudis*; cf. Ps 115:16-17 (116:16-17).

[45] Augustine, Conf 5.1.1; ed. O'Donnell, 46: *Accipe sacrificium confessionum mearum de manu linguae meae quam formasti et excitasti, ut confiteatur nomini tuo, et sana omnia ossa mea, et dicant, Domine, quis similis tibi?*; cf. Ps 34:10 (35:10).

[46] Augustine, Conf 9.1.1; ed. O'Donnell, 231.

[47] Augustine, Conf 1.5.5–6; ed. O'Donnell, 4; cf. Ps 34:3 (35:3) and Ps 18:13-14 (19:12-13).

[48] Augustine, Conf 7.10.16; ed. O'Donnell, 82.

your servant and the son of your handmaid. Break my chains, so that I might offer to you with absolute freedom the sacrifice of praise. Accept it, I pray, from my tongue which you formed and excited so that it might acknowledge your name; let your love be poured over my bones, that they might say: Lord, who is like you? Let them speak, and you, answer: say to my soul: "I am your salvation." But speak so that I might hear it. Here before you, Lord, are the ears of my heart: open them. And say to my soul: "I am your salvation." I will run to follow that voice, and I will reach it. Do not hide your face from me. Narrow is the house of my soul, that you should enter it; let it be widened by you. It is in ruins; rebuild it. There are things that offend your eyes; I confess that and know it. But who will clean it? Or to whom, other than you, shall I cry: "Cleanse me of my hidden faults, O Lord, and from strange sins deliver your servant"? O eternal truth, and true charity, and dear eternity.

Five different Augustinian texts (at least) are here assembled. The synthesis is a product of traditional transmission over a course of centuries. Augustine's invocations have by this time entered the public domain. His is a style, a voice, that has been integrated throughout Christian culture; it is a prayer-attitude which pertains to many different moments in religious life rather than to any one context or named individual. Many passages from Augustine hold a near-sacred, parascriptural authority. Along with their presumed intimate familiarity to the devout reader, this licenses the freedom to recombine and even rewrite them.

In the process of *meditatio*, the reader reads and prays through Augustine's reading/prayer of the psalms. The first-person-singular voice of "David" is transferred successively to Augustine, to the compiler of the prayer, and to the final recipient(s) of the prayer book. Each reader in turn assumes this generalized persona, and with it the first-person plural designating a community whose presence is felt over time—in history—as well as across any distance in space. Also assumed is the speaker's relationship to the second-person singular—God—acknowledged as present to each and every participant in the dialogue.

The dramatic simplicity of Augustine's rhetoric, deliberately chosen and underpinned by his rigorously objective inquiry, adapts itself perfectly to the environment of the prayer book designed for laity. The paratactic style, consisting of short, disconnected phrases, reduces grammatical complexity to a minimum. The repeated words and parallel structures take on the rhythm of responsive liturgy. The psalm verses quoted by Augustine are among those most familiar to all. These means address the needs of a nonclerical (albeit aristocratic) reader whose latinity in the Carolingian period and afterward might have been presumed to be minimal. What is sought and found here is poverty of spirit: "My house is too narrow; let it be widened by You" (*Confessions* 1.5). The reader—who has made due confessions and learned humble utterances for each moment of the daily routine—could readily adopt the Augustinian wording and apply it to his or her own personal concerns.

This prayer summarizes various features of the prayer books and offers a striking illustration of *lectio divina* as it could be performed by a lay person or by any solitary individual. The text is assumed by the reader individually and personally. It is a "living word" spoken by God as well as to him. God takes the initiative and inspires the reader to respond; the prayer flows through the text, as it were, in both directions. It has a sacramental efficacy—a capability of placing the reader in a live presence and in communion with the church—on the same level as participation in a fully "ecclesial" liturgy.

Chapter Five

The Extension of Meditation

Compilations document instances of reading-reception. The examples that we have examined so far are relatively conservative and even scholarly, as the meticulous attributions of sources given by Defensor and by Bede might suggest. The eleventh-century spiritual revival brings to the genre a renewal of subjectivity: a more intensely personal response to reading, followed by a lengthening extension of the thought processes that the reading inspired. The compiler ventures now some distance beyond the conservation of authoritative texts in order to rediscover their meaning in practice. From this point onward, *meditatio* evolves toward freer "meditations," in the modern sense of the word, confided now to writing in a relatively assertive, self-dramatizing rhetorical style.

Two works, written respectively at the beginning and at the end of the eleventh century, will serve to illustrate these tendencies: the *Confessio theologica* of John of Fécamp and the *Prayers and Meditations* of Saint Anselm. The former compilation records reflections relatively closely derived from abundantly quoted patristic and scriptural texts. The latter absorbs its sources into an originally composed poetic prose, resonating with scriptural and liturgical rhythms. Both works are dramatically voiced by a first-person-singular *persona* expressing and generalizing the situation of the writer; both orient their reflections to specific readers: prominent lay personalities whose roles in the dialogue are likewise generalized. In their differences and similarities, the two works explore potentialities of the act of reading that will be more fully realized in the generations that immediately follow them.

John of Fécamp's *Confessio theologica*

"Between Saint Gregory and Saint Bernard no one, in the Middle Ages, ascended the heights of mystical life with more conviction than did this forgotten monk."[1] André Wilmart's high praise honors John of Fécamp as an important transitional figure in the history of literary spirituality. Until the beginning of the twentieth century, however, he had been virtually forgotten. His writings, although abundantly recopied, had been attributed variously to Augustine, Alcuin, Anselm, and others. Wilmart undertook to disentangle the tradition, and this labor was completed by Jean Leclercq in collaboration with Jean-Paul Bonnes.[2] It was in his studies of John of Fécamp and Peter of Celle, which were published in the same year (1946), that Leclercq first explored concepts of textual traditionalism which he later generalized in *The Love of Learning and the Desire for God*.

Born in the region of Ravenna toward the end of the tenth century, John presumably entered monastic life at a young age. He came into contact with the Cluniac reform movement in the person of William of Volpiano, whom he followed to Dijon. John was appointed prior of Fécamp around 1010, then abbot in 1028; he remained in charge of that abbey until his death in 1078. His small physical stature earned him the nickname "Jeannelin" and paradoxically heightened the admiration of his contemporaries for his spiritual gifts. He lived during a period of rapid change in Normandy and was involved all his life in political and administrative responsibilities, and he wrote in various places of his longing for solitude and the repose of contemplation.

The *Confessio theologica*[3] (dated before 1018) is modestly conceived by its author as a "little compilation" (*defloratiuncula*). It is much more than that, however, as the reader soon discovers; emerging from the tradition of the *florilegia* and the prayer books, this work powerfully extends the movement of reading into prayer, and from prayer into writing. To whom was it written? To God,

---

[1] A. Wilmart, *Revue de d'ascétique et de mystique* 18 (1937), 7.

[2] Leclercq and Bonnes, *Un maître*.

[3] A critical edition of the *Confessio theologica* is provided in Leclercq and Bonnes, *Un maître*, 109–83. My parenthetical references by chapter and line number are to this edition. For a translation into French, see Philippe de Vial, *Jean de Fécamp: La confession théologique*, Sagesses chrétiennes (Paris: Éditions du Cerf, 1992). English translations given here are my own.

following the example of Augustine's *Confessions*, and to himself, as he implies in the concluding *recapitulatio*: *Ut breue et manuale uerbum de Deo mecum semper haberem* ("So that I might always have the word of God with me, in brief and handy form"). The book would serve to rekindle the author's ardor whenever that grows cold (Conf theo 3.1274–76). Other possible external readers are implied elsewhere in the text, as in the address which concludes the first section: *Tu qui haec vel legis vel oras vel confiteris* (Conf theo 1.332). John recomposed material from the *Confessio* in a *Libellus de scripturis et uerbis patrum* dedicated to an unnamed nun and rededicated in 1063 or 1064 to the Empress Agnes, the widow of Henry III of Bavaria. Much of the same material was recast yet again in a *Confessio fidei* written for the author's personal use.[4]

The two words of the title of *Confessio theologica* require interpretation. John's *Confessio* is a *profession* of faith, following the example of Augustine. It is not a "confession" of specific sins. John adopts the Augustinian mode of invoking God by addressing his prayer to God in writing.[5] Concerning the adjective *theologica*, Leclercq stresses that John's confession is not "theological" in the restricted sense of the term as used following Abelard; rather, it is used with the broad understanding by which ancient poets were termed *theologi*, that is, "divinely inspired."[6] In broad terms, the title signifies John's intent to found his personal profession upon orthodox doctrine, understood both intellectually and spiritually on a high level. The work is divided into three parts: the first—the most "theological" in the modern sense—makes a statement of faith, focused on the nature of God and the Trinity; the second offers thanksgiving for the redemption by Christ; the third, the longest section, develops the theme of longing for heaven, expressed in repeated prayers for the gift of tears of contrition.

A programmatic statement at the beginning of the second part relates the *Confessio* to the earlier compilations. This section, John announces, is about the "grace by which we were redeemed" and the "perfection of faith," which are both necessary for salvation:

---

[4] Leclercq and Bonnes, *Un maître*, 31–44.
[5] Leclercq and Bonnes, *Un maître*, 53–56.
[6] Leclercq and Bonnes, *Un maître*, 76–78.

> Sed quia oportet nos et recte credere et bene vivere (unum enim
> sine altero nihil perfectionis habet), ideo multa verba orationi
> congrua addita sunt. Dicta mea dicta sunt patrum. Sic ista quae
> dicimus lege ut putes te patrum verba relegere, et toto mentis
> adnisu quas vales actiones gratiarum tuo redemptori alacriter
> sinceriterque persolve. (Conf theo 2.3–9)

> But since we must both believe rightly and live well—for the
> one without the other has no perfection—therefore many
> words that are suited for prayer have been added. My words are
> the words of the fathers; read then those that I say so that you
> will think that you are rereading the words of the fathers, and
> with the utmost striving of your mind, eagerly offer heartfelt
> thanksgiving to your redeemer.

A declaration of correct belief cannot be sufficient in itself; it must
be fulfilled in "living well." That wholly traditional imperative,
echoing Isidore of Seville and many others, here justifies John's
intention to supplement his profession of faith by "adding" phraseology for prayer and thereby translating theology into spirituality.

Dicta mea dicta patrum ("My words are the words of the Fathers"). John of Fécamp quotes extensively from Augustine's *Confessions* and from Gregory's *Moralia* and *Homilies on Ezekiel*. He
begins where Augustine begins: *Quomodo invocabo Deum?* How
does one invoke or call God to "be present," since God is already
in the writer—just as the writer is in God—and the writer would
not "be" at all without God the Creator? John transcribes nearly
verbatim the opening paragraphs of the *Confessions*, including
the series of epithets describing God: *Summe, omnipotentissime,
misericordissime.* To this he seamlessly joins a passage of descriptive
phrases taken from Gregory: *Qui solus uiuificas omnia; qui creasti
omnia. Qui ubique es, et ubique totus. Qui sentiri potes et uideri non
potes* (Hiez 1.8.16: "You who alone give life to all things, who created all things; you who are everywhere, and everywhere whole;
who can be felt and who cannot be seen"). Similarly, in the third
part of the *Confessio* he cites long passages from books 12 and 13
of the *Confessions* in which Augustine further justifies the act of
invocation and describes God's eternal dwelling place, the goal of
the human pilgrimage.

These quotations, set down at length, were copied seemingly from writing rather than from memory.[7] What were his immediate sources? He might readily have consulted collections of patristic texts found in the monastic library at Fécamp.[8] Augustine's invocations in the *Confessions* were, of course, well-known, often cited, and recopied, as in the prayer quoted above (pp. 129–31). In the context of the *Confessio*, the long quotations appear, in any case, as *other* writing, distinct stylistically as well as conceptually from their surroundings. John refers to Augustine and Gregory indistinctly as "the words of the Fathers," as the authoritative voice of the church. He has copied pages into his book in order to have them in "brief and handy" form, available to be (re)read by himself and eventually by another reader. These writings are, so to speak, the theology in his confession; he does not assume them as his own.

The prayer books surveyed above would have been another important source of material and inspiration. Each of the three sections of the *Confessio* ends with a prayer found in one or another of the *libelli*, and the third section both begins and ends in this manner. His reflections in the course of each section are framed by the prayer from which they take their final form and meaning. The general discourse of the prayer books informs the work throughout. John writes in short, grammatically simple sentences and often reverts to *anaphora* and other rhetorical repetitions characteristic of liturgy: *Gratias tibi ago pro sancta incarnation. . . . Gratias tibi ago pro passione* (Conf theo 2.71–4: "I give thanks to you for the holy Incarnation. . . . I give thanks to you for the Passion"); *Da mihi cor contritum, cor purum, cor sincerum, cor deuotum, cor castum, cor sobrium* (Conf theo 2.375–6: "Give me a contrite heart, a pure heart, a sincere heart, a devout heart, a chaste heart, a sober heart"). In this manner, moving from objective doctrine to personal, spiritual realization, he guides his reader to experience and "savor" the scriptural and patristic texts that he provides.

---

[7] Whether or not John had in fact memorized these passages cannot be determined with certainty. He does pray in several places for a "tenacious memory"; see Conf theo 3.424–5; 3.957–64.

[8] Leclercq and Bonnes, *Un maître*, 63, n.1 and n. 3.

In contrast to the long paragraphs from Augustine, he cites Scripture in short phrases, apparently from memory, weaving together exact and approximate quotations, allusions, and reminiscences from many different sources. He draws most frequently from the Psalms and secondarily from the epistles, the Gospel of John, the Song of Songs, Job, Jeremiah, and other books of the Bible. Patristic writings and the prayer books are also frequently cited in this manner. The tissue or "chain" of Scripture may extend unbroken for a page or more, flowing seamlessly thereafter into John's own prose. John is a master of this traditional literary art, and Leclercq's *apologia* for it is clearly apt: John is not quoting "phrases borrowed from another"; his references are fully personally assumed.[9] He is "speaking Bible" with the spontaneity of one speaking his own language—"drawing from his own well," as he is mandated to do by Cassian and the monastic tradition.

It is a reading-prayer, a movement of reading into prayer, impelled by the expressed or implied wish to become qualified to "sing with" or "say with" the psalmist (or other writer) the words that are read and that have ideally been memorized and internalized in action. *O Domine, tribue mihi ut "laudet te cor meum et lingua mea et omnia ossa mea dicant: 'Domine quis similis tui?'"* (Conf theo 3.150: "O Lord, grant to me that 'my heart might praise you, and that my tongue and all my bones might say: "Lord, who is like you?"' Cf. Augustine, Conf 9.1.1, and Ps 34:10 [35:10]). Here John is actually quoting Augustine quoting the psalm. John is reading the Psalm through Augustine's reading, devoutly asking to be able to "say it with" him. Similarly, throughout the *Confessio* John asks for the gift of tears, as it were, in order to "weep with" the psalmist: "As a deer longs for flowing streams, so my soul longs for you, O God. My soul thirsts for God, for the living God. When shall I come and behold the face of God? My tears have been my food, day and night . . ." (Ps 41:1-3 [42:1-3]). John returns frequently to this favorite text and compares the tears of the psalmist with those of Hannah before the birth of Samuel (1 Kgs 1:9-18), with those of Job and Jeremiah, with those of Mary Magdalen standing before the empty tomb of Jesus (John 20:11), with the water drawn

---

[9] Leclercq and Bonnes, *Un maître*, 56–60; cf. Leclercq, *Love of Learning* 94.

from the rock (Exod 17), and not least with the water of baptism. These typological associations are drawn from the prayer books and from longstanding tradition.[10] Whereas for the psalmist tears most often express the bitterness of privation, John, in the role of a Christian penitent, actively seeks them as a grace, as an ablution or an irrigation, as a melting of the hardened heart:[11]

> Veni, Domine, et noli tardare. Scinde duritiam cordis mei ut emanet fons iste cuius desiderio nimis aestuat anima mea. Da mihi irriguum inferius et irriguum superius. Da benedictionem de rore caeli et de piguedine terrae, ut lacrimae meae fiant mihi panis die ac nocte. (Conf theo 2.468–73)

> Come, Lord, do not delay. Cut through the hardness of my heart, so that that fountain might erupt, which my soul passionately desires. Give me the lower and higher irrigation. Give me the blessing of the dew from heaven and the fatness of the earth, so that my tears may be my bread day and night [cf. Ps 41:4 (42:4) and *Precum libelli* 90].

> Opto enim, et tota mente mea peto dari mihi panem lacrimarum, quem manducem nocte ac die, dum dico fluctuanti animae: Quare tristis es misera? (Conf theo 3.1107)

> For I wish, and beg with all my mind to be given the bread of tears, which I might eat day and night, while I say to my anxious soul: "Why, wretch, are you sad?" [cf. Ps 41:4-6 (42:4-6)]

The desire for tears, the longing of the deer for the stream (Ps 41:2 [42:1]), is further linked to the psalmist's wish for dove's wings, with which to fly upward to heaven (Ps 54:7 [55:6]):

> Quando apparebo ante faciem tuam [Ps 41:3 (42:2)]? . . .
> Quando, quando transibo in illam admirabilem sempiterni

---

[10] Cf. John's "Oratio pro lacrimis," in *Libellus turonesnsis*, in Wilmart, *Precum libelli*, 101.

[11] Psalm 41 (42) is similarly inflected in the collect which follows the psalm in the *Libellus Turonensis* (Wilmart, *Precum libelli*, 138) and in the *Officia per ferias* (PL 101:583): *Tribue ut dum te visibili lacrimarum imbre pasti requirimus, invisibiliter te intra pectoris nostri tabernaculum collocemus.*

gaudii domum? Quemadmodum desiderat ceruum ad fontem
aquarum, ita desiderat anima mea ad Deum fontem uiuum [Ps
41:2 (42:1)]. Quis dabit mihi pennas sicut columbae, et uolabo,
et requiescam [Ps 54:7 (55:6)]? (Conf theo 3.181–89)

When shall I appear before your face [Ps 41:3 (42:2)]? . . .
When, when shall I cross over into that admirable dwelling of
perpetual joy? As the deer longs for the flowing stream, so my
soul desires God, the living fountain [Ps 41:2 (42:1)].[12]
Who shall give me wings like a dove's, so that I might fly upward and be at rest [Ps 54:7 (55:6)]?

Lire c'est méditer et c'est prier.[13] Leclercq rightly insists on the equivalence of these terms—reading, meditation, and prayer—although
they are not synonyms. There is a flow from one phase to the next, a
continuum or process of becoming, which should be further specified. *Lire et méditer*—*meditatio*, in a word—become prayer through
a movement of active, personal implication in the reading; John
identifies with the psalmist, or rather with the first-person singular
subject of the psalms; he inflects their meaning as he recognizes his
own experience in them. At the same time, his personal identity
is transcended and generalized. Not without effort, not without a
struggle through the darkness of faith, he gropes toward what is not
yet perfectly realized. Where John perceives a gap between his own
state of mind and that of the psalmist, he prays—notably in his repeated prayer for the response and release of tears—to align himself
with the text, to feel emotionally as well as perceive intellectually
what the text expresses. Meditation on the Psalms leads John out
of this world into an internal Jerusalem, the city of contemplation:
*Ingrediar in interiora mentis meae, et transcendens eam, curram in latitudinem
ditissimae patriae tuae* (Conf theo 3.791: "I will enter into the interior of my mind, and transcending that, I will run in the breadth of
your bountiful land"). The chains of scriptural quotations serve as a
wall, deployed sometimes as though with an intent to keep out any
thought, any writing that is *not* Scripture. Reading and praying the

---

[12] John reads: *Sitivit anima mea ad Deum fontem vivum*, rather than *fortem vivum*
as in the Vulgate.

[13] Leclercq and Bonnes, *Un maître*, 101.

psalms, John places himself inside the texts as in a protected interior space, in their presence, surrounded by them:

> Unde mihi ualde libet de te loqui, de te audire, de te legere, de te scribere, de te conferre, ut sub dulcem umbram since-ritatis tuae ingressus, ab huius saeculi aestibus in tui refrigerii temperamento abscondar. Huius rei gratia umbrosum montem et condensum ascendo, amoena prata perlustro, uiridissimas sententiarum herbas legendo carpo, frequentando rumino, exarando congrego, ut suauitatem dulcedinis et caritatis tuae reponam in alta sede memoriae meae. (Conf theo 3.418–25)
>
> ───────────
>
> It pleases me greatly to speak of you, to hear you, to read you, to write of you, to discourse about you, so that, having come into the soft shadow of your sincerity, I might hide myself in your refreshing coolness from the hot blasts of this world. By that grace I go up a densely shaded mountain, I wander through pleasant meadows, I pick out in reading the green herbs of your sayings, I visit frequently and ruminate, digging in I gather to-gether, so that I might put up the sweetness of your goodness and charity in the deep-set place of my memory.

Lire c'est méditer et c'est prier. Should we add: *et c'est écrire?* Can the *Confessio* be described as a prayer in writing? It is prayer-compilation, having some generic resemblance to the examples studied above, but it is set forth not as an anthology or as a service manual, but as one continuous utterance, addressed by a first-person-singular subject writing directly to God. Although the activity of writing this text may be a prayer, in theory at least, the resultant text itself, once detached from the writer, is not. It is certainly a representation of a prayer; it may perhaps be a record of a prayer that John once uttered; it stands "on the record" as a confession/profession of faith whose permanent validity the writer continues to acknowledge. But the text remains to be actualized by the eventual reader (who may be John himself at a later time). To be a prayer it must be spoken or heard, restored to a personal presence, and indeed performed.

John summons his reader accordingly: *Tu qui haec vel legis vel oras vel confiteris* (Conf theo 1.332: "You who read these things or pray them or confess them")—"you" are to "lift up your mind" and adore in spirit the God who is Spirit; you are to read what John has written and compiled as though rereading the "words of the Fathers," and "eagerly, sincerely, with all the effort of your mind, pour out thanksgiving to your redeemer." Later versions of the *Confessio*, those dedicated to an unnamed nun and to the Empress Agnes, will carry an injunction in prefatory letters that they should read this book "reverently and with due fearfulness," and not approach it in a spirit of temerity or impiety. This book is not a commentary. Its purpose is spiritual, not didactic. We are warned against any detached mode of reading and drawn into fully active, personal engagement.

The reader's participation is modeled by the first-person-singular speaker of the prayer. This textual "I" is not, of course, identical to the historical John of Fécamp (although Leclercq's reading tends to equate the two). "John" is a generalized *persona* who demonstrates the devotional attitude that the eventual reader should adopt upon (re)reading the Biblical and patristic texts that he quotes. He is staged in the text as the protagonist in an allegory.[14] We follow his quest as he makes his initial statement of belief, gives thanks for redemption, and passionately prays for deliverance from this world; he encounters several important secondary figures—his soul, his tears, God—and so proceeds toward the internal heavenly city. He looks forward to being released by death into heaven itself. The *persona* is not bounded by the particular circumstances of the writer; even more so than its Augustinian forebear, it is an identity made available to the reader to assume as his or her own.

There is, however, a self-conscious literary dimension to the *Confessio* which would tend to detach the text from a live devotional act. John's writing deploys the style of prayer for aesthetic effect, notably in the use of anaphora, parallelisms, vocative epithets, and other rhetorical ornaments derived from the *libelli precum*. He is aware of the insufficiency of his expressive resources before God—*dico quod ualeo, sed non dico quod debeo* (Conf theo 3.886: "I say what I can, but I do not say what I ought")—but he also obeys

---

[14] Brian Stock comments, "One of the privileged partners of silence and contemplation is allegory. . . . During these brief interludes, mentally recreated personifications clarified the role of moral, emotional and psychological forces in the individual's ethical orientation" (*After Augustine*, 17).

a religious imperative, inherited from Augustine, to praise God as best he can: *Vae tacentibus de te!* (Conf 1.4.4: "Woe to those who are silent about you!"). He wishes that he could praise God with the voice of the angelic chorus, or at least, we sense, with the voice of Augustine. He prays that God might hear not merely what he says, but what he wishes to say. Implicitly, he prays for eloquence, for inspiration, for that same numinous power of feeling which would also bring him the gift of tears.

As much as for another reader, John writes for himself. Having received the teaching of the church on faith, he copies out authoritative paragraphs by Augustine and Gregory in order to *see* them and *have* them: *Desideraui intellectu uidere quod credidi. Deus accende in me magis magisque scientiae lumen* (Conf theo 1.233; cf. Augustine, *De trinitate* 15 and 18: "I desired to see with the understanding what I believed. God, light in me more and more the light of knowledge"). He steps thereby beyond acceptance on faith and hope—mediated in Pauline terms by hearing (*fides ex auditu,* Rom10:17)—toward a fully grasped, clearly visualized comprehension "in fact" (*in re*): *Corde credo, ore confiteor, quia uera sunt omnia quae illa* [sc. *ecclesia*] *credit, confitetur et docet. Certe uidebimus in re quod tenemus in spe* (Conf theo 1.6: "I believe in my heart, I confess with my mouth, for those things are true which the church believes, confesses and teaches. Certainly we will see in fact what we possess in hope").[15] What he seeks is the removal of all obstacles and intermediaries in order to experience the presence of God in immediacy: *Ut ipso cordis palato sentiam, gustem et sapiam, quam dulcis et suavis es, Domine* (Conf theo 3.1094–5: "Let me feel and taste and savor on the palate of my own heart how sweet you are, Lord"). Writing to God actualizes the spiritual (invisible, immaterial) reality of his presence; John prays as he writes, and as he rereads his own text, he repeats the act of prayer. He surrounds himself with God's presence in words; in speech, hearing, and reading, but most tangibly in writing, he is constructing the protected space of contemplation, his interior Jerusalem.

---

[15] Cf. Rom 8:24: "Hope that is seen is not hope. For who hopes for what he sees? But if we hope for what we do not see, we wait for it with patience"; and 2 Cor 5:7: "We walk by faith, not by sight."

John of Fécamp's *Confessio* combines various dimensions of compilation, not without some uncertainty of resolution. It is a work of conservation; it is also a ruminative *meditatio* on the psalms and on Augustine's *Confessions*. John seeks to build a "theological" bridge between the retention/transmission of doctrine and a personally engaged act of prayer; he writes both for the use of a devout reader and for his own benefit. The *Confessio* is, finally, a work of literature, highly self-aware and not exempt from preciosity. John's writing claims our attention, generates its own logic and momentum, and realizes itself in terms of aesthetics on the page. We sense that this text may potentially be detached from the live presence of a prayer act and read for its own sake.

John does forestall merely aesthetic reception, offering careful instructions to the readers of his *Libellus de scripturis et verbis patrum* as to the spirit in which his compilation should be read. In the dedicatory letters to an unnamed nun and to the Empress Agnes,[16] he advises that this text is "to be read reverently, and meditated with due fearfulness." It should not be approached rashly or pridefully, he warns, but rather with tears and deep piety, for only then will one taste the sweetness that lies within it. "Read it frequently," he concludes, "especially when you feel that your mind has been touched by the desire for heaven." The implication is that this reader will have the freedom to approach the book at will, as inspired by the Holy Spirit. *Lectio divina* is now to be rediscovered by a solitary individual in an unregimented situation, removed from the monastic routine.

---

[16] "Lettre à une moniale," in Leclercq and Bonnes, *Un maître* 207; the identical passage is found in the "Lettre à l'impératrice Agnès," 214–15: *In quo reperies magna ex parte caelestis theoriae dulcia verba, quae reuerenter legenda sunt et cum timore debito meditanda, ne forte de temeritate iudicetur qui tepidus et indeuotus accesserit. Unde sciendum est quod huius libelli lectio illis praesertim debetur qui mentes suas carnalibus desideriis et terrenis concupiscentiis obtenebrari non sinunt. Quando autem ista leguntur cum lacrimis et deuotione nimia, tunc mitis lector ipso cordis palato sapit quid dulcedinis intus lateat. Si ita est, immo quia ita est, eloquiorum diuinorum archana et sublimia uerba tangere non praesumat superba et fastiosa mens, ne forte labatur in errorem. . . . Illi uero soli secundum Deum sapientes, qui profunda pollent humilitate, tantum capiunt quantum Spiritus Sanctus eis reuelare dignatur. Haec ergo frequenter lege, et tunc praecipue cum mentem tuam caelesti afflatam desiderio uides.*

Saint Anselm of Canterbury's *Orationes sive meditationes*

The *Orationes sive meditationes* of Saint Anselm of Canterbury (1033–1109) make significant further steps in this same direction.[17] This collection is among his earliest writings. It was originally compiled "at the request of several brothers" during the decade of the 1170s. In 1072, he sent six of the prayers and one meditation, together with a selection from the Psalter, to the Princess Adelaide, a daughter of William the Conqueror; this collection would have included *Meditatio* 1, *Orationes* 13, 16, and probably 8, 9, 10, and 11.[18] Three prayers to the Virgin Mary were sent in 1073–4 to a friend, the monk Gundolf of Bec.[19] Other prayers and meditations were added in subsequent years, among them *Meditatio* 3, "On Human Redemption," written in 1099 as a devotional reflection on the conclusions he had reached in *Cur Deus homo*.[20] In 1104 he sent the entire collection—leaving out, however, the Psalter selection—to the Countess Matilda of Tuscany.

In a short preface to *Orationes sive meditationes*, Anselm instructs his readers:

> Orationes sive meditationes quae subscriptae sunt, quoniam ad excitandam legentis mentem ad dei amorem vel timorem, seu ad suimet discussionem editae sunt, non sunt legendae in tumultu, sed in quiete, nec cursim et velociter, sed paulatim cum intenta et morosa meditatione. Nec debet intendere lector ut quamlibet earum totam perlegat, sed quantum sentit sibi deo

---

[17] Franciscus Salesius Schmitt, ed., *S. Anselmi Cantuariensis archiepiscopi opera omnia* (Stuttgart: Frommann, 1968), 2:2–91; Ward, *Prayers and Meditations*. Parenthetical references are to the Schmitt edition (by Prayer or Meditation number and by line number) and to Ward's translation (by page number).

[18] On the development of the collection and its reception history, see R. W. Southern, *Saint Anselm: A Portrait in a Landscape* (Cambridge: Cambridge University Press, 1990), 91–112, and Ward, *Prayers and Meditations*, appendix, 275–77. Southern cites a 1072 letter to the Princess Adelaide (Ep. 10, Schmitt 2:113–14) identifying the contents of the collection sent to her.

[19] Anselm briefly describes the composition of the three Marian prayers in a letter to Gundolf (Ep. 28, Schmitt 2:135).

[20] In *S. Anselmi Cantuariensis archiepiscopi opera omnia*, vol. 2, ed. Franciscus Salesius Schmitt (Stuttgart: Frommann, 1968).

adiuvante valere ad accendendum affectum orandi, vel quantum illum delectat. Nec necesse habet aliquam semper a principio incipere, sed ubi magis illi placuerit. Ad hoc enim ipsum paragraphis sunt distinctae per partes, ut ubi elegerit incipiat aut desinat, ne prolixitas aut frequens eiusdem loci repetitio generet fastidium, sed potius aliquem inde colligat lector propter quod factae sunt pietatis affectum. (Prol 2–12)

The purpose of the prayers and meditations that follow is to stir up the mind of the reader to the love or fear of God, or to self-examination. They are not to be read in turmoil, but quietly, not skimmed or hurried through, but taken a little at a time, with deep and thoughtful meditation. The reader should not trouble about reading the whole of any of them, but only as much as, by God's help, he finds useful in stirring up his spirit to pray, or as much as he likes. Nor is it necessary for him always to begin any one always at the beginning, but wherever he pleases. With this in mind the sections are divided into paragraphs, so that the reader can choose where he wishes to begin and leave off, and not get bored by too much material or by the repetition of the same passages; rather let him gather from them some feeling of prayer, for the sake of which these prayers have been composed. (Ward, 89)

Anselm's instructions, like those of John of Fécamp, project a surprisingly modern vision of the reader he addresses: a literate, reflective individual with a book in hand in a private setting, in which he or she may browse at leisure and at will. This reader profile would have been realized in fact by the Empress Agnes or the Princess Adelaide or the Countess Matilda—devout, aristocratic lay women, actively involved in the church-state politics of the time; one recalls especially the role played by Matilda at Canossa.[21] In such disciples, not unlike

---

[21] On Matilda of Tuscany, see Valerie Eads, "The Very Model of a Medieval General: A Website Devoted to the Career of Matilda of Tuscany," http://www.the-orb.net/encyclop/culture/women/matilda.html; on the relations of Matilda and her mother, Beatrice, with Pope Gregory VII, see H. E. J. Cowdrey, *Pope Gregory VII, 1073–1085* (Oxford: Clarendon Press, 1998), 296–307. The bishop Anselm of Lucca, whom Gregory VII had appointed as Countess Matilda's spiritual guardian, composed five prayer-texts for her that are comparable to those of Anselm of Canterbury. See André Wilmart, "Cinq textes de prière composés

the Roman ladies who had studied with Jerome centuries before, the writers assume a high level of self-discipline and maturity. In his letters to them, Anselm maintains a careful balance between deference to their rank and the assertion of his own spiritual authority. Apparently he trusts them to guide themselves by what "pleases" them (*delectat, placuerit*)—not, of course, as a dilettantism, but with the due seriousness of a devotional exercise.

Like Alcuin before him, Anselm is concerned with the quality of his readers' attention. The various prayers and meditations will emphasize the fear of God, the love of God, and the process of penitential introspection; these three orientations remain distinct in Anselm's mind, even as he draws them into close and necessary relationship. These texts are not to be read hurriedly, he stresses, not in noisy public circumstances, but in quiet and privacy, with a focused concentration befitting the complexity of ideas they convey and the depth of emotional realization they are designed to elicit.[22] A letter to Adelaide echoes the preface by urging her to keep in mind, as she reads, "the attitude of humility, and the feelings of fear and love that should accompany the sacrifice of prayer."[23] The rededication of the collection to the Countess Matilda reiterates, *non sunt legendae cursim nec velociter, sed paulatim cum intenta et morosa mediatione* (Prol [*alia recensio*] 8: "They are not to be read hastily but little by little, with intent and lingering meditation").

It is nonetheless an interrupted reading that Anselm foresees. The reader is encouraged to browse in the book, as inspired by the Holy Spirit, who moves one to pick it up and who guides the hand that opens and closes it. The writer has personally supervised a layout in paragraphs for ease of access. He sees no point in reading

---

par Anselme de Lucques pour la Comtesse Mathilde," *Revue d'Ascétique et de Mystique* 19 (1938): 23–72.

[22] R.W. Southern comments, "Whereas in the comparable prayer of an earlier generation everything is immediately clear, in Anselm there is much that is too subtle, too complex and too personal to be understood without a close concentration which is possible only in the seclusion of an inner chamber. The environment of prayer has shifted decisively from the church to the chamber, and from communal effort to severe and lonely introspection" (*Portrait in a Landscape*, 102).

[23] Ep. 10 (Schmitt 2:113–14).

any text completely through; on the contrary, he directs his reader to *let go* of the text the moment he or she feels the desire to pray.[24] In the rededication to the Countess Matilda, he suggests even that she might use his prayers merely as models, in order to compose others more appropriate to her own situation:

> Placuit celsitudini vestrae ut *Orationes*, quas diversis fratribus secundum singulorum petitionem edidi, sibi mitterem. In quibus quamvis quaedam sint quae ad vestram personam non pertinent, omnes tamen volui mittere, ut, si cui placuerint, de hoc exemplari eas possit accipere. (Prol [*alia recensio*] 1–6)

> It has seemed good to your highness that I should send to you these prayers, which I edited at the request of several brothers. Some of them are not appropriate to you, but I want to send them all, so that if you like them you may be able to compose others after their example. (Ward, 90)

Anselm calls for an intensity of meditation on his writings, which ultimately—and paradoxically—do not matter. It is not the content or the integrity of Anselm's own texts which is to be valued, but rather the presence of the Spirit that they recall and imply. The written prayers will serve to "stir up the mind of the reader to the love or fear of God," in preparation for the *real* prayers which will take place when one puts down the book and lifts one's eyes.

Anselm's directions both rejoin and depart from earlier concepts of spiritual reading. A scriptural text would always be pre-

---

[24] Cf. Ep. 28 to Gundolf (Schmitt 3:135–36). The concept of interrupted reading will be taken up by twelfth-century writers. William of Saint-Thierry writes, "The reading should stimulate the feelings and give rise to prayer, which should interrupt your reading, not so much hampering it as restoring to it a mind ever more purified for understanding" (*The Golden Epistle*, trans. Theodore Berkeley, CF 12 [Kalamazoo, MI: Cistercian Publications, 1971], 52). God's response to prayers similarly occurs as an interruption, according to Guigo II: "The Lord does not wait until the end of the prayer, but rather interrupts it in the middle of its course, and hastens to meet the soul who desires him" (*The Ladder of Monks*, trans. Edmund Colledge and James Walsh, CS 48 [Kalamazoo, MI: Cistercian Publications, 1981], 74). Interjected prayers and interrupting objective theological discussion frequently occur in patristic writings, as they do in Anselm's *Proslogion*.

sented as infinite, inexhaustible; everything one personally might need is to be found in the psalms, according to *De psalmorum usu*.[25] There is a power (*virtus*) that shines *through* the sacred text and reaches the reader even before one understands the words; full understanding would be an ultimate goal, which the reader might approach but never actually reach in this life. One is summoned, in any case, to "assiduous" concentration on the text, which lies always before one's gaze, and it is always understood that the true fulfillment of reading is found not in intellectual understanding but in action, as Cassian teaches (Conf 10.11.5). From this traditional pedagogy Anselm retains *intenta et morosa meditatio* and the experiential appropriation which should follow it.

Anselm's *Prayers*, however, are not to be received as Scripture. He quotes the Bible sparingly and the Fathers not all; he sends his writings to his readers under his own name as their author—not indeed to claim personal credit but, on the contrary, to disclaim authority and to distinguish his texts from the liturgy.[26] He evokes the traditional images of rumination, but focuses them not on words but on ideas and feelings. Where Cassian had celebrated the timeless freshness of the Psalter,[27] Anselm fears, rather, that repetition of familiar passages may dull devotion, *ne prolixitas aut frequens eiusdem loci repetitio generet fastidium* (Prol 10–11: "lest prolixity or frequent repetition of the same passages generate boredom"). He proposes, accordingly, to refound meditation and prayer on a basis of doctrinal understanding applied to a reader's own self-examination (*ad suimet discussionem*). He has not forgotten Gregory's metaphor: "Holy Scripture is offered to the eyes of the soul as a mirror, in which our interior face is seen; here we may recognize our ugliness

---

[25] *In psalmis invenies tam intimam orationem, si intenta mente perscruteris, quantum non potes per teipsum ullatenus excogitare . . . in psalmis quoque invenies omnium rerum, quae tibi accidunt, intimam gratiarum actionem. . . . Omnes enim virtutes in psalmis invenies, si a Deo merueris, ut tibi revelet secreta psalmorum* (*De psalmorum usu*, PL 101: 465–66).

[26] As Southern notes (*Portrait in a Landscape*, 100), the absence of anonymity is self-abasing in intention; for later generations, on the contrary, Anselm's name acquired prestige and authority, attracting spurious additions to the *Prayers and Meditations* collection.

[27] Cassian, *Conferences*, 14.13.5; SCh 54:200.

and our beauty."[28] The text reads the reader as much as the reader reads the text. Anselm's writings are not Scripture, but even so, he suggests that they might possess a similar reflective capability.

The nineteen Prayers (*Orationes*) are addressed variously to God, Christ, the Virgin Mary, Saint Paul, Saint John, and others. The three *Meditationes* take the form of soliloquies on moral and theological topics (e.g., "A meditation to stir up fear," "Lament for lost virginity," and "On Human Redemption"). Like the Carolingian *libelli precum*, and more nearly like John of Fécamp's *Confessio*, Anselm's texts were written as prayers for another's use. They were in fact presented to prominent, pious laity, as has been noted. They are voiced as the first-person-singular utterances of a generalized *persona* at prayer, who may be identified equally with the writer or with the reader. They are not based on the Psalter or the liturgy; neither are they specifically personal or pertinent to given personalities or circumstances.

In the tradition of the *libelli precum* and other writings destined for laity, the emphasis throughout Anselm's *Prayers* is strongly penitential. Anselm's prayer (the one who prays) finds himself enveloped and suffocated, as though buried alive in the state of sin; having described that state, he declares that he is unable to voice his consciousness in a prayer: *Hoc erat certe quod orare nec poteram nec sciebam. Hoc erat vere, quia me omni rei execrabilem intelligebam et velut insensibilis non dolebam. . . . O deus, quis orabit pro mortuo isto?* (Or 10.127–8: "Certainly neither could I pray, nor did I know how. This was true, because I understood that I was cursed by all things, and I did not grieve, as if unfeeling. . . . O God, who will pray for such a dead man?" [Ward, 149]). The writer has, however, analytically diagnosed this condition, and he uses a heightened, dramatic, and poetic language with which to express it feelingly.

Throughout the *Prayers*, rhymed phrases set off parallel constructions and sharp antitheses: *Ille dereliquit deum permittentem, ego fugi deum prosequentem. Ille perstat in malitia deo reprobante, ego in illam cucurri deo revocante. Ille obduratus ad punientem, ego obturatus ad blandiendem* (Or 8.39–42, Ward 129: "[Lucifer] deserted God, and God let him go; I fled from God, and God came with me. He persisted in evil, cast off by God; I ran toward evil, when God was calling me back. He hardened himself against punishment, I closed myself off from kindness"). Surface ornamentation is deployed in abundance: *annominato, polyptoton,* anaphora, anadiplosis, chains of gerund phrases (e.g., *indigendo desideratis, desiderando imploratis, implorando impetrates* [Or 7.12–13: "in need, you desire, desiring you implore, imploring you obtain"]), adverb-adjective exchanges (e.g., *miserabiliter mirabilis et mirabiliter miserabilis* [Med 1.21: "marvelously wretched and wretchedly marvelous"]), and rhetorical questions. These and other school figures serve to heighten emotional impact while drawing attention to the texts as works of verbal art. Modern readers like Benedicta Ward have found this style "mannered and elegant to a fault."[29] It does sharply contrast with the rigorous discourse of Anselm's theological writings, such as the *Monologion* or *Cur Deus homo.* Where the latter works, theoretical and scientific in character, were addressed to monks and prelates on Anselm's own clerical, intellectual level, the *Prayers and Meditations* offer affective, devotional expressions conceived for laity and/or initially for monks under Anselm's abbatial supervision. There is a vernacularizing tendency to be felt in the paratactic rhythm of the rhymed parallel phrases. This manner of writing anticipates the French octosyllabic couplet that became current in the twelfth century.[30] It is an oral style designed for reading

---

[29] Ward, *Prayers and Meditations,* 57.

[30] Jocelyn Wogan-Browne has suggested persuasively that Clemence of Barking's late-twelfth-century Anglo-Norman verse "Life of Saint Catherine" may have drawn concepts and phrasings from Anselm's *Cur Deus homo* (*Saints' Lives and Women's Literary Cuture: Virginity and its Authorizations* [Oxford: University Press, 2001], 227–45). The *Meditatio redemptionis humanae* might possibly have been Clemence's more immediate source; her octosyllabic couplets seem to echo the paired rhymed phrases in the *Meditatio: In omnibus his non est divina natura humiliata, sed humana est exaltata. Nec illa est imminuta, sed ista est misericorditer adiuta. Nec humana natura in illo homine passa est aliquid ulla necessitate, sed sola libera voluntate* (Med 3.102–05). Clemence of Barking writes, *Par poesté, nient par nature, / Devint li faitres criature. . . . Sa nature pas ne muad, / mais nostre par soe honurad. / La sue ne pot estre enpeirie, / Mais la nostre par soe essalcie* (*The Life of St. Catherine by Clemence of Barking,* ed. William Macbain [Oxford: Anglo-Norman Text Society, 1964], vv. 837–38, 961–64).

aloud and conducive to the interrupted, meditative reception that Anselm's prefaces have foreseen.

Most often, prayers take the form of a dramatic allegory. The writer typically begins with an apostrophe to a saint—Mary, John the Baptist, Peter, Paul, and others—and introduces himself as a third person: "a very grave sinner" (Or 9.11), or "a guilty worm, a wretched little human creature" (Or 8.8–9), or, more analytically, as "my heart," "my mouth," "my mind," or "my soul" (Or 7.6–7). Alternatively, the one who prays apostrophizes his own faculties ("exert yourselves, viscera of my soul" Or 7.9) and denounces his sins and shortcomings in a similar personified direct address:

> Tibi, O genetrix vitae, o mater salutis, o templum pietatis et misericordiae, tibi sese conatur praesentare miserabilis anima mea, morbis vitiorum languida, vulneribus facinorum scissa, ulceribus flagitiorum putrida. . . . Peccata mea, nequitiae meae, si habetis animam meam vestro veneno peremptam: vel cur sic facitis eam vestra foeditate horrendam, ut miseratio non possit aspicere illam? (Or 5.8–10, 17–19.)

> To you [Mary], author of life, mother of salvation, shrine of piety and mercy, to you my wretched soul longs to present herself, sick as she is with the disease of vices, wounded by crimes, putrid with the ulcers of sin. . . . O my sins, my wicked deeds, since you have destroyed my soul with your poison, why do you make her horrid with your foulness, so that pity cannot bear to look on her? (Ward, 108)

With the shifting play of apostrophes and personifications, Anselm brings persons (the reader, saints, God) and psychological states (reason, my sins, my heart) into dramatic confrontations. The attribution of the third-person singular to the soul or self is a particularly powerful strategy (e.g., "To you [Mary] . . . my wretched soul longs to present herself, sick as she is with the disease of vices"). In such moments, the generalized first-person writing/praying persona takes a higher mediating position: "I" am fully cognizant of "my" soul's sins and suffering and can speak more freely and eloquently for "her" (my soul) than she can for herself (Jean-Jacques Rousseau will adopt a similar strategy in the first paragraph of the *Confessions*). Led by identification with the writer's first-person voice, the reader would ideally articulate his or her own situation more passionately, more "utterly," so to speak, than would be possible without the support that the text provides. The "Prayer to Saint Paul" (Or 10) offers an inclusive example of Anselm's dramatic technique. The Sinner confronts the Judge and finds both good and evil spirits giving witness against him. He denounces his Sins (personified but not actually specified), who have enticed him into the trap, as despair closes around him; he is all but dead (spiritually), about to be sold to the "merchants of hell" (Or 10.64). He cannot pray; that is to say, in Anselm's analysis, he cannot emotionally grasp what he knows and intellectually understands: *Sic enim esse veritas ostendit, et tamen affectus non sentit. Sic ratio docet, et cor non dolet. Sic video quia est, et heu, nequeo liquefieri totus in lacrimas, quia sic est. Si hoc possem, forsitan sperarem, sperando orarem, orando impetrarem* (Or 10.41–4: "The truth shows itself thus, and yet I do not feel it. Thus reason teaches, yet my heart does not feel pain. I see that this is so, yet alas! I am unable to dissolve in tears because it is so. If I could do so, perhaps I could hope, and hoping pray, and praying receive" [my translation]). He appeals to God to show him a way or lead him to an intercessor. He appeals then to Jesus and Saint Paul, evoking Scripture and pleading with them in terms of the logic of their respective roles, as is traditional in intercessory prayer: "Jesus, why did you give yourself up to death, if not to save sinners? Paul, what else did you teach throughout the world?" (Or 10.78–9). But the logic of sin, leading to insensibility and to despair, closes down the appeal to faith, as the Sinner remembers that "faith without works is dead"; he must now seek not merely to be reconciled but to be resuscitated. But even then he recalls that God said to Paul, "My grace is sufficient for you" (2 Cor 12:9) and that Paul was "all things to all men" (1 Cor 9:22). The Sinner's conclusion is that Paul has the power to intercede for him, and God has the power to revive him; the Sinner must persist in prayer against all logic, relying on the maternal as well as paternal natures of Saint Paul and Jesus to regenerate him:

> *Paule, mater, et te ipse genuit. Pone ergo mortuum filium tuum ante pedes Christi, matris tuae . . . Christe, mater . . . Calor tuus mortuos vivificat, attactus tuus peccatores iustificat. Agnosce, mater, filium tuum mortuum vel per signum crucis tuae et per vocem confessionis tuae.* (Or 10.218–34)

Paul, mother, Christ bore you too. Place therefore your dead
son before the feet of Christ, your mother . . . Christ, mother
. . . your warmth revives the dead, your touch justifies sinners.
Acknowledge, mother, your dead son at least by the sign of the
cross and the voice of [his] confession." (My translation)

This is not liturgy. Nor, presumably, are these texts the actual
personal prayers of Anselm or of his reader. They propose *reading
experiences* that will lead to actual prayers; they are written, as we
have noted, in a dramatic, paratactic, quasi-vernacularizing style,
replete with auditory ornamentation, designed for reading—or indeed declaiming—aloud. The emotionalism of the poetry reposes,
however, on firm doctrinal bases, unsparing self-examination on
the reader's side (as prompted by the exemplary self-accusation of
Anselm's praying *persona*), and precise theological concepts arrayed
in deductive sequence.

The balance between affective and intellectual realization is
perfectly struck in the final piece in the collection, the *Meditatio redemptionis humanae* (Med 3). In this essay written near the
end of his life, Anselm evokes the devotional consequences of
the redemption, which he had expounded theoretically in *Cur
Deus homo*. The reader is summoned in the opening paragraph to
apply the studious "ruminative" processes of traditional *meditatio*
to ideas and feelings: *Mande cogitando, suge intelligendo, gluti amando
et gaudendo* (Med 3.10–11; Ward 230): "Chew by thinking, suck
by understanding, swallow by loving and rejoicing"). He begins
with a catechetical question: "What is the strength and power of
your salvation, and where is it found?" (Med 3.13; Ward 230). It
is to be found in Christ, he answers, but he proceeds to question,
What power is to be found in the weakness, humility, and obscurity
of the crucified man? Following then the sequence of ideas laid
out in *Cur Deus homo*, he reflects that Christ gave himself freely,
under no compulsion, not even under obedience to the Father,
but in the awareness that the gift would be pleasing to him; and
that Christ's spontaneous act, a payment made by one who did not
owe it, repays the debt of original sin that mankind owed to the
Creator. The gratuity of Christ's act, Anselm finds, is the source
of its redemptive power. But that gift can only be received by

the person who accepts it with the right penitential spirit (Med 3.124: *cum digna paenitentia*) and with the right *feeling* (*cum digno affectu:* Ward translates, "with the love it deserves" [234]). That is the purpose of the *meditatio* Anselm proposes, and again he calls on the reader to ruminate not on words but on the idea of the redemption, as received in the Eucharist: *Hoc mandat, o homo, hoc ruminet hoc sugat, hoc glutiat cor tuum, cum eiusdem redemptoris tui carnem et sanguinem accipit os tuum* (Med 3.132–34: "Chew on this, O Man, ruminate this, suck this, let your heart swallow this, when your mouth receives the body and blood of your redeemer").

Consider, ponder, see, remember—Anselm's imperatives urgently call on the involvement of the reader, who has to rejoice in the freedom that has been granted and to recall fearfully and penitentially the weight of sin that had dragged him irresistibly downward, which the redemption has lifted from his neck. The discourse of this *meditatio* alternates between the expository manner of *Cur Deus homo* and the rhetorical intensity of the *Prayers*; or, rather, we observe a fusion of the two styles, dramatizing the logical argument with the play of balanced, rhymed antitheses: *In omnibus his non est divina natura humiliata, sed humana est exaltata. Nec illa est imminuta, sed ista est misericorditer adiuta. Nec humana natura in illo homine passa est aliquid ulla necessitate, sed sola libera voluntate* (Med 3.102–05: "In all these things, the divine nature was not humiliated, but human nature was exalted. The divine was not diminished, but the human was increased. Nor did the human nature of that man suffer anything from necessity, but only from free will" [my translation]).

"I pray you, Lord, make me to taste through love what I taste through knowledge. Let me feel emotionally [*per affectum*] what I perceive through understanding" (Med 3.196–97). This plea could be Anselm's own as well as the reader's; it could be taken as the motto for the whole *Prayers and Meditations* collection. He proposes a reading experience which liberates *meditatio* from rumination of words, in favor of the intellectual and emotional exploration of their meanings and wider implications; he breaks through, as it were, the textual ceiling into a space of meditation in the modern sense of the term.

Chapter Six

Reading the Song of Songs

Perhaps more than any other book of the Bible, the Song of Songs compels the reader to reflect upon the act of reading. The poem presents itself as a dramatic dialogue; at almost every turn of phrase the reader must ask, Who is speaking here—in this manner!—and to whom? One must identify the *personae* present and imaginatively conceive their relationships to each other, to the human and divine authors, and to oneself. As with the psalms, we are invited at times to identify with one or more of them, and at times we are implicitly warned against that presumption. Like other hermetic books of the Bible, such as Ezekiel or Apocalypse, the Song deploys a puzzling panoply of poetic images, including fruits, flowers, animals, and geographical and seasonal evocations, defying interpretive ingenuity. Moreover, unlike any other biblical book, the Song expresses itself in a language of erotic love. How can this text belong to the canon of Sacred Scripture? What reading strategies must be used to approach it, and how may one learn or become qualified to do so?

The populous field of Latin commentaries on the Song comprises at a minimum some sixty texts composed between the third and the twelfth centuries, and many more thereafter. Modern scholars have mapped this territory,[1] which I will not attempt to explore comprehensively within this chapter. Several recent, focused studies offer valuable insights and points of departure. E. Ann Matter traces the formation of Song commentary as a literary genre defined by form as well as by content, generative of a recognizable, historically enduring tradition.[2] She highlights in

---

[1] For basic studies, see Friedrich Ohly, *Hohelied-Studien: Grundzüge einer Geschichte der Hoheliedauslegung des Abendlandes bis um 1200* (Wiesbaden: Franz Steiner, 1958), and Marvin H. Pope, *Song of Songs: A New Translation and Commentary*, The Anchor Bible (New York: Doubleday, 1977).

[2] E. Ann Matter, *The Voice of My Beloved: The Song of Songs in Western Medieval Christianity* (Philadelphia: University of Pennsylvania Press, 1990).

particular the use of fourfold exegesis (*littera, allegoria, tropologia,* and *anagogia*), which she derives originally from Cassian's *Conferences* (cf. p. 19, n. 32 above) and finds most systematically developed in the twelfth-century *Expositio* of Honorius of Autun. Denys Turner traces the preoccupation with *eros/desiderium* in monastic Song commentaries to the influence, however indirect, of speculative Christian Neoplatonism as mediated through Denys the Pseudo-Areopagite.[3] Turner's essay introduces an anthology of illustrative texts in English translation, including the *Expositio* by Gregory the Great, the *Compendium* by Alcuin of York, and other works from the twelfth and thirteenth centuries. Closest to my own project is the critical survey by Ann W. Astell.[4] Beginning with Origen, she describes a technique of interpretation that predominates throughout the earlier medieval commentaries, consisting primarily in the translation of the poem's imagery into spiritual meanings. She finds a radically contrasting "reliteralization" taking place in the twelfth-century expositions, in conjunction with a new interest in spiritual psychology.[5] She observes that Bernard of Clairvaux, William of Saint-Thierry, and their contemporaries sought to redeem the affective powers of the soul, those connected to the bodily senses so richly evoked in the literal text of the Song. Beyond *translation* of vocabulary, she argues that the twelfth-century exegetes sought to *transfer* the experience evoked in the poem to its (purportedly true and original) spiritual domain. This important and well-founded distinction is directly relevant to the study of reading. I believe, however, that the issue originates rather earlier in the history of Song interpretation than Astell implies. I find also that she perhaps minimizes the degree of division and ambivalence that any given

---

[3] Turner, *Eros and Allegory.*

[4] Ann W. Astell, *The Song of Songs in the Middle Ages* (Ithaca, NY and London: Cornell University Press, 1990).

[5] Astell, *The Song of Songs,* 8: "When twelfth-century commentators approach the Song of Songs, their exegesis moves beyond an exposition of hidden meaning (*allegoria*) to tropological exhortation—that is, they apply the interpreted text to the concrete life situation of their auditors and use the affective force of the Song's literal imagery to move them to virtuous action. In the process the allegory is reliteralized, joined again to the letter from which it was derived."

commentator will exhibit in the course of his search for a valid meditative reading methodology.

In the following pages I propose to read four pivotal works individually and in some detail: Origen's *Commentarium* and his *Homiliae* on the Song, illustrating very different reading experiences founded on the same interpretations of the scriptural texts; the *Expositio* of Gregory the Great, whose humane psychology of reading anticipates the explorations of the twelfth-century writers; and finally the *Sermones super cantica canticorum* by Bernard of Clairvaux, the uncontested masterwork summarizing the tradition and the diversities within it. My study necessarily leaves many important works out—notably the commentaries by Honorius of Autun, Rupert of Deutz, and William of Saint-Thierry. I find, however, that with Origen, Gregory, and Bernard we follow, as it were, the backbone of the tradition; their varying solutions to fundamental hermeneutical problems create a coherent discussion, one that focuses upon conceptions of the reader's role.

Origen's *Commentary* on the Song of Songs

Origen's *Commentary* (dated 240–44), originally ten books, survives mainly in a Latin translation by Rufinus (410) and consists of a prologue and a commentary as far as the fifteenth verse of book 2.[6] The *Commentary* is followed by two *Homilies* (ca. 244) which cover the Song through 2:14; these survive in a Latin translation by Jerome (dated 383; the Latin translation of the *Homilies* thus precedes that of the *Commentary*).[7]

The *Commentary* on the Song may be said to apply the methodology of *On First Principles*, *mutatis mutandis*—changing many

---

[6] Surviving Greek fragments are excerpted in PG 17:253–88 and included in a commentary ascribed to Procopius of Gaza (PG 87.2:1545–1780).

[7] Origène, *Commentaire sur le Cantique des cantiques*, ed. and trans. L. Bésard, H. Crouzel, M. Borret. SCh 375–76 (Paris: Éditions du Cerf, 1991–92); *Homélies sur le Cantique des cantiques*, ed. and trans. Olivier Rousseau, 2nd ed., SCh 37bis (Paris: Éditions du Cerf, 1966). English translation by R. P. Lawson, *The Song of Songs: Commentary and Homilies*, Ancient Christian Writers 26 (Westminster, MD: Newman Press, 1957). My English translations reflect both Lawson's wording and that of the French translations in the SCh editions.

things that needed to be changed. Origen retains the tripartite construction of the scriptural text, following the Platonic model of body, soul, and spirit: the first, "physical" reading by which the simplest readers may be nourished and edified; the second, "psychic" level associated with moral instruction; and third, the spiritual interpretation, leading to the intuition of celestial realities and the life to come (Prin 4.2.4; SCh 268:310–12). The *Commentary* follows this scheme,[8] but in a different order, placing the spiritual reading in second position. Usually, Origen offers an initial paragraph on the first level and then develops an extensive spiritual interpretation in which the Bride and Bridegroom are taken to figure the church and Christ, respectively. Finally, almost as an afterthought, he concludes with a note on the individual soul in relation to the Word of God, usually taken to mirror the ecclesiological dialogue which is his principal concern. This procedure arguably provides an example of the "theological" order described by de Lubac—*littera, allegoria, tropologia*—in which the psychological or moral application follows from the development of doctrine, rather than the reverse.[9] But here as in *First Principles*, Origen devotes little attention to the individual soul, and the result is that his exposition reduces in practice to just two levels, the physical and the spiritual.

Origen had foreseen in *First Principles* (Prin 4.2.9; SCh 268:336) that the understanding of the text might be strategically impeded by stumbling blocks and interruptions (*offendicula quaedam vel intercapedines intellegentiae*), and by *inpossibilia quaedam et inconvenientia*—impossible or unsuitable things deliberately inserted by divine Wisdom in order to force the reader to seek the higher path of allegory. The erotic discourse of the Song would be of the order of *inconvenientia*, including things that do not actually block understanding, but rather open all too wide a pathway to misreading. The optimistic view, expressed in *First Principles*, that even an untrained reader would sense the presence of sacred mysteries beneath the textual surface, seemingly gives way to a

---

[8] See Lawson, Origen, *The Song of Songs*, introduction, 9–10.

[9] de Lubac, *Exégèse médiévale*, 1.1:202–07; *Medieval Exegesis*, trans. Sebanc, 1:146–50.

fear lest the reader, as yet "incapable of hearing the names of love purely and with chaste ears," might tend to "deflect" his reception (his "hearing") of the text away from the interior or spiritual self toward the exterior or carnal one (Cant Prol 1.6; SCh 375:84). Accordingly, he advises such a reader to refrain altogether from reading this potentially dangerous "little book."

What, or how, does one hear with "chaste ears"? How does one recover the original meaning of this text, the "things written well and spiritually by the ancients" (Cant Prol 2.3; SCh 375:92: *ea quae a veteribus bene et spiritualiter scripta sunt*)? Origen's method is to search widely throughout both Testaments, comparing the given difficult passage with others, discovering recurrent vocabulary, themes, and turns of rhetoric, in which he can recognize the characteristic manner of the divine Author. Here he applies to the Song a distinction between the interior and exterior person based on Genesis 1:26 and 2:7, conflated with Paul's conceptions of the old and new man (Rom 6:6; Eph 4:22-24; Col 3:9). Related to this construction is the usage of "homonyms" that he finds in the Song:

> Scripturis divinis per homonymas, id est per similes appellationes, immo per eadem vocabula, et exterioris hominis membra et illius interioris partes affectusque nominantur eaque non solum vocabulis, sed et rebus ipsis invicem comparantur. (Cant Prol 2.6; SCh 375:94)

> The divine Scriptures name by homonyms, that is to say by similar terms, or rather even by the same words, the external members of the body and the parts and dispositions of the interior person; and not only the words but also the realities they designate are reciprocally compared. (Cf. Lawson, 26)

The names of the members of the body in the Song, he reasons, must refer metaphorically to the workings and dispositions of the soul (Cant Prol 2.9; SCh 375:98: *efficientiae animae affectusque*), as in locutions found throughout the Bible such as "The eyes of a sage are in his head" (Eccl 2:14), or "Their throat is as an open sepulcher" (Ps 5:9), or "Your foot will not stumble" (Prov 3:23).

Origen's approach to the Song does follow from his polemic in *First Principles* against retaining the *proper* meaning of words—their "somatic" or "fleshly" meaning, as he accurately terms it—where a metaphor is intended, even on the literal level of interpretation. We recall his argument (see above, chap. 2, p. 45) that the Jews failed to recognize the coming of Christ because some messianic prophecies were not literally fulfilled—for example, that prisoners would be released (Isa 61:1) or that a wolf (a four-footed animal) would lie down with a lamb (Isa 11:6). Origen asks, "Who is so silly as to believe that God, after the manner of a farmer, 'planted a paradise eastward in Eden', and set in it a visible and palpable 'tree of life'. . . ? And when God is said to 'walk in the paradise in the cool of the day', and Adam to hide himself behind a tree, I do not think anyone will doubt that these are figurative expressions" (Prin 4.3.1; SCh 268:342–44). Simpleminded readers, however—those who cannot distinguish between the respective attributions of the interior and exterior person—have been confused by the Song in exactly this manner, he argues in the *Commentary*, "deceived by similarities of nomenclature, they take refuge in inept fables and vain fictions" (Cant Prol 2.14; SCh 375:100–102: *vocabulorum similitudinibus falsi ad ineptas quasdam se fabulas et figmenta inania contulerint*). In *First Principles*, Origen had allowed that "simple" readers could indeed learn and benefit from the first-level reading of most scriptural texts. They must, however, be excluded or prevented from reading the Song (and several other hermetic texts, including the beginning of Genesis and the first chapters of Ezekiel); only by means of a sophisticated, systematic, and reverent translation could a "chaste hearing" of the originally intended meanings of the vocabulary be recovered.

"The names of the members may in no wise be applied to the visible body, but must be referred to the parts and powers of the invisible soul" (Cant Prol 2.11; SCh 375:100). What he proposes is a systematic translation of terms: not a merely verbal exercise, but one which would take into account the realities that the words represent, in a comparison between physical and spiritual faculties (Cant Prol 2.6; SCh 375:94: *non solum vocabulis sed et rebus ipsis comparantur*).[10] On "For your breasts are better than wine" (Song 1:1),

---

[10] Astell, *The Song of Songs*, 29, contrasts Origen's approach with that of Hugh of Saint-Victor and other twelfth-century expositors: "Hugh holds that 'historia' always means *something more* than what it says (as a temporal foreshadowing,

he translates the breasts—taken to be those of the Bridegroom, not the Bride—as the *principale cordis*, (Cant 1.2.3–9; SCh 375:192–96: the "ground principle of the heart" in Lawson's translation, 63): *Cor tuum, o sponse, et mens, id est dogmata quae intra te sunt, vel doctrinae gratia, superat omne vinum quod cor hominis laetificare solet* (Cant 1.2.6; SCh 375:194: "Your heart, O Spouse, and your mind, that is to say, the dogmas that are within you, or the grace of your doctrine, surpasses the 'wine' that ordinarily 'gladdens the heart of man'"). On Song 1:9, "Your cheeks are fair like the turtledove's, your neck like necklaces," he refers to Paul's discussion of the members of the body of Christ (1 Cor 12:14-18, 27); the cheeks are those parts of the face where one recognizes the nobility and modesty of the soul, and they designate then those members of the church who cultivate nobility, chastity, and purity (Cant 2.7.6; SCh 375:396); the neck carries the sweet "yoke" of obedience to Christ (Cant 2.7.10; SCh 375:398); the eyes of the Bride are like doves (Song 1:14) because she now understands the divine Scriptures not after the letter but after the Spirit, and sees in them spiritual mysteries, for the dove is the emblem of the Holy Spirit.

The same translation technique is applied to the various terms denoting love itself: *amor, dilectio, caritas, cupido,* and the verb *adamare*. Sometimes, Origen finds, the Scriptures purposefully use the more "respectable" (*honestior*) terms, *dilectio* or *caritas*, instead of *amor*, in order to avoid drawing the reader into error; sometimes, on the contrary, the Scriptures use the term *amor* where no occasion for fault is present, as in the "love of wisdom" (Wis 8:2). Origen does conceive of a passionate spiritual or mystical love felt by the individual soul, "wounded" indeed by the beauty of the Word of God (Cant Prol 2.17; SCh 375:102–04). This love is experienced likewise by the church in her desire to be united to Christ: *Hunc ergo amorem loquitur praesens scriptura, quo erga Verbum Dei anima beata uritur et inflammatur, et istud epithalamii carmen per Spiritum canit, quo ecclesia sponso caelesti Christo coniungitur ac sociatur* (Cant Prol 2.46; SCh 375:122–24: "The Scripture before us, therefore, speaks of this

---

factual allegory, type or *figura*). For Origen, on the other hand, the text generally means *something else* . . . the literal Song is for Origen a kind of code requiring decipherment, not a prefiguration of other nuptials."

love with which the blessed soul is kindled and inflamed toward the Word of God; it sings by the Spirit the song of the marriage whereby the church is joined and allied to Christ the heavenly Bridegroom"). Origen finally identifies this love with *caritas* and concludes that the differences in vocabulary do not actually matter, as long as this understanding is maintained: God is love/charity, and it is "something similar" to that love that he requires from us (Cant Prol 2.29; SCh 375:112).

At the deepest level, Origen's concept of reading rests on a theory of correspondences between earth and heaven, between visible and invisible things, based on Paul (Rom 1:20 and 2 Cor 4:18). Things on earth, he speculates, were created by God following heavenly "patterns" (Cant 3.13.8–9, SCh 376:625; Cant 3.13.27–28, SCh 376:629; trans. Lawson 216–19) to which they continue to bear a certain likeness; the same relationship governs things recorded in the Scriptures. Our five physical ("exterior") senses correspond likewise to spiritual ("interior") faculties; the physical senses must be mortified and the spiritual senses must be trained (*exercitatus*) by the reader of the Song, through scholarly study (*eruditione*) and sustained effort (*industria*), in order to develop the discernment of good and evil (Cant 1.4.18; SCh 375:232; cf. Heb 5:15). Origen's Bride is the figure for this reader, who is, ideally, scholarly and ascetic. Her opening cry, *Osculetur me ab osculis oris sui*, signals the end of apprenticeship; she had previously received interpretations ("kisses," in the plural in Origen's citation) from the mouths of teachers, but now that she has begun to discern obscurities and unravel parables and riddles for herself, now that she herself is able explain what she reads in terms appropriate to understanding (*competentibus intelligentiae lineis explicare*), she must now long for direct, unmediated communications from the Word himself (Cant 1.1.11; SCh 375:184). That desire indicates, in fact, that she has begun to receive them.

Origen's *Homilies* on the Song of Songs

As Origen's *Commentary* on the Song may be understood as an application of his *First Principles*, so the two *Homilies* may be seen to apply further the concepts and techniques developed in the *Commentary*. In this final stage of a closely-connected three-part sequence, Origen carries forward his interpretations of the Song into an enactment of the reading process. His conception of the scriptural text remains essentially unchanged. But we discover here, at last, a fully dramatized dialogue between the commentator, in the role of a preacher, and his auditor(s), singular and plural. The presentation in the *Homilies* is relatively succinct, omitting much of the encyclopedic supporting material deployed in the *Commentary*. Where the latter work had focused interpretation on the church as the Bride of Christ, the *Homilies* address the individual soul in an intimate discourse that is emotionally warm and directly didactic. Accordingly, Jerome, in the prologue to his Latin translation, infers that the *Homilies* were composed mainly for beginners—for "little readers as yet nourished with milk" (*parvulis adhuc lactantibus*). That assessment should not be retained at face value. Jerome oversimplifies the complexity and inclusivity of a work that takes all levels of reading into account, reflecting the multi-leveled construction of the Scripture itself as Origen perceives it.

The Scriptures are not mere *fabulae* or *narationes*, he repeatedly reminds us (Hom 1.4; SCh 37bis:80), but mysteries; they contain always "something secret" (*aliquid secreti*). The style, as he asserted in *First Principles*, alerts readers that they must indeed advance beyond flesh and blood to reach understandings that will be worthy of God. Beyond the initial intuition, we must seek "something hidden" and develop the reading through a process of struggle. *Necesse est . . . omni labore contendere* (Hom 1.2; SCh 37bis:74). *Diligenter observa . . . quaere et invenies scripturam diuinam non frustra et fortuitu unumquemque usurpare sermonem* (Hom 1.8; SCh37bis:96: "Carefully observe . . . seek and you will find that the divine Scripture does not use words by chance or carelessly"). The reader is invited to adopt Origen's own scholarly, ascetic vocation in searching through the Scriptures to learn the vocabulary and rhetorical habits of the Author in order to elucidate the given passage. In this manner, one develops the "chaste ears" and the "eyes of a dove" as in the Song (1:15): *Ingrediens ad interiora cordis tui et alios oculos mente perquirens . . . Illud enitere, labora, contende, ut sancte intelligas universa quae dicta sunt* (Hom 2.4; SCh 37bis:118: "Entering into the interior of your heart, seek other eyes with your mind . . . try to reach this, labor, struggle to understand in a sacred manner all the things which have been said"). The reader must labor systematically to translate physical language into spiritual meaning. This essential message has been stated and analyzed at length in the *Commentary*; here, however, the nuance is more optimistic, more inclusive, in that he provides not only for expert readers—who already know how to "hear spiritually" the Scriptures—but also for those who do not yet know but who desire to do so.

The didactic direct address does suggest, as Jerome notes, the stance of a preacher facing a present congregation of beginners. We know little or nothing, however, about the original audience for these homilies, or about the conditions of their oral delivery. The texts that have come down to us do conform clearly to the homiletic genre, one abundantly represented throughout the literature, for example, by Augustine's sermons on the psalms, Gregory's *Homilies on Ezekiel* (discussed above in chap. 2), and ultimately by the *Sermons* on the Song of Songs by Bernard of Clairvaux. The homily is a dialogic form, one responsive to present local needs and to the immediate inspiration of the spirit. As such, it is suited to elite auditors—as in Bernard's sermons—as well as to beginners, and it is uniquely appropriate to the dialogue of the Song: the conversation between preacher and listener(s) parallels that between the Bridegroom and the Bride, and also that between either of the latter two and the youths and the maidens who accompany them, respectively.

Repeating the description of the four roles in the drama (*fabula*), as given in the *Commentary*, Origen opens here the possibilities for the reader to assume them: "Listen to the Song, hasten to understand it and to say what the Bride says, so that you may hear what she herself has heard" (Hom 1.1; SCh 37bis:70: *Audi canticum canticorum et festina intelligere illud et cum sponsa dicere ea, quae sponsa dicit, ut audias, quae audivit et sponsa*). But if you cannot enact the conversation on that highest level, Origen continues, you should join the group of youths, or else, if that is still impossible, join the maidens who accompany the Bride. This concept of active, participative reading—reading as role-playing—recurs throughout Christian spirituality, as we have seen in previous chapters. It is not far removed from the literary impersonation exercises prescribed in the antique classroom (e.g., as recorded by Quintilian). Origen, trained in classical rhetoric, stands in a pivotal transitional position, very near the headwaters of the Christian literary tradition.

His authoritative speech, as a preacher to the auditor(s), parallels that of the Bridegroom to the Bride. At other times, he assumes and models the Bride's role or humbles himself further as a sinner among others; in that case, he positions himself outside the text, seeking a point of entry. At times his role doubles or divides between the scholar who examines the text and the (potential) participant in it, as in a curious passage where he expresses the wish that that "my spouse might be enfolded in the Bridegroom's tighter embrace" (Hom 1.2; SCh 37bis:76: *utinam contingat, ut et meam sponsam artior sponsi amplexus includat*). *Meam sponsam* is clarified by the following paragraph in which he wishes that the Bridegroom might come to "my soul become his Bride" (Hom 1.3; SCh 37bis:78: *Si autem et ad meam animam factam sponsam suam uenire dignabitur*). How beautiful must she become then, he muses, how ardent must be her love, to attract him to her, so that he would say to her what he says to the perfect Bride!

In a famous passage, one that may have inspired Bernard of Clairvaux—and many later mystical experiences as well—Origen describes the mysterious comings and goings of the Bridegroom. "He does this often throughout the poem," he comments, observing the text first from the point of view of a detached reader. But he then seems to forgo his customary scholarly procedure of explication by concordance, in favor of a reference to a personal experience recognized in reading. This text, he categorically declares, cannot be understood otherwise:

> Deinde conspexit sponsum, qui conspectus abscedit. Et frequenter hoc in toto carmine facit, quod nisi quis ipse patiatur, non potest intelligere. Saepe, Deus testis est, sponsum mihi adventare conspexi et mecum esse quam plurimum; quo subito recedente, invenire non potui quod quaerebam. Rursum igitur desidero eius adventum et nonumquam iterum uenit; et cum apparuerit meisque fuerit manibus comprehensus, rursus elabitur. (Hom 1.7; SCh 37bis:94)

> Then she looks for the Bridegroom, who, as soon as she has glimpsed him, departs. And he does this often throughout the poem, something that only someone who has experienced it can understand. Often, God is my witness, I have felt the Bridegroom come to me, and stay with me quite long; but

when suddenly he withdrew, I could not find what I sought.
Then again I desire his coming and sometimes he returns; and
as soon as he appears and I hold him in my hands, again he slips
away. (Cf. Lawson 279–80)

The Bride's role is discovered in the first two verses of the
Song. She appears first as a reader of texts who has met the criteria
of Origen's scholarly-ascetic pedagogy; she has become erudite in
biblical studies, keenly insightful and skillful in translating physical
metaphors into spiritual meaning. She longs impatiently, however,
for an end to mediated communications filtered through prophets
and evangelists. Her cry in the first verse ("Let him kiss me . . .") is
a prayer for a direct contact. That prayer is answered as soon as (or
even before) it is fully formulated by the Bridegroom who appears,
in Origen's reading, in the second verse. There she "ceases praying"
and speaks directly to him, acknowledging his presence: "For your
breasts are better than wine." That moment captures an essential
incidence of the spiritual reading experience: the interruption of
reading by an interlocutor—Origen cites Isa 65:24: *Adhuc loquente
te dicam, ecce adsum* ("Even while you are still speaking, I will say,
'here I am'")[11]—a break in the linear process of text-reception,
suddenly opening into dialogue. Christian meditative readers have
always savored such moments. Thus Cassian notes that one may feel
the "power" of a scriptural text before one understands it (Conf
10.11.5); the communication of understanding may well follow
the reading much later, perhaps during sleep. The Spirit of Wisdom
informs the reading unpredictably—*spiritus ubi vult spirat*—and
indeed the Bride-reader's sudden, passionate response mirrors the
movement of the Spirit, as Bernard will emphasize and celebrate.

The Bride is unique: like a lily among thorns, she does not
walk behind him, among the maidens, but by his side, *proxima
mea*. Her singular, confident beauty comes from her closeness to
the Word of God. She alone is admitted to his chamber. Even so,
she remains an accessible object of our emulation: *tu sponsa, tu
ecclesiastica anima* (Hom 1.10; SCh 37bis:100)—an individuality
realized in identification with the corporate church personality.

[11] The modern Vulgate text reads, *Eritque antequam clament, ego exaudiam; adhuc
illis loquentibus, ego audiam.*

In umbra eius concupiui et sedi (Song 2:3: "In his shadow I desired, and sat"). The preterite rather than present tense of the verb *concupiui* suggests to Origen a previous state when "we," the Bride, could not yet converse directly with the Bridegroom; since then, we have moved indeed from the "shadow" of death to the "shadow" of life (Hom 2.6; SCh 37bis:126). The word *umbra* inspires a complex, free-associative reading; the nativity of Christ began *ab umbra*, as an "overshadowing" in the annunciation scene in Luke 1:35, and it ended *in veritate*. The reader-as-Bride is called upon to recapitulate that history in a present spiritual experience: *Non solum autem in Maria ab umbra eius natiuitas coepit, sed et in te, si dignus fueris, nascitur sermo Dei. Fac igitur, ut possis capere umbram eius et, cum umbra fueris dignus effectus, ueniet ad te* (Hom 2.6; SCh 37bis:126: "Not only in Mary did his nativity begin from a shadow, but also in you, if you become worthy, the word of God will be born. Act then, so that you may receive his shadow, and when you have become worthy of the shadow, he will come to you").

A similar construction governs Origen's interpretation of Jesus's acts of healing. The spiritual reading of those acts would mean seeing Jesus in action not only at the time when these deeds were done in the flesh, but also today, in continuous presence: *uidens Iesum omnem languorem et infirmitatem non solum eo tempore, quo carnaliter facta sunt, fuisse medicatum, sed hodieque medicantem, et non tantum tunc ad homines descendisse, sed hodieque descendere et esse praesentem* (Hom 2.4; SCh 37bis:118: "seeing Jesus healing all illnesses and infirmities, not only at the time when these deeds were done in the flesh, but also today, and descending to men and being present not only at that time but also today"). In such passages, Origen's concept of the first level of reading as "somatic" or "fleshly" (*carnaliter*)—equated with the "historical" reading and contrasted always with the spiritual—proves its value and usefulness. This construction is especially appropriate to the Song and its physical vocabulary: "somatic" and "fleshly" are clear and precisely suitable terms for the first-level reading, which Rufinus and later commentators will designate as "literal," not without considerable confusion, as we have seen.

Origen's influence will remain pervasive throughout the medieval commentaries on the Song. A number of topics drawn from the prologue to the *Commentary* recur as obligatory references throughout the tradition. One of these concerns the superlative in the title *Canticum canticorum* as analogous to *sancta sanctorum*, *saecula seculorum*, and other Biblical phrases (the later tradition will add, significantly, *rex regum et dominus dominantium* [King of Kings and Lord of Lords]). The Song of Songs then is taken to be the highest, final step in a graduated series of biblical songs, seventh in a list given by Origen. The medieval commentators follow also Origen's placement of the Song as the third and final book in the series by Solomon: Proverbs, Ecclesiastes, and Song of Songs, corresponding in Origen's analysis to the ethical, physical (or natural), and "enoptic" (contemplative) modes of exposition. The three patriarchs, Abraham, Isaac, and Jacob, prefigure allegorically this division; Solomon, whose name is glossed as "peaceful," figures as a type of Christ. Also retained in medieval tradition is Origen's listing of the four *dramatis personae*—namely, the Bridegroom, the Bride, the youths, and the maidens—situated in relationship to roles to be taken by the reader.

More generally, the medieval commentators agree with Origen that the Song is not suitable for beginners. How to attain the level of spiritual maturity that this text seems to require? How to understand the discourse of love with its physical vocabulary? How to construe the relationship between the reader and the Bride, whose role we are invited to emulate, or ideally to assume altogether? Explicit discussions of these issues reveal persistent underlying questions posed by Origen's allegorical method and by his use of Biblical concordance, as tested in readings of the individual verses of the Song. Even after his name had become associated with (mostly unrelated) controversies, and so remained unacknowledged, we may follow the evolution through medieval tradition of a generally "Origenist" mode of analysis, based on a denial of the possibility of a first-level reading and on the systematic translation of the text into terms deemed spiritually meaningful. That approach, based on an objective concept of the Song text, is patented in Origen's *Commentary*. His *Homilies*, however, open another way of reading in which the text is, in effect, recreated in the experience of the reader, who is invited to take an active part in the dialogue. For this approach, which will be developed extensively in the twelfth-century commentaries, Gregory the Great offers an early authoritative confirmation.

Gregory's *Exposition* on the Song of Songs

The authenticity of the *Exposition* by Gregory the Great on the Song of Songs[12] was long questioned. It was attributed to the eleventh-century writer Robert de Tombelaine and also to Richard of Saint-Victor, who attached Gregory's prologue to his own commentary on the Song.[13] But once the textual question had been resolved, scholars no longer hesitated to recognize the characteristic style and preoccupations that link this work to the *Moralia in Job* and the *Homilies on Ezekiel*. Gregory emphasizes in all things the nurturing pedagogy of the Holy Spirit, and in that respect his *Exposition* is not far removed from Origen's *Homilies* on the Song. But Gregory makes a significant departure from Origen's hermeneutics: he does not categorically reject the physical reading as Origen does—that is, he does not take it as a stumbling block that would force the reader to seek higher ground through the process of translating its terms. Gregory proposes, on the contrary, a more forgiving, humane observation of the reading process:

> Postquam a paradisi gaudiis expulsum est genus humanum, in istam peregrinationem uitae prasesentis ueniens caecum cor ab spiritali intellectu habet. Cui caeco cordi si diceretur uoce di-uina: "Sequere deum" uel "Dilige deum," sicut ei in lege dictum est, semel foris missum et per torporem insensibilitatis frigidum non caperet quod audiret. Idcirco per quaedam enigmata sermo diuinus animae torpenti et frigidae loquitur et de rebus, quas nouit, latenter insinuat ei amorem, quem non nouit.

---

[12] Grégoire le Grand, *Commentaire sur le Cantique des cantiques*, ed. and trans. Rodrigue Bélanger, SCh 314 (Paris: Éditions du Cerf, 1984). Parenthetical references are to this edition. English translation by Turner, *Eros and Allegory*, 215–55. The translations given here are my own, but I have consulted those of Bélanger and Turner. See also *Gregory the Great: On the Song of Songs*, trans. and intro. Mark DelCogliano, CS 244 (Collegeville, MN: Cistercian, 2012).

[13] For a summary of the question, see the introduction by Rodrigue Bélanger to the SCh edition, 15–21. Astell, *The Song of Songs*, 36–38, attributes Gregory's text to "Pseudo Richard of St. Victor."

Allegoria enim animae longe a deo positae quasi quandam machinam facit, ut per illam leuetur ad deum. Interpositis quippe enigmatibus, dum quiddam in uerbis cognoscit, quod suum est, in sensu uerborum intellegit, quod non est suum, et per terrena uerba separatur a terra. Per hoc enim, quod non abhorret cognitum, intellegit quiddam incognitum. Rebus enim nobis notis, per quas allegoriae conficiuntur, sententiae diuinae uestiuntur et, dum recognoscimus exteriora uerba, peruenimus ad interiorem intellegentiam.

Hinc est enim, quod in hoc libro, qui in Cantiicis canticorum conscriptus est, amoris quasi corporei uerba ponuntur: ut a torpore suo anima per sermones suae consuetudinis refricata recalescat et per uerba amoris, qui infra est, excitetur ad amorem, qui supra est. Nominantur enim in hoc libro oscula, nominantur ubera, nominantur genae, nominantur femora; in quibus uerbis non irridenda est sacra descriptio, sed maior dei misericordia consideranda est: quia, dum membra corporis nominat et sic ad amorem uocat, notandum est quam mirabiliter nobiscum et misericorditer operatur, qui, ut cor nostrum ad instigationem sacri amoris accenderet, usque ad turpis amoris nostri uerba distendit. Sed, unde se loquendo humiliat, inde nos intellectu exaltat: quia ex sermonibus huius amoris discimus, qua uirtute in diuinitatis amore ferueamus. (Exp 1–3; SCh 314:69–70)

Ever since the human race was expelled from the joys of paradise, it has entered into the pilgrimage of this present life, with a heart grown blind to spiritual understanding. If the divine voice said to this blind heart, "Follow God," or "Love God," as is stated in the law, the heart now in exile, numbed with the torpor of insensibility, would not grasp what it hears. Accordingly, the divine discourse addresses the sluggish, frozen soul through certain enigmas, and through the things that it knows, inspires in it a love that it does not know.

To the soul far distant from God, allegory provides, as it were, a machine to raise her to him. By means of enigmas in which the soul recognizes something that is her own, she understands in the meanings of the words something that is not her own, and by earthly words she is separated from earth. Thus indeed, since she has no aversion to the known, she understands something unknown. With things known to us, by which allegories are composed, the divine discourses are cloaked, and, as we recognize the exterior words, we come to understand their interior meaning.

This is why, in the book entitled Song of Songs, words seemingly of physical love are spoken: so that the soul may be rubbed and warmed out of her torpor by expressions familiar to her, and by words of lower love be aroused to a love which is higher. Thus kisses are named in this book, and breasts, cheeks, and thighs are named. By these words the sacred discourse is not trivialized; rather is the mercy of God to be contemplated here. For as he names the members of the body and so calls us to love, we must notice how marvelously and mercifully he works with us. In order to enflame our heart and inspire us with sacred love, he lowers himself even to using words of our base love. But as he humbles himself in speech, he raises us in understanding: for from the expressions of this love we learn with what force we should burn with the love of God.

For the human soul in exile, numbed and cold, the apprehension of eroticism in words is validated by Gregory as a warming, as the beginning of a return to spiritualization. He refers directly, I believe, to Origen's prologue to the *Commentary*,[14] taking issue with the Alexandrian's observation of the "homonyms" in Scripture (Cant Prol 2.6; see above, p. 160), specifically the names of the members of the body. Where Origen insists that these terms are no more than metaphors for spiritual faculties, requiring immediate translation, Gregory proposes rather that the reader should conserve the feelings that they arouse and transfer them from the physical to the spiritual plane; in the evocation of "this" (our physical) experience of love, we are to "learn"—the pedagogy is typically Gregorian—the quality of passion with which we should "burn" (*ferveamus*) for the love of God.

This analysis offers justification, as Origen's does not, for the Holy Spirit's use of erotic language. Gregory does not, of course,

[14] Quite possibly, Gregory had access to the Latin versions of Origen's *Commentary* and *Homilies* on the Song. He refers in his *Exposition* to several classic Origenian topics: the analogy between the title, *Canticum canticorum*, and the phrases *sancta sanctorum and sabbata sabbatorum* (Exp 6); the place of the Song of Songs following and surpassing all other biblical songs (Exp 7); and its place following Proverbs and Ecclesiastes as the third of the books of Solomon (Exp 9), corresponding to moral, natural, and contemplative life, respectively. A number of verbal echoes have also been noted by Bélanger in the introduction to the SCh edition, 44–46.

advocate actual sexual experience. He focuses rather on the pivotal movement of verbal reception as the reader "recognizes" (*novit/cognoscit/recognoscimus*) familiar and welcome words of love. The action of the allegorical "machine" then moves the reader from a recognition of the "external" words to an understanding of their "internal" meaning. What is ultimately "recognized" here is the marvelous, merciful working of the Holy Spirit, who lowers himself in words in order to raise us in understanding. That perception brings about, finally, the transfer from the physical to the spiritual, from the known to the unknown.

The communication of Scripture replicates, for Gregory, the Incarnation: "Though he was in the form of God . . . he emptied himself, taking the form of a servant, being born in the likeness of men" (Phil 2:6-7). Gregory returns to this underlying thought later in the *Exposition*, commenting on "for your breasts are better than wine" (Song 1:2): we could not "grasp" (*capere*) divine wisdom, a "lactation" in the breasts of God—that is, we could not conceive it or internalize it, emotionally or spiritually—until God took a human form that we could "recognize": *sapientiam . . . quam enim in diuinitate sua capere minime poteramus, in incarnatione eius agnosceremus* (Exp 13; SCh 314:90: "the wisdom . . . that we could not at all grasp in its divinity, we do recognize in his incarnation"). Again, on "your name is as oil poured forth" (Song 1:3): *Unguentum effusum est diuinitas incarnata. . . . Effudit se unguentum, cum se et deum seruauit et homo exhibuit* (Exp 21; SCh 314:102: "The oil poured forth is divinity incarnated. . . . He poured himself out when he conserved his divine identity, and manifested himself as a man").

In what follows, Gregory returns to the essentials of Origen's hermeneutics, as developed in the latter's *First Principles* and in the *Commentary*. Gregory, however, expounds these ideas in a characteristic profusion of mixed metaphors. Following Origen, he perceives the divine discourse as "clothed" in figures (*aenigmata, exteriora verba*)—put on as a vestment—as the body encases the soul, as the chaff encloses the grain (Exp 4; SCh 314:72). Origen, in *First Principles* (4.2.8; SCh 268:334, in the Latin of Rufinus), had referred to the *indumentum litterae*, the garment of the letter, the veil placed over the spiritual meanings, constituting the "body of Scripture": *indumentum quoddam et uelamen spiritualium sensuum*

. . . *et hoc est quod diximus scripturae sanctae corpus)*. We are called to search through this outer text and penetrate into its interior. *Debemus*, Gregory repeats. *Necesse est.* We must not remain on the outside, attached to the wording, lest the "machine" of allegory hold us down rather than lift us as it is intended to do. In another metaphor, Gregory suggests that to cling to the exterior words of Scripture would be analogous to perceiving the colors in a painting but refusing to see—to recognize—the object represented. We must learn to read with the eyes of doves, as Origen put it; Gregory echoes that thought: even while speaking of the body, we become as though out of the body (Exp 4; SCh 314:72: *extra corpora fieri*). Called to attend the wedding feast dramatized in the Song, we must put on the appropriate wedding dress (*id est digna caritatis intelligentia*). It is the reader now, in this mixed metaphor, who puts on the garment; failing to do so, we would be expelled into the outer darkness of blind ignorance.

As he completes the prologue, Gregory acknowledges what have become the classic Origenian topics, as noted above: the superlative in the title (*Canticum canticorum*), its place with respect to other biblical songs, and its position following the books of Proverbs and Ecclesiastes in the canon. In passing, Gregory develops a theme that will be of the greatest importance to Bernard of Clairvaux years later—namely, that the superiority of this Song over all others resides in that it is not occasioned by specific circumstances, but rather by love itself, by union with God. Gregory adds that God is at times feared as a lord, honored as a father, and loved as a spouse, and it is the latter relation which is highest and held dearest (Exp 8; SCh 314:80–82; cf. Bernard of Clairvaux, *Sermons* on the Song of Song 1.7–8 and 83.4).

The surviving texts of Gregory's *Exposition*, following the prologue, cover just the first eight verses of the Song, book 1. Following Origen, for a given verse Gregory normally proposes an ecclesial interpretation first, followed by its application to the individual soul. Both readings are not always possible. Certain verses recall to Gregory the history of the church and the movements of groups of people within it or outside it. At times the verse will seem to lead in contrary or unrelated directions (e.g., Exp 35, 38, 40; SCh 314:122, 126,128, on Song 1:5: "They made me keeper of the vineyards, but my own vineyard I have not kept"). Not always is the individual subordinated to the general; it is the single soul that most completely embodies the unity of the church, and in the progress of that soul toward mystical contemplation, Gregory finds the perfected realization of the Song's erotic metaphor, calling forth the deeper reading.

Bernard of Clairvaux's *Sermons* on the Song of Songs

The *Sermons* on the Song of Songs by Bernard of Clairvaux[15] stand in relation to other commentaries on the Song as the Song itself, according to Bernard, stands in relation to other biblical songs: this work (properly referred to in the singular) is the "fruit of all the others" (SC 1.11; SBOp 1:7), the culmination of an already millennial tradition of textual interpretation. Bernard's allegiance to this tradition is unquestionable, yet he makes few or no recognizable references to his immediate predecessors (Rupert of Deutz, Honorius of Autun, and others).[16] He does return at key moments to Origen's *First Principles*, to Origen's *Commentary* on the Song, and to Gregory's *Exposition*. We do not know whether or when he

[15] Bernard of Clairvaux, *Sermones super Cantica canticorum*, ed. Jean Leclercq, Charles H. Talbot, and Henri M. Rochais, 2 vols. (Rome: Editiones Cistercienses, 1957–58); *Sancti Bernardi opera*, 7 vols. (Rome: Editiones Cistercienses, 1957–74). My parenthetical references cite this edition, abbreviated SBOp henceforth, by sermon, paragraph, and page numbers. English translations are my own, but I have consulted those of Killian Walsh, Irene Edmonds, and M. Corneille Halflants, in *Bernard of Clairvaux, On the Song of Songs*, 4 vols., CF 4, 7, 31, 40 (Kalamazoo, MI: Cistercian Publications, 1971–80). The essential background studies are by Jean Leclercq, collected in the *Recueil d'études sur saint Bernard et ses écrits*, 3 vols. (Rome: Edizioni di Storia e Letteratura, 1962–69). Of these, see especially "Les Sermons sur les Cantiques ont-ils été prononcés?" *Recueil* 1:193–212, (translated into English in *On the Song of Songs* 2:vii–xxx); "Les étapes de la rédaction," *Recueil* 1:213–44; and "Aux sources des sermons sur les Cantiques," *Recueil* 1:275–78. For a study of Bernard's Latin style and rhetoric, see the introduction by Christine Mohrmann to Vol. 2 of the critical edition, "Observations sur la langue et le style de saint Bernard," *Sancti Bernardi opera* 2:ix–xxxiii. The classic study of Bernard's theology is that of Etienne Gilson, *La théologie mystique de saint Bernard* (Paris: Vrin, 1947). For a succinct summary, see Bernard McGinn, *The Growth of Mysticism*, 158–224.

[16] On Bernard's presumed sources see Jean Leclercq, "Aux sources des sermons sur les Cantiques."

might have gained access to these texts. But directly or indirectly, he derives from them leading themes and methodologies of spiritual interpretation. He draws, moreover, on Origen's *Homilies* on the Song, and on other works by Gregory—namely, the *Moralia on Job* and the *Homilies on Ezekiel*—in his rediscovery of the sermon as the literary form best suited to his exegetical and literary project.

Bernard began writing the *Sermons* in 1135 or 1136. By this time he had reached a stage of maturity with a confidence in his own insights, reinforced by his growing power and influence in church affairs. He had approached several of the major themes of the *Sermons* in previous writings, in *De gratia et libero arbitrio* (*On Grace and Free Will*, 1128), and especially in *De diligendo Deo* (*On Loving God*, ca. 1130). There he proposes a four-step progression leading from human self-love, the first step, to a total self-emptying into the love of God at the top of the ladder. This treatise includes a re-transcription of letter 11, written earlier (1125) to the Carthusians, in which Bernard distinguishes between love and other human affections; that discussion is extended and completed in the *Sermons* (especially SC 7 and SC 83, see below, pp. 193–94, n. 34). Bernard may have also coauthored with William of Saint-Thierry a *Brevis commentatio in Cantica canticorum*.[17]

Throughout the rest of his life, Bernard continued writing on the Song through many interruptions and spiritual sea changes.[18] By the time of his death in 1153, he had composed eighty-six sermons, commenting on the Song as far as the first verse of chapter three. The commentary was eventually completed by his disciples Gilbert of Hoyland, Geoffrey of Auxerre, and John of Ford. Bernard's *Sermons* make up, however, a "complete" work in another sense—as a record of his own interaction with the Song, which necessarily ends with the end of his life.[19] This "work" is

---

[17] PL 184:407–36. On this debated attribution, see E. Ann Matter, *Voice of My Beloved*, 131 and n. 27.

[18] Jean Leclercq summarizes the stages of composition in "Les étapes de la rédaction."

[19] Sermon 83 presents a synthesis of the doctrinal conclusions he had reached in the course of his study. This sermon was written around 1148 according to Leclercq's estimate ("Les étapes de la redaction," 232). By this time Bernard doubtless realized that he would never finish the commentary.

unified by the personality of the writer and shaped by the trajectory of his intellectual and spiritual evolution. It is—among many other things—a journal of a reading experience, one of the most eloquent indeed in all of European literary history. To follow that record "day to day," as it were, would be to retrace his pathway, labyrinthine and seemingly directionless at times, through the "forest of allegory" in order to discover what cannot be mapped in the abstract or perceived from above.

The *Sermons* are properly described as a "monastic literary sermon-series."[20] From the available internal and external evidence, Jean Leclercq concludes that they were not originally delivered orally but composed and transmitted in writing.[21] Bernard undoubtedly spoke to his monks on occasion about the Song, but as Leclercq observes, the rhetorical and theological complexity of these *Sermons* contrasts with Bernard's manner in more informal talks whose transcriptions have come down to us. The *Sermons* have the character of literary compositions, or rather of *a* literary composition, cast in what subsequently became a characteristically Cistercian form.[22]

The work maintains, however, a fiction of orality throughout. Like Origen's *Homilies* on the Song, Bernard's *Sermons* take the form of a *live* reading in process, rather than that of a finished "commentary." *Vobis, fratres*, he begins (SC 1.1; SBOp 1:3); he regularly evokes a present monastic assembly. He refers to the previous night's vigils (SC 36.7; SBOp 2:8), field work to be done, visitors arriving (SC 3.6; SBOp 1:17), and other typical details of coenobitic life. The pressure of time curtails each "day's" sermon, which is to be continued on the following day; he alludes to questions the monks have raised and scolds them for falling asleep; he calls upon them to consult the "book of experience" in order to confirm his moral teachings and apply them to practical life.

The persona of abbot-preacher is vividly realized in this dialogue in an ever-changing panoply of moods. He is authoritative, concerned above all with the instruction of his flock, following

[20] Emero Stiegman, "The Literary Genre of Bernard of Clairvaux's *Sermones super cantica canticorum*," in *Simplicity and Ordinariness: Studies in Medieval Cistercian History* 4, CS 61 (Kalamazoo, MI: Cistercian Publications, 1980), 79.
[21] See Jean Leclercq, "Les Sermons sur les Cantiques ont-ils été prononcés?"
[22] Stiegman, "The Literary Genre," 71.

the great example of Gregory. He would have us understand that he has shouldered the burdens of his ministry, forgoing the peace of contemplation in response to the imperatives of active charity. He is called to preach and commanded to give out all that he has received from the inspiration of the Holy Spirit; often he will respond to the suggestions that come to him by free association, trusting the Spirit to provide coherence rather than seeking to impose a human logic or order. He believes that if he were to hold back or put aside ideas for later, he would receive no more (SC 82.1; SBOp 2:292). He deplores his own unworthiness chiefly in order to demonstrate the virtue of humility that he is striving to teach. In moments of depression or uncertainty (e.g., SC 54.8; SBOp 2:107), he reaches out for the emotional support of his hearers (SC 77.8; SBOp 2:266). More than once has he been favored with the visits of the Word (here he possibly echoes Origen), and after much hesitation he recounts this personal experience, again ostensibly for didactic purposes (SC 74.5; SBOp 2:242). Personal circumstances and current church issues claim his attention: the death of his brother Gerard evokes an expression of profound grief (SC 26); he angrily denounces recent heresies (SC 75) and refutes new and unorthodox teachings—for example, those of Gilbert de la Porrée (SC 80). Approaching the text of the Song, he is eager, optimistic, impetuous, and delighted with its sensuous beauty; he is also baffled by it in places, and occasionally he vents impatience with its obscurities.

Dialogic formats had been used, of course, since antiquity to frame philosophical discussions. The dramatic conventions inherited from Plato and Cicero had been continuously applied by the church fathers. Cassian's *Conferences*, to cite but one important example, are presented as dialogues featuring the author, John Cassian, and his companion, Germanus, who interview various anchorites encountered on a journey through Egypt. Bernard's imitation of orality serves in wholly traditional fashion to enliven his discourse.[23] More profoundly, it expresses essential aspects of

---

[23] Early modern commentators were in fact deceived by Bernard's oral fiction. Leclercq cites Vacandard's *Vie de saint Bernard* (1895) among other studies preceding his 1955 article, "Les sermons sur les cantiques ont-ils été prononcés?"

the reading process as Bernard conceives it. He is not addressing an individual "silent reader"—that is, a visual reader—but rather one who will "hear" him in the assumed virtual presence of a group. This implied reader is a participating member of the church communion, and he remains so even in physical solitude and silence. Bernard addresses him both singly and collectively, in both the second-person singular and second-person plural, as does the psalmist; Bernard uses the first-person plural to include himself in the congregation (and refers to himself alone in the first-person singular).[24]

The reader is called upon to "hear" the sermon, that is, to adopt the listening attitude—the attitude of faith, the posture of obedience. Bernard often quotes Psalm 44:11 (45:11): "Hear, daughter, and see," and especially Paul: "Faith comes from hearing" (Rom 10:17); "We walk by faith, not by sight" (2 Cor 5:7). Bernard accordingly declares: *Auditus ad meritum, visus ad praemium* (SC 28.5; SBOp 1:195: "Hearing is connected with deserving, sight with the reward"). Hearing is associated with effort, the labor of prayer, and thought, by which the hidden things of God—"what the eye has not seen, nor the [physical] ear heard, nor the heart of man conceived" (1 Cor 2:9)—are communicated "by faith, as if wrapped in a covering and kept under seal" (SC 28.9; SBOp 1:198). The faculty of sight, in this world, will most often be deceived by appearances. True vision is reserved for the next world, when "we shall see face to face" (1 Cor 13:12); but even now, as a reward of faith, we gain partial and indirect glimpses of the divine, *per speculum in aenigmate* (1 Cor 13:12: in a mirror dimly)—that is, Bernard implies, chiefly through the study of Scripture.

The sermon, in the Gregorian tradition, is a "reading aloud" of a passage of Scripture: a reading to other readers, a reading and interpretation directed to them, performed with them. Bernard instinctively reaches out to that reciprocity, for "where two or three are gathered together in my name" (Matt 18:20) he knows that the Holy Spirit will be present to inspire him. He seeks, however,

---

[24] In "Les sermons sur les cantiques ont-ils été prononcés?", 198–99, Leclercq somewhat exaggerates the importance of the second-person singular as implying individual reading. Bernard clearly subscribes to the traditional understandings summarized by Peter Damian in *Dominus vobiscum*; see above, p. 124.

to extend his congregation geographically beyond the walls of Clairvaux and temporally beyond the present moment. He seeks universality and permanence and therefore resorts to writing; he maintains in imagination, however, the live interaction with the home audience, trusting that their presence to him would not be confined in physical space and time.

The form he adopts is the sermon-series, developed into a commentary. He follows the Scripture in its own order, verse by verse and chapter by chapter, in *lectio continua*. That systematic (and occasionally arbitrary) procedure contrasts with the discontinuous selection of scriptural pericopes that normally occurs in day-to-day sermons following the church calendar. Where the daily sermon responds to the calendar and to local congregational needs, the commentary finds its *raison d'être* in the sequential order and (ideally) in the completeness of its exposition. Still, Bernard imaginatively refers to the frame of each "day's" discourse, containing each sermon within a comparable duration (averaging five to seven pages each in the critical edition), enclosing each between an introduction and a concluding doxology. A basic rhythm of one verse from the Song per sermon is felt to be the norm, but the discussion most often overflows from one sermon to the next, prompting elegant apologies for the interruption in the thought (e.g., in SC 36.7; SBOp 2:8: *facientes finem ubi non erat finis* ["making an end where there was no end"]) and promises concerning its continuation on the "morrow."

Bernard's Reading Project

Parate fauces! (SC 1.1; SBOp 1:3: "Prepare your jaws!"). With that challenge Bernard introduces his undertaking, conceived at the outset in the terms of the traditional patristic alimentary metaphor. Like the prophet Ezekiel of old, Bernard's monks are invited to "eat this book!" (Ezek 3:1).[25] It will be "solid food" rather than "milk" (1 Cor 3:1-2; Heb 5:12-14), appropriate for mature minds, not for novices. It is a loaf of bread, "splendid and tasty" (SC 1.1; SBOp 1:3: *splendidus sapidusque*), nourishing and

---

[25] Cf. Gregory, Hiez 1.10.3; discussed above, p. 63.

indeed "crusty" under the tooth. *Proferatur, si placet, et frangatur* (SC 1.1; SBOp 1:3: "Let us bring it forth, if you please, and break it"). It is the eucharistic host, which the celebrant brings forth and breaks over the altar. "This is my body."[26] *Adest paterfamilias: cognoscite Dominum in fractione panis. . . . O piissime, frange esurientibus panem tuum, meis quidem, si dignaris manibus, sed tuis viribus* (SC 1.4; SBOp 1:4–5: "The father of the family is present: recognize the Lord in the breaking of bread. . . . O most loving Lord, break your bread for the hungry, in my hands if it should please you, but by your power").

Not without a certain violence, as we shall see, will the reading process be accomplished. But in the first sermon Bernard's view is as yet optimistic. There is a freshness, an exuberance, in his approach to the first verse of the Song. He has many questions to raise concerning this utterance; he trusts absolutely that they will be answered in due course:

> Dic, quaeso, nobis, a quo,de quo ad quemve dicitur: *Osculetur me osculo oris sui?* Aut quale est istud ita subitaneum et factum repente de medio sermonis exordium? Sic quippe in verba prorumpit, quasi quempiam loquentem praemiserit, cui consequenter respondentem et hanc introducat personam, quaecumque est ipsa quae osculum flagitat. . . . Et quidem iucundum eloquium, quod ab osculo principium sumit, et blanda ipsa quaedam Scripturae facies facile afficit et allicit ad legendum, ita ut quod in ea latet delectet etiam cum labore investigare, ne fatiget inquirendi forte difficultas, ubi eloquii suavitas mulcet. Verum quem non valde attentum faciat istiusmodi principium sine principio, et novitas in veteri libro locutionis? Unde constat hoc opus non humano ingenio, sed Spiritus arte ita compositum, ut quamvis sit difficile intellectu, sit tamen inquisitu delectabile. (SC 1.5; SBOp 1:5)

> Tell us, I beg you, by whom, about whom, and to whom it is said: "Let him kiss me with the kiss of his mouth?" And why this suddenness, this abrupt beginning of the speech in the middle?

----

[26] The eucharistic metaphor for interpretation may have been originally introduced by Ambrose, as J. Leclercq notes in "Aspects littéraires de l'oeuvre de saint Bernard," *Recueil* 3:88.

The Song erupts into words, as though implying a previous speaker to whom she is responding—whoever she is who asks for a kiss. . . . What a joyous discourse is this, which begins with a kiss! The pleasant face of the Scripture easily prompts and entices one to read, so that it becomes a delight to search out its deeper meaning; one never tires of the inquiry, difficult as it is, where one is charmed by the sweetness of the language. Who could possibly help noticing this beginning without a beginning, this novelty of speech in the old book? Clearly this work was composed by no human skill but by the artistry of the Spirit, difficult to understand and yet delightful to investigate.

Bernard's initial inquiry focuses on rhetoric, on the manner of discourse rather than the matter. He notes that the Song erupts into speech, without the benefit of a proper *exordium*. This *principium sine principio* breaks a rule of composition accepted in all known classrooms since Cicero. New speech in an old book! Joyous speech, which takes its beginning from a kiss. What is the meaning of its abruptness? Who could it be who speaks in this manner, and to whom?

Bernard will return more than once to these questions. In the meantime, he takes a frank delight in the sweetness of the scriptural discourse (*eloquii suavitas*), which indicates to him that the text was indeed composed by no human hand but by artistry of the Spirit.[27] Origen had also observed the "elevated style" of Scripture,[28] mainly characterized by mysteries and obscurities. But Bernard's remark implies a more trusting attitude: he does not anticipate stumbling blocks, but rather expresses confidence at the outset that the "pleasant face," or "inviting surface," of Scripture

---

[27] Cistercian scholars have long commented on the apparent contrast between Bernard's attitude to the visual arts, expressed particularly in the *Apology to Abbot William*, and his literary manner. For example, see Emero Stiegman, "A Tradition of Aesthetics in Saint Bernard," in John Sommerfeldt, ed., *Bernardus Magister: Papers Presented at the Nonacentenary Celebration of the Birth of Saint Bernard of Clairvaux*, CS 135 (Spencer, MA: Cistercian Publications, and Cîteaux: Comentarii Cistercienses, 1992).

[28] The reverent reader must necessarily sense, according to Origen, that the Scriptures were written in a more than human, divinely elevated style (Origen, *On First Principles* 4.1.6 [SCh 268:282]; *ex semetipso sentiet non humana arte nec mortali eloquio sed divino, ut ita dixerim, coturno libros esse conscriptos*).

(*blanda facies*) will not prove deceptive, and that it will lead him to a true understanding of its deeper meaning.

Sermon 1 thus takes the form of a prologue derived from that of Origen in the *Commentary*.[29] Bernard evokes here many of the classic Origenian topics and applies them to monastic spiritual life. The Song, he recalls, is the third in order of Solomon's books, following Proverbs and Ecclesiastes; acceding to the Song, one will ideally have learned from the two preceding books to discipline one's life and to understand the vanity of this world (SC 1.2; SBOp 1:3). Origen's observation of the superlative in the title Song of Songs—parallel, Bernard notes, to "King of Kings and Lord of Lords"—prompts a summary of Origen's list of biblical songs preceding "the" Song: the Israelites sang to celebrate their escape from Egypt; Deborah, Judith, Samuel's mother, and many prophets also sang on given occasions—when a victory was won, a peril avoided, or whenever they received benefits they desired. And "you" too—Bernard turns to his imaginary monastic assembly—looking back on your own experience, you will recall many occasions when you sang to the Lord songs of praise and due gratitude for specific graces received. But Solomon, the presumed writer of the Song of Songs, was "unique in wisdom, surpassing in wealth and renown, secure in peace; he stood in no need of any particular benefits that would have inspired him to sing those songs" (SC 1.7; SBOp 1:6). The Song of Songs is a metasong, so to speak, sung on a level of abstraction higher or deeper than the others. Its subject is sacred Love, as Gregory and all others had perceived. It is motivated by no specific need or circumstance, Bernard emphasizes; he conceives the Song text as arising from the absolute gratuity that he will ascribe to Love itself, an emotion purer than fear or reverence because it is unmixed with any other motivation. Bernard shows here a deeper affinity with Gregory than with Origen (cf. Gregory, Exp 8 and 18, p. 174 above), and he will return frequently to this essential theme throughout the *Sermons*, notably in sermons 7 and 83.

---

[29] For a detailed comparison, see Luc Brésard, "Bernard et Origène commentent le Cantique," *Collectanea Cisterciensia* 44 (1982): 111–30, 183–209, 293–308. Bernard does not name Origen in the first sermon. Where he does so (e.g., in sermon 54), it is with extreme caution or frank denunciation.

Bernard does not retain the distinctions Origen makes among terms for love—*amor, dilectio,* and *caritas*—which, as even Origen concedes, mean the same thing in the last analysis. Love is everywhere the same in essence, for Bernard; there are differences in degree, and it may involve different objects—none, of course, as worthy of love as Love itself. Bernard seems relatively untroubled by sex. Nor is he overly concerned with excluding the unqualified "carnal" reader. At the outset, he addresses an audience limited a priori to elite Cistercian monks, in whom he urbanely recognizes a spiritual aristocracy to which he himself belongs. They were presumably recruited as adults, and they would have brought to Cîteaux a certain experience of love in the world which they must now transfer to the love of God. They are not the older men addressed by Origen, people who have ceased altogether to feel the "affections of material nature" (Cant Prol 6). Bernard's monks, he implies, are young adults capable of *desiderium,* indeed no longer children or novices but men who have attained a kind of sexual maturity of the spirit—a mind that has attained "nubile years" and is now "ripe for marriage with the heavenly Spouse" (SC 1.12; SBOp 1:8: *Ad nubiles quodammodo pervenerit annos . . . facta nuptiis caelestis sponsi idonea*).

Allegorical Analysis

The bread must be broken; the scriptural book interpreted (objectively) and experienced (subjectively). Objectively: the text is to be broken *open*—its content must be disclosed and revealed. Broken *into*—in order to extract meaning, in all the traditional metaphors, as the wheat is taken out of the chaff, as the kernel from a nut, as the marrow from a bone (SC 73.2; SBOp 2:234), as honey from the comb (SC 7.5: SBOp 1:34). Broken *apart*—analyzed, disassembled ("deconstructed") as necessary: *Non oportet ne unum quidem iota, quando et minutias iubemur colligere fragmentorum, ne pereant* (SC 1.6; SBOp 1: 1:5: "Not one iota should be lost [cf. Matt 5:18], since we are commanded to gather up the tiniest fragments"). Bernard's will be what we now call a "close reading": as after the Eucharist, as after the feeding of the four thousand, all the crumbs must be gathered up (Matt 15:37, Mark 8:8). Subjectively:

the text is to be "tasted" *in palato cordis;* "chewed," ruminated, meditated, and memorized; "swallowed," "digested," and internalized so that it ultimately "nourishes" the soul and is integrated into the reader's active life.

For each verse of the Song, Bernard devotes an initial paragraph to the *littera*, imagining the scene depicted, relating it to its immediate context, and conscientiously questioning its vocabulary and grammar. He proceeds then to expound its spiritual meaning allegorically (in terms of Christian doctrine) and morally (in regard to its implications for human psychology and conduct). Allegory and morality are always closely intertwined. The emphasis awarded to each and the order of their discussion vary considerably from verse to verse. The form of the presentation remains at all times flexible, with ample room allowed for digressions and free associations.

Bernard reads the Song text closely, questioning details of phrasing, often proposing possible alternative wordings by way of contrast. Why in verse 1 does the Bride ask to be kissed "with the kiss of his mouth" as if lovers kissed by other means than the mouth, or with mouths other than their own? And why not simply say "Let him kiss me *with his mouth*" (SC 1.5; SBOp 1:5)? Bernard finds reasons: "Let the mouth that kisses signify the Word who assumes flesh; the mouth that receives the kiss signifies the flesh that is assumed; the kiss, however, that is composed of both, is the person that is formed by both, Christ the mediator between God and man" (SC 2.3; SBOp 1:10). But may an individual aspire to that mystical kiss which signifies reconciliation? In the spirit of humility, Bernard adds two other, preparatory kisses—namely, of the feet of Christ (penitence) and of his hands (perseverance)— before returning to the kiss of the mouth (contemplation); he further identifies the feet as Mercy and Judgment (SC 6.6; SBOp 1:29), the hands as Liberality and Fortitude (SC 7.1; SBOp 1:31), before abandoning the game.

Here and elsewhere Bernard freely adds terms to the verse under discussion. The procedure is justified usually by associations that he finds elsewhere in Scripture. In sermon 23 on "The King has brought me into his storerooms (*cellaria*)" (Song 1:3), he adds to the storerooms the garden and the bedroom from later in the

Song (Song 3:4 and 5:1) in order to posit three basic terms: the garden is taken to represent the historical sense of Scripture, the storeroom its moral sense, and the bedroom the mystery of contemplation. He then subdivides these into threes: the garden of history contains the creation, the reconciliation, and the renewal of heaven and earth; the storerooms of the moral sense contain a room of spices (discipline), one of ointments (nature), and one of wine (grace); the bedroom includes a place of instruction, a place of experience, and finally a place of contemplation, completing the symmetrical, tripartite scheme.[30]

Beneath the artificiality of the allegorical scheme lies a concern to derive a general hermeneutics, that is to say, a set of concepts and techniques that would enable him to cope with the bewildering imagery of the Song on a more than *ad hoc* basis. In the later sermons, those numbered in the sixties and seventies, the optimism of the first sermon yields to a mounting irritation with obscurities, as Bernard's demand for understanding becomes more insistently focused.

In principle, "hearing leads to sight," as Bernard explains (SC 41.2; SBOp 2:29–30). The hearing of the scriptural text (i.e., the reading of it, its reception by faith) inspires the creation in the imagination of spiritual images (*spirituales similitudines*) through which divine wisdom is communicated to the mind (SC 41.3; SBOp 2:30).[31] The images are based on familiar experiences and earthly "things that have been made" (Rom 1:20); in these, as in a puzzling mirror (*per speculum in aenigmate*), the light is tempered to the human understanding, which could not yet bear to gaze at it

---

[30] Sermon 23 is analyzed in detail by J. Leclercq, "Aspects littéraires," *Recueil* 3:56–64; for a more recent reading, see M. B. Pranger, *Bernard of Clairvaux and the Shape of Monastic Thought: Broken Dreams*, (Leiden, New York, and Köln, 1994), 51–84. Still more elaborate is the allegory of Pharaoh's chariots in sermon 39; see J. Leclercq, "L'art de la composition dans les sermons de saint Bernard," *Recueil* 3:150–58.

[31] In sermon 41 on Song 1:11 ("We will make you ornaments of gold, studded with silver"), Bernard develops an allegory derived from Origen, *Commentary*, book 2. For a comparative study, see Luc Brésard, "Bernard et Origène," 127–30. Bernard construes the ornaments as earrings, with the gold figuring divine wisdom and the silver the gift of eloquence in preaching.

"face to face" (1 Cor 13:12). Bernard's view of spiritual pedagogy, Gregorian in essence, foresees a progress from the known to the unknown (cf. SC 51.7; SBOp 2:88), from earthly images and words of human language to a (partial) intuition by faith of the divine. The difficulty Bernard encounters is that the text of the Song can evoke physical images (*corporea phantasmata*) as well as spiritual ones, and at such times the puzzling mirror of its poetry becomes a wall which must be broken through. Confronted with apparent "stumbling blocks," Bernard seems to revert to Origenian herme-neutics. "Behold, he comes, leaping upon the mountains, bounding over the hills" (Song 2:8: *Ecce iste venit, saliens in montibus, transiliens colles*); what should we imagine here, he inquires—a giant "cap-tured by the love of a girlfriend" (*mulierculae amore captum*), bound-ing over mountains to return to her embraces (SC 53.3; SBOp 2:97)? The core of the problem is not, actually, eroticism; it is that the "physical image" seems trivial, unworthy of the spiritual song, whose meaning must then be sought on another level. What, then, are these spiritual mountains and hills, and in what sense does the Bridegroom leap upon or over them? Over the course of three sermons, Bernard gropes with alternative explanations, attempting to refer the Scripture to other Scripture; perhaps the mountains are those in which the ninety-nine sheep were left behind while the shepherd searched for the one that was lost (Matt 18:11-12)? Or are these the holy mountains where Jerusalem is said to be founded (Ps 86:1[87:1])? Or the living, rational mountains and hills that "break forth into singing," according to Isaiah 55:12? But are we to then visualize mountains feeding on mountains and sheep on sheep?

Lost in the forest of allegory, Bernard ends sermon 53 with the consoling thought that occurs at similar moments, that at least "it is good for us to be here" (Matt 17:4) resting in the mountains, searching into secrets and contemplating things of beauty. On the next "day," he proposes a new explanation focused on a difference in prepositions: the Bridegroom leaps *in* or *upon* the mountains (*in montibus*) but *over* the hills (*transiliens colles*). The hills, then, represent powers of the air, fallen angels, barren in their pride, that the Lord passed over and did not visit when he came down to the valleys on earth. Bernard then applies this part of the image to himself: he has been guilty of pride, the Lord has turned away in anger, and

that is the reason for the languor of soul and dullness of mind that
has invaded him, he confesses, over the last two days.

> Hinc ista sterilitas animae meae, et devotionis inopia quam pa-
> tior. . . . Non sapit psalmus, non legere libet, non orare delectet,
> meditationes solitas non invenio. Ubi illa inebriatio Spiritus?
> Ubi mentis serenitas, et pax, et gaudium in Spirito Sancto? (SC
> 54.8; SBOp 2:107)

> This is the cause of the sterility of soul and the poverty of devo-
> tion from which I suffer. . . . The psalm has no taste, reading dis-
> pleases, prayer does not delight me, I cannot find my accustomed
> meditations. Where is that intoxication of the Spirit? Where is
> my serenity of mind, and peace and joy in the Holy Spirit?

This may possibly be the voice of Bernard himself, referring to the
apparently unsatisfactory questioning in progress. But, more cau-
tiously, the modern critical reader recognizes here the voice of the
preaching *persona*, "Bernard," addressing the imaginary assembly
for whose benefit he immediately turns his distress into a lesson in
humility, and advises his monks to imitate him in that regard (SC
54.9; SBOp 2:108). Not until the next sermon (SC 55.1; SBOp
2:111–12) does he make the poetic connection between the leaping in or over mountains and hills and the image of the beloved
who leaps "like a gazelle or a fawn" in the next verse (Song 2:9:
Similis est dilectus meus capreae hinnuloque cervorum): the fawn then
evokes for him the Christ child, the gazelle the keen vision of the
sure-footed animal—mercy and judgment, respectively.

Bernard does not attempt to conceal his hesitations or uncertainties. He dramatizes, on the contrary, his own struggles as a
fearless interpreter who ventures into the thick of difficulties in
quest of truth. His unconcealed fumbling truly illustrates, in any
case, several features of his reading methodology. He has made
the commitment that "not a single iota," no tiniest detail of the
text, should pass unnoticed. He has inherited from Origen and
the exegetical tradition the doctrine that absurdity on the literal
level is to be resolved by spiritual allegory. Analytical to a fault, he
breaks each verse down into its components, interpreting or rather
translating them separately, as though refusing to "see" the poetic
figure as a whole. In the example just summarized, he appears—or

pretends—to not perceive the synonymy of mountains and hills, or that of the fawn and the gazelle, and only belatedly does he link the "leaping" in verse 8 to the two animals in verse 9. Similarly, in the reading of Song 2:13, "My dove in the clefts of the rock, in the crannies of the wall . . . ," he disassembles the image: the clefts in the rock are Christ's wounds, the wall is the communion of saints, in which the devout mind hollows out resting places ("crannies") by study and prayer.[32] Often he will fail to recognize synecdoche, a frequently used figure in the Song. "The voice of the turtledove . . ." (Song 2:12); why only one, he inquires? Why not turtledoves? (SC 59.6; SBOp 2:138). Again in the next verse, "The fig tree has put forth its green figs," he does not perceive the tree as a singular-for-plural figure, and insists that only one tree is designated, meaning only one people, the Jews, whose early fruits are green, that is, worthless (SC 60.3; SBOp 2:143).

Bernard is oddly literal-minded, a paradoxical result of his concern with allegory. Does he not accept, with Augustine (*De doctrina* 3.16), that the scriptural authors made free use of figurative language, as did the classical poets? Bernard's particular difficulty may reside in the natural and agricultural imagery, the flora and fauna that enliven the lyricism of the Song. His understanding of animals and vegetables is often practical rather than poetic, derived from bookish scientific lore about the "real" world: the voice of the turtledove is usually mournful, he claims, not "sweet" (SC 59.3; SBOp 2:136–37); the "fawn" and the "gazelle" have different behaviors and faculties in nature; he observes that the "apple tree among the trees of the wood" (Song 2:3) is actually small and insignificant in the comparison (and what does that mean? SC 48.3; SBOp 2:68). He perhaps follows a method like that advised by Hugh of Saint-Victor, who teaches that the word must be carefully related to the thing it designates before one attempts to interpret the meaning of the thing (*De scripturis*, PL 175:13). More pervasively, we sense Bernard's discomfort with the "pagan" subhuman world, an intolerance no doubt closely related to his famous denunciation in the *Apology to William of Saint-Thierry* of the animal imagery sculpted on

---

[32] J. Leclercq, "Aux sources," *Recueil* 1:290–01, lists sources for this traditional interpretation.

Cluniac column capitals. He feels an urgent hermeneutic imperative to translate animal and vegetable figures into properly spiritual
terms appropriate to the human and divine dialogue. Echoing 1
Cor 9:9, he demands, "Is it for vineyards that God is concerned?"
(SC 30.2; SBOp 1:211); "God is concerned with men, not with
trees" (SC 60.2; SBOp 2:142); "Is God concerned with bushes?
The man-God is concerned with men, and he counts our progress
as his fruit" (SC 63.5; SBOp 2:164).

The image of the little foxes that destroy the vines (Song 2:15)
prompts a particularly vehement attack:

> Ante omnia sane, ut communem et usitatum litterae sensum
> ab hac explanatione penitus respuamus, utpote ineptum et in-
> sulsum, indignum plane qui recipiatur in Scriptura tam sancta,
> tam authentica. Nisi quis forte ita vecors et animo stolidus sit, ut
> pro magno habeat didicisse ex ea, instar filiorum huius saeculi,
> curam gerere terrenarum possessionum, custodire et defen-
> sare vineas ab incursantibus bestiis, ne forte contingat amittere
> fructum vini. . . . Non estis tam rudes, neque adeo spiritualis
> expertes gratiae, ut ita carnaliter sapiatis. (SC 63.1; SBOp 2:161)

> First of all, let us totally reject from this interpretation the
> common and familiar meaning of the literal text as unsuitable
> and tasteless, unworthy indeed to be received in such holy and
> authentic Scripture. Unless one were so foolish and obtuse in
> mind, like the children of this world, as to think it a great mat-
> ter to have learned from it how to manage earthly possessions,
> how to guard and defend vines from the incursions of beasts,
> in order not to lose the fruit of the vine. . . . You are not so
> uncouth, nor so lacking in spiritual grace, that you would "taste"
> the verse in this carnal manner.

The literal reading is denounced as *ineptum* ("absurd," "imperti-
nent," "unsuitable"), *insulsum* ("tasteless," "insipid" [etymologi-
cally, "unsalted"]), and therefore *indignum* ("unworthy") of Holy
Scripture. This critique sharply contrasts with the trusting attitude
expressed in sermon 1. Apparently, his early hope of progressing
smoothly from the *littera* into its deeper meaning has not been
realized. He has been delighted by the Bride's utterance; the discourse of vineyard management he finds tasteless. "It is good to be

here" in the text perhaps, but he can no longer rest content with that. Where earlier authorities had, at such moments, counseled patience and humility, a matter of giving the Spirit time to work below the conscious level—during sleep perhaps[33]—Bernard is characteristically impatient with obscurities and intolerant of intermediaries. He deplores the prolonged state of exile in which he must continue to accept the spiritual repast wrapped in "the husk of the sacrament, the bran of the flesh, the chaff of the letter, the veil of faith" (SC 33.3; SBOp 1:235):

> Quidni eruam dulce ac salutare epulum spiritus de sterili et insipida littera, tamquam granum de palea, de testa nucleum, de osse medullam? Nihil mihi et litterae huic, quae gustata carnem sapit, glutita mortem affert! (SC 73.2; SBOp 2:234)

> _____

> Why should I not dig out the sweet and healthful feast of the spirit from the sterile and tasteless letter, like the grain from the ear, the nut from the shell, the marrow from the bone? I will have nothing to do with this letter! It has the taste the flesh, and if swallowed it brings death!

"The letter kills, the Spirit brings life" (2 Cor 3:6). *Spiritus autem vivificat* ("the Spirit vivifies or enlivens"); is not understanding the essence of life?

> Annon vita intellectus? "Intellectum da mihi, et vivam," ait Propheta Domino. Intellectus non remanet extra, non haeret in superficie, non instar caeci palpat forinseca, sed profunda rimatur, pretiosissimas solitus exinde veritatis exuvias tota aviditate diripere ac tollere sibi, et cum Propheta dicere Deo: "Laetabor ego super eloquia tua, sicut qui invenit spolia multa." Nempe ita "regnum veritatis vim patitur, et violenti rapiunt illud." (SC 73.2; SBOp 2:234)

> _____

> Is not life understanding? "Give me understanding, and I shall live," says the prophet to the Lord. Understanding does not remain outside, it does not grope along the surface, like a blind man, but searches out the depths, often bringing up precious spoils of truth, and carries them away with all eagerness, and says

[33] Cf. Cassian, Conf 14.10.4.

to God with the prophet: "I will rejoice over your discourses like a man who finds many spoils." So indeed "the kingdom of heaven suffers violence, and the violent bear it away."

This passage brings out with singular clarity the true ferocity contained within the traditional alimentary metaphor for interpretation. "Prepare your jaws!" (SC 1.1; SBOp 1:3). The bread of Scripture must be opened up, torn apart, chewed, tasted in its sweetness, digested in order to receive its nutrition. Here the immediate goal is knowledge: spiritual understanding, *intellectus*, derived from a correct exegesis of the scriptural text. But if and when Bernard arrives at that, something else will still be needed: a quality of experiential immediacy that he associates with the Bride and describes in terms of an erotic metaphor for reading, rather than an alimentary one. It is her voice that he continues to listen for, and her example that he hopes eventually to follow.

The Voice of the Bride

The Bride's voice is the first that Bernard hears at the beginning of his reading project. Her confidence and impetuosity reassure him throughout, and they inspire much of his finest writing. He returns at frequent intervals to his initial questioning: who is it that speaks in such a manner? Of whom is she speaking, and to whom?

The Bride personifies both the "soul thirsting for God" (SC 7.2; SBOp 1:31) and the church espoused to Christ. She bursts out, in the first verse of the Song, without the benefit of a proper *exordium*. She needs no introduction, for she has no need to "capture benevolence" as Cicero had prescribed; indeed, she is not writing but speaking, and not orating but responding in a dialogue to someone already present. She fears no rejection because her Bridegroom, as we are to learn, loved her first. Bernard describes her attitude by means of a *priamel*, that is, a list of contrasting examples:

> Sed pono diversas affectiones, ut ea quae proprie sponsae congruit distinctius elucescat. Si servus est, timet a facie domini; si mercenarius, sperat de manu domini; si discipulus, aurem parat magistro; si filius, honorat patrem: quae vero osculum

postulat, amat. . . . Non petit libertatem, non mercedem, non
hereditatem, non denique doctrinam, sed osculum, more plane
castissimae sponsae ac sacrum spirantis amorem, nec omnino
valentis flammam dissimulare quam patitur. Vide enim quale
praeripiat sermonis exordium. Magnum quid a magno petitura,
nullo tamen, ut assolet, utitur blanditiarum fuco, nullis circum-
volutionibus ad id quod desiderat ambit. Non facit proemium,
non captat benevolentiam, sed ex abundantia cordis repente
prorumpens, nude frontoseque satis: "Osculetur me," ait, "osculo
oris sui." (SC 7.2; SBOp 1:31)

I will describe various affective relationships, so that the one that
is proper to the Bride will appear more clearly. The slave fears
his master, the wage earner hopes for gain from his employer,
the learner gives attention to his teacher, the son honors his
father. But the one who asks for a kiss, she is a lover. . . . It is
not for liberty that she asks, not for wages, not for an inheritance
or even knowledge, but for a kiss. It is obviously the request of
a Bride who is chaste, who breathes forth a love that she cannot
at all disguise. For see how she does away with *exordium*. She is
about to ask much from a great person, but she resorts to no
cosmetic flattery or circumlocution, she makes no preamble, she
does not conciliate [*non captat benevolentiam*]—but straight from
the abundance of her heart, barefaced, shamelessly, she bursts
out: "Let him kiss me with the kiss of his mouth!"[34]

The Bride's boldness contrasts with the admonition of the
Benedictine Rule: "Whenever we want to ask some favor of a
powerful man, we do it humbly and respectfully, for fear of presumption. How much more important, then, to lay our petitions
before the Lord God of all things with the utmost humility and
sincere devotion" (RB 20.1-2). Bernard rejects this cautious, traditional advice because the Bride is not asking for a "favor"; she
is in love, and she seeks only love in return. Her love is "chaste"
but indeed erotic in nature. It is chaste in the sense that it is

-----

[34] An early version of this discussion had been proposed in letter 11 (SBOp
7:52–60), written to the Carthusians in 1125, and Bernard returns to it at key
points in the *Sermons* on the Song of Songs, notably in the *summa* of sermon 83. Letter 11 is reproduced at the end of *On loving God*: "A man can
acknowledge that the Lord is powerful, that the Lord is good to him, and that

ontologically pure, unmixed with ulterior motives. Her outcry is gratuitous. It arises from no particular circumstance; accordingly, it comes without preface, *ex nihilo*, or rather *ex abundantia cordis*, uncontrollably, straight from the overflow of the heart.

To whom is the Song addressed? To whom is the Bride speaking? These are important, related questions that lurk in Bernard's mind throughout the course of the *Sermons*. In sermon 7, Bernard hypothesizes that the Bride must be speaking to angels, members of the Bridegroom's household; in a spirit of "modesty" she would seek to conciliate intermediaries rather than directly approach the Bridegroom himself (SC 7.4; SBOp 1:32–33). That careful reading conflicts, however, with the passionate poetics of her outburst, noted with enthusiasm in the previous paragraph (SC 7.2; SBOp 1:31, quoted above). For Bernard, the Bride personifies the Pauline virtue of confidence (*fiducia*, Greek *parresia*, "free speaking, bold speaking"),[35] a spiritual freedom springing from an instinctive consciousness of her own purity (SC10.9, SBOp 1:53; and SC 32.8, SBOp 1:231). Hesitations and uncertainties would be excluded from this state of mind. Growth in grace brings expansion of confidence. "You will love with greater ardor, and knock on the door with greater assurance, in order to gain what you perceive to be still wanting to you" (SC 3.5; SBOp 1:17). The boldness of the Bride is

---

the Lord is simply good. The first is the love of a slave who fears for himself; the second is that of a hireling who thinks only of himself; the third is that of a son who honors his father. He, therefore, who fears and he who covets do so for themselves. Charity is found only in the son. It does not seek its own advantage" (Bernard of Clairvaux, *Treatises II: The Steps of Humility and Pride, On Loving God*, trans. Robert Walton, CF 13 [Kalamazoo, MI: Cistercian Publications, 1980], 126). In this letter, Bernard finds that the love of the son for the father is superior to the self-interest of the slave or the hireling; in *Sermons* on the Song of Songs 7, he goes further and places the Bride's love still higher than that of the son.

[35] For a survey of this theme in New Testament epistles, see the web site http://www.a-zbiblicalconcepts.org/confidence.htm. "Such is the confidence that we have through Christ toward God. Not that we are competent of ourselves to claim anything as coming from us; our competence is from God" (2 Cor 3:4-5). We have, Paul continues, the hope of eventually seeing the glory of God, and "Since we have such a hope, we are very bold, not like Moses who put a veil over his face" (2 Cor 3:12-13); "We have boldness and confidence of access through our faith in him" (Eph 3:12).

the "magnanimity" of the great souls who approach God with high hearts and who can dare great things:

> Quid optabilius caritate, qua fit ut, humano magisterio non contenta, per temet, o anima, fiducialiter accedas ad Verbum, Verbo constanter inhaeras, Verbum familiariter percuncteris consultesque de omni re, quantum intellectu capax, tantum audax desiderio? (SC 83.3; SBOp 2:299)

> _____

> What is more desirable than love, by which, O soul, not content with human teaching, you yourself may confidently approach the Word, cling to him with constancy, question him familiarly, and consult him on every matter, since you are as capable in understanding as you are audacious in desire?

This confidence is unimpaired, moreover, by the sense of inequality between her and her lover. "But what a disparity it is! . . . What comparison can there be between such different persons?" She is undismayed: "Such is the daring of a pure heart, a good conscience, and an unfeigned faith!" (SC 68.1–2; SBOp 2:197). Her faith teaches her that indeed "he loved her first" (1 John 4:10). And her self-assurance will be confirmed finally in sermon 83, where Bernard gives, as it were, his *summa* of the question:

> Solus est amor, ex omnibus animae motibus, sensibus atque affectibus, in quo potest creatura, etsi non ex aequo, respondere Auctori, vel de simili mutuam rependere vicem. . . . Nam etsi minus diligit creatura, quoniam minor est, tamen si ex tota se diligit, nihil deest ubi totum est. (SC 83.4; 83.6; SBOp 2:300–02)

> _____

> Love is the only one, among all motions or senses or affections of the soul, in which the creature can respond to its creator, however unequally, and repay him in kind. . . . For even if the creature loves less, because she is less, yet if she loves him with her whole self, there is nothing lacking where there is all.

Absolute lover that she is, the Bride will be intolerant of intermediaries. To whom, then, is she speaking? Bernard faces this question in sermon 67 on Song 2:16: *Dilectus meus mihi, et ego illi* ("My beloved is mine and I am his"). It is a pivotal moment in his inquiry. In the sermons immediately preceding this one, he has contended with little foxes and tangled vines, with difficulties of interpretation—not always successfully, as we have seen—and with controversial issues raised by contemporary heresies (SC 65–66). He now listens once again to the Bride's own discourse. *Simplex vox videtur, quoniam suaviter sonat* (SC 67.1; SBOp 2:189: "Her utterance seems simple, for it sounds sweet"). As always, it is the *sound* of her voice that he mainly hears. Her words are "sweet," deceptively simple, and deeply mysterious (SC 67.1; SBOp 2:188).

Of whom she speaks is obvious, he finds, but not *to* whom, since the third-person reference to the Bridegroom suggests that he himself is absent here (SC 67.2; SBOp 2:189). Could she be conversing with handmaidens? Bernard is ready now to reject that rational supposition in favor of a bolder idea: she is not talking to anyone else but only to herself, for indeed her phrase is "truncated" and incoherent, and it is not a communication of an intelligible message to an auditor. *Nescimus quid loquitur, quia non sentimus quod sentit. . . . Affectus locutus est, non intellectus, et ideo non ad intellectum* (SC 67.2–3; SBOp 2:189–90: "We do not know what she is saying, because we do not feel what she feels. . . . It is a feeling which has spoken, not understanding, and not to the understanding [of a hearer]").

> Ad quid ergo? Ad nihil, nisi quod mirabiliter delectata, et affectata vehementer ad desideratos affatus, finem illo faciente, nec tacere omnino quivit, nec tamen quod sensit exprimere. Neque enim ut exprimeret sic locuta est, sed ne taceret. (SC 67.3; SBOp 2:190)
>
> ---
>
> For what purpose, then, does she speak? For none, but only because she is marvelously loved and profoundly moved by what he has said, fulfilling her desire. As he finishes speaking, she cannot wholly keep silent, and neither can she express what she feels. Nor has she spoken in this manner to express any thought, but simply to break her silence.

Habent suas voces affectus, per quas se, etiam cum nolunt, produnt, he continues (SC 67.3; SBOp 2:190: "Feelings have their own language, by which they reveal themselves, even against their will"). Fear has trembling, grief has weeping, those in pain scream, lovers have cries of joy; these are not rational or premeditated discourses. So it is with the love of God, and here Bernard performs a virtuoso variation on an Ovidian theme:

Sic flagrans ac vehemens amor, praesertim divinus, cum se intra se cohibere non valet, non atttendit quo ordine, qua lege, quave serie seu paucitate verborum ebulliat, dummodo ex hoc nullum sui sentiat detrimentum. Interdum nec verba requirit, interdum nec voces omnino nullas, solis ad hoc contentus suspiriis. Inde est quod sponsa sancto amore flagrans, idque incredibili modo, sane pro captanda quantulacumque evaporatione ardoris quam patitur, non considerat quid qualiter eloquatur, sed qudquid in buccam venerit, amore urgente, non enuntiat, sed eructat. (SC 67.3; SBOp 2:190)

So it is with passionate, violent love, especially divine love: since it cannot contain itself, it pays no attention to the order, grammar, succession, or scarcity of words in which it bursts out, as long as it feels no impediment to its expression. At such times it needs no words or even speech, it is content with sighs alone. Thus the Bride, ablaze with a holy love, in incredible fashion, pays no heed to what she says or how she speaks. Doubtless in order to catch some exhalation of the passion she feels, she belches forth, rather than enunciates, whatever comes into her mouth at the urging of love.

How to understand, or rather, how to receive this unintelligible utterance, not intended for our ears? *Ructus est!* It is a "belch!" (SC 67.4; SBOp 2:190). With that homely image—one could never accuse Bernard of preciosity—the Cistercian abbot means perhaps to correct the element of sentimentality in the preceding passage. He proceeds conscientiously, linking the word *ructus* to other scriptural "eructations" and particularly to David's in Psalm 44.2 (45.1): *Eructavit cor meum verbum bonum* ("My heart overflows with a goodly theme"). The "belch" is a logical extension, after all, of the alimentary metaphor. It gives out a good or bad odor, Bernard notes, according to the quality of the vessel it comes from (SC 67.4; SBOp 2:191). Bernard the preacher takes then the posture of humility. As a repentant sinner, he must patiently await the moment when he will truly "taste and see" God face to face; in the meantime, he will remain content to sniff the "fragrance" of the breath of the Bride, receiving a perception of divinity indirectly and from afar.

The Bride's speech comes from no context; it bursts out from nowhere, without preamble, and remains, as it were, suspended in

midair: *Pendet oratio; immo non pendet, sed deficit* (SC 67.2; SBOp
2:189: "Her speech hovers; or rather, it does not hover, it ceases").
Her outcry is free of notional content. There is nothing to understand here. Conventional exegesis fails, scientific scrutiny is fruitless
(SC 67.1; SBOp 2:188–89). Bernard listens then for a tone of voice,
a melody, a song indeed (*suaviter sonat*), rather than an exposition.
The Bride speaks, or rather sings, in the "language of love," expressing not words but "feelings" (*affectus*):

> Unde in epithalamio hoc non verba pensanda sunt, sed affectus.
> Cur ita, nisi quod amor sanctus, quem totius huius voluminis
> constat esse materiam, non verbo sit aestimandus aut lingua,
> sed opere et veritate? Amor ubique loquitur; et si quis horum
> quae leguntur cupit notitiam adipisci, amet. Alioquin frustra ad
> audiendum legendumve amoris carmen, qui non amat, accedit:
> quoniam omnino non potest capere ignitum eloquium frigidum
> pectus. Quomodo enim graece loquentem non intelligit qui
> graece non novit, nec latine loquentem qui latinus non est, et
> ita de ceteris, sic lingua amoris ei qui non amat barbara erit, erit
> sucut aes sonans aut cymbalum tinniens. (SC 79.1; SBOp 2:272)

Thus in this marriage song it is not words which are to be
pondered, but feelings. Why so, if not that holy love, which is
the subject of this whole volume, is not measured by words or
in language, but by deeds and truth? Love speaks everywhere,
and if anyone seeks to understand what one reads, one must
love. It would be vain for anyone who does not love to attempt
to read or hear this poem of love, for a cold heart cannot at all
comprehend its fiery eloquence. Just as one who does not speak
Greek cannot understand it spoken, and neither can anyone
who is not Latin understand spoken Latin, and so with other
tongues, so also the language of love will sound barbarous to an
unloving ear, like a noisy gong or a clanging cymbal.

Bernard reverses here 1 Cor 13:1: "If I speak in the tongues of
men and angels, but have not love. . . ." For Bernard, it is love
itself that will sound "like a noisy gong or a clanging cymbal," like
a barbarous vernacular, to one who does not speak its language.

  Sola unctio docet: only divine anointing can teach this idiom;
sola addiscit experientia: only by direct, personal experience can one
learn it (SC 1.11; SBOp 1:7).

Experti recognoscant, inexperti inardescant desiderio, non tam cognoscendi quam experiendi. Non est strepitus oris, sed iubilus cordis; non sonus labiorum, sed motus gaudiorum; voluntatum, non vocum consonantia. Non auditur foris, nec enim in publico personat: sola quae cantat audit, et cui cantatur, id est sponsus et sponsa. (SC 1.11; SBOp 1:7–8)

Those who have experienced it should recognize its sound, and those who have not should burn with desire, not so much to learn about it as to experience it for themselves. It is not a noise in the mouth, but a gladness in the heart; not a sound on the lips, but a surge of rejoicing; a harmony of wills, not voices. It is not heard outside or sounded in public; only she who sings hears it, and he to whom it is sung—the Bride and the Bridegroom.

The Bride's song, the Song itself, is not even heard "outside." No external words or sounds register; no visions appear to the physical or imaginative eye. "The Word is spirit and the soul is spirit. *Habent linguas suas*: they have their own modes of speech by which they communicate and indicate their presence to each other" (SC 45.7; SBOp 2:48).

Sola experientia. Only experience can teach spiritual listening comprehension. The experience must indeed precede reading, as Cassian had taught (Conf 10.11.4–6), in order for the reader to "recognize" in the Song the reality that he or she already knows. One cannot learn "about" the Song; it is accessible only to an active participant who becomes or aspires to become the Bride, the singer herself. Only the singer hears the Song, and the one to whom it is sung. One must, in effect, step into the text to hear it. By means of exegesis one may seek to break through its literal surface to reach its inner meaning—*intellectus*, "spiritual understanding," the wheat within the chaff, the kernel in the nut, the marrow in the bone . . . *experientia*, however, lies deeper still, and that is what Bernard "recognizes" when it erupts to the surface of text, into the music of the Bride's outcry.

Reading the Song, Bernard recalls his own mystical encounters, and he reflects upon them in several oft-quoted pages of the *Sermons.* Paradoxically, as scholars have noted, it would appear that his most personal expressions flow not only from previous experience, but also from previous reading. There are reminiscences of Origen in his description of the unpredictable visitations of the Bridegroom to his soul; he admits that the Word has come to him "many times," but he has never felt the moment of entry; he had occasional presentiments of his coming and remembered the event afterwards (SC 74.5; SBOp 2:242; cf. Origen, *Homilies* 1.7).[36] God's visit to the soul is preceded by the surge of desire (SC 31.4; SBOp 1:221) and felt as an interior presence: *non figuratum, sed infusum, non apparentem, sed afficientem . . . non sonans, sed penetrans* (SC 31.6; SBOp 1:223: "not in a figure, but infused; not appearing, but felt . . . not sounding but penetrating"). When after vigils and prayers the Word appears, "suddenly he is gone again, just as we think we hold him fast. But he will present himself anew to the soul that pursues him with tears, he will let himself be embraced but not detained, and suddenly again he slips out of our hands" (SC 32.2; SBOp 1:227). Bernard's sense that God is within him, yet uncontained within him, recalls Augustine's invocation in the *Confessions* (SC 1.2–3; SBOp 1:3–4; cf. SC 3.6; SBOp 1:17):

> Ascendi etiam superius meum, et ecce supra hoc Verbum eminens. Ad inferius quoque meum curiosus explorator descendi, et nihilominus infra inventum est. Si foras aspexi, extra omne exterius meum comperi illud esse; si intus, et ipsum interius erat. . . . Nullis denique suis motibus compertum est mihi, nullis meis sensibus illapsum penetralibus meis: tantum ex motu cordis, sicut praefatus sum, intellexi presentiam eius. (SC 74.5–6; SBOp 2:243)

> I have ascended to the highest in me, and look! the Word is towering above that. In my curiosity I have descended to explore my lowest depths, yet I found him even deeper. If I looked outside myself, I saw him stretching beyond the furthest I could see; and if I looked within, he was yet further within. . . . It was not by any movement of his that I recognized his coming; it was not by any of my senses that I perceived he had penetrated the depths of my being. Only by the movement of my heart, as I have told you, did I perceive his presence.

---

[36] The parallel passages from Origen's homily and Bernard's sermon 74 are studied by J. Leclercq, "Aspects littéraires," *Recueil* 3:90, and Luc Brésard, "Bernard et Origène," 301.

In such passages, literature and personal recollection flow inseparably together. Bernard "experiences" the Song rather than reading its objective text. It is an intersubjective interaction which occurs, one which confirms the belief that the sacred text addresses him individually as well as the church collectively, that it refers to what he himself has felt and understood, and that it "intends" him to give out again every thought that it gives him (SC 82.1; SBOp 2:292). That trust impels him to follow the trail of free associations that the text inspires, from the wording of a verse to a related doctrinal idea, to scriptural evocations, to allegorical and moral interpretations, to their confirmation in extratextual, spiritual life. His sermons retain the spontaneity and unpredictability of an auditory event. What he records is a live reading in process, in the present tense, rather than the result of such a reading transcribed after the fact. He reads the Song from within, as a participant in the drama—potentially as a protagonist, ultimately as its singer or as its author. He seeks, in effect, to marry himself to the text, paralleling the wedding of the soul and the Word. The marriage must be consummated. Reading is an *act*. He would be ideally a "nubile" reader, that is, of marriageable age, sexually/spiritually mature, for "the singing and hearing of the Song are not suitable for novices" (SC 1.12; SBOp 1:8). Intellectual cognition will not suffice. Bernard would take possession of the text and be possessed by it. That desire drives the muscular violence of his exegesis, which is the masculine aspect, so to speak, of his reading. He will boldly attack the sacred Scripture, rejecting its wording, adding and subtracting terms, rewriting it where necessary to make it his own—such is the *fiducia* inherited from Paul, the audacity he learns from the Bride. At other times, where the Bridegroom seems absent, he longs for understanding, as she does for reunion. And where exegesis fails altogether, he must then "feel" the wording (or "taste" or "smell" it), he must open himself as a Bride to the *affectus* of the poetry, the sound of the Song, rather than grasping for its meaning. He "contemplates" the Song text then and responds in prayerful celebration:

> O suavitatem! O gratiam! O amoris vim! Itane summus omnium, unus factus est omnium? Quis hoc fecit? Amor, dignitatis nescius, dignatione dives, affectu potens, suasu efficax. Quid violentius? Triumphat de Deo amor. Quid tamen tam non

violentum? Amor est. Quae ista vis, quaeso, tam violenta ad victoriam, tam victa ad violentiam? (SC 64.10; SBOp 2:171)

O sweetness! O grace! O power of love! And so the highest of all things is made one with all? Who has done this? Love, unconscious of its own dignity, rich in mercy, mighty in affection, effective in persuasion. What could be more violent? Love triumphs over God himself. But what could be so nonviolent? Love is so. What is this force, I ask, that is so violent in victory, and so unresisting to violence?

With Bernard the tradition of *lectio divina* arrives at perhaps its ultimate extension or point of culmination.[37] Bernard had inherited from the fathers the alimentary metaphor for textual meditation and interpretation; from the Song itself he adapts the erotic metaphor to the same process. He thereby transforms reading into an "embrace of souls" (SC 1.12; SBOp 1:8: *complexus animorum*), that is to say, an exchange rather than a one-way transmission, a reciprocity in which the text "experiences" the reader as well as vice versa. Bernard's reading brings into actuality the capabilities of Scripture that Cassian and Gregory had only speculatively foreseen: the flexibility of the text, its responsiveness to the reader individually and to the church collectively (in both cases imaged by the Bride); its ability to "mirror" the reader, changing as he or she changes; its openness, unboundedness, accessibility to penetration; the continuity of its flow into and out of the reader's "real" life. Scripture as Bernard conceives it is not finite, not imprisoned within objectivity nor confined to the written page. Intellectual understanding alone cannot comprehend such a text; the *affectus* and even the physical body must also be wholly committed. Reading, for Bernard, will be a true marriage, or it will be nothing.

---

[37] The Song commentary tradition continued, of course, in Latin and in the vernacular through the later Middle Ages into the early modern period. On Richard Rolle and later medieval English lyric, see Astell, *The Song of Songs*, 105–76. In Spain, the tradition may be said to culminate in the *Meditaciones sobre los Cantares* by Teresa of Ávila and in the poetry by John of the Cross.

Chapter Seven

The Twelfth-Century Integration

"After centuries of Christian reading, the page was suddenly transformed from a score for pious mumblers into an optically organized text for logical thinkers."[1] In these provocative terms Ivan Illich describes the twelfth-century "transition from monastic to scholastic reading." He is surely correct in insisting on the importance of this cultural change, which preceded by some twelve generations the invention of the printing press. Illich seems to exaggerate, however, the suddenness and absoluteness of the phenomenon. A progressive development of reading technology over many centuries had already made texts increasingly available and legible, enabling the nascent scholastic movement. Looking back over the writings of Anselm and John of Fécamp, and still further back to Cassiodorus and Jerome, we perceive that the provision for reading fluency had been a constant concern throughout the early Middle Ages. Word separation, pioneered by Irish scribes as early as the seventh century, had become the norm on the continent well before the year 1100.[2] Privileged readers like Jerome's disciples, or like Anselm's patron the countess Matilda of Tuscany, had long enjoyed free access to texts designed for visual perusal, and they were encouraged to browse in them at will. The practice of individual, silent reading became more widespread through the course of the twelfth century, but it did not bring about the immediate end of ruminative, oral, and literary meditation. We have seen that Bernard of Clairvaux continued to stage his exposition of the Song before an imagined present, listening assembly. Abelard, Hugh of Saint-Victor, John of Salisbury, and other early schoolmen

[1] Illich, *In the Vineyard of the Text*, 2.

[2] Saenger, "Silent Reading," 367–414, describes the gradual adoption of word separation on the European continent from the ninth century onward (375–77).

clung to the traditional reading disciplines, even as they began to systematize discussions of the ideas that such reading could generate. On all sides the need was felt to reaffirm a commitment to the act of reading as a bulwark against confusion, in anticipation of the cultural changes on the horizon.

Meditatio and *Meditationes*

All authorities reaffirm the value of intensive scrutiny of the texts and correspondingly criticize superficiality in all its forms. There is no point in reading without understanding: "Understanding does not remain outside," writes Bernard, "it does not grope along the surface, like a blind man, but searches out the depths, often bringing up precious spoils of truth, and carries them away" (SC 73.2; SBOp 2:234). The Carthusian prior Guigo II echoes Bernard's wording.[3] William of Saint-Thierry finds "the same gulf between attentive study and mere reading as there is between friendship and acquaintance with a passing guest, between boon companionship and chance meeting."[4] Guigo II reiterates, "What is the use of spending one's time in *lectio continua*, running through the lives and sayings of holy men, unless we can extract nourishment from them by chewing and digesting this food so that its strength can pass into our inmost heart?" (Scala 13; SCh 163:108). What matters is retention, by which one "carries away" the kingdom of heaven. Teaching, both in the cathedral school and in the monastery, continues accordingly to rely on memorization, as in John of Salisbury's well-known description of the classroom of Bernard of Chartres: "Each student was daily required to recite part of what he had heard on the previous day. Some would recite

---

[3] Guigo II writes, *Meditatio non remanet extra, non haeret in superficie, altius pedem figit, interiora penetrat, singula rimatur* (*Scala Claustralium* 5). On Guigo II, see below, n. 17, and pp. 224–30.

[4] William of Saint-Thierry, *Epistola ad Fratres de Monte Dei*, 121, in Guillaume de Saint-Thierry, *Lettre aux Frères du Mont-Dieu (Lettre d'or)*, ed. Jean Déchanet, SCh 223 (Paris: Éditions du Cerf, 1975), 238. *The Golden Epistle: A Letter to the Brethren at Mont Dieu*, trans. Theodore Berkeley, CF 12 (Kalamazoo, MI: Cistercian Publications, 1971), 52.

more, others less. Each succeeding day thus became the disciple of its predecessor."[5]

All agree that reading should ideally initiate a process of integration into understanding and experience. The fulfillment of reading is generally seen to take place in distinct graduated stages. John of Salisbury lists four steps in all: *lectio*, the perception of a written text; *doctrina*, "learning," in which the reader synthesizes the text under study with texts and concepts already present in memory; *meditatio*, a reaching further toward things as yet unknown, or a penetration into hidden recesses of meaning; and *assiduitas operis*, putting understanding into experiential practice (*Metalogicon* 1.23; McGarry 64–65). John's basically academic approach envisions scientific knowledge and understanding as its goals. Guigo II directs the development of reading more exclusively toward spirituality, in the four steps familiar to students of *lectio divina*: *lectio*, *meditatio*, *oratio*, and *contemplatio*. Hugh of Saint-Victor offers five steps, effectively combining intellectual and religious orientations: *lectio*, *meditatio*, *oratio*, *operatio*, and *contemplatio*. I shall study these terms in more detail in the following pages. Let me note for the present that despite the distinct vocations of the three authors, their systems of reading-extension are more alike than they are different. Hugh and Guigo II both assign critical importance, and especially thorough discussions, to the second term, *meditatio*; John of Salisbury covers this same phase under two headings, *doctrina* and *meditatio*. Terminology aside, the theorists all agree to institute, immediately following the first apprehension of a text, a task of focused scrutiny and reflection, "guided by one's own reason" (*ductu propriae rationis*), as Guigo II states (Scala 2; SCh 163:84).

Meditatio can take various directions. Most traditional would be the work of interpretation of the text, following the allegorical methods prescribed by the fathers, as we have seen applied in commentaries on the Song of Songs. The familiar alimentary metaphors, "mastication," "rumination," and "digestion," are evoked, as always; more particularly characteristic of the twelfth century, perhaps, is the view of this activity as a conscious, voluntary, rational

---

[5] John of Salisbury, *Metalogicon* 1.24, trans. Daniel D. McGarry (Gloucester, MA: Peter Smith, 1971), 67.

"scrutiny," in which the reader "penetrates" (*penetrat*) and "investigates" (*rimatur*), seeking to "extract" hidden meaning. Rupert of Deutz and Ælred of Rievaulx both liken the struggle to understand to the wrestling of Jacob with the angel: *Labor magnus et difficilis.*[6] Bernard, as we have seen, finds himself occasionally baffled in this effort, fearful of engaging in a transgressive "curiosity" concerning mysteries beyond his reach (e.g., in SC 67.1).

A newer approach to meditation, focused primarily on the literal/historical level of Scripture, is explored by Ælred of Rievaulx in his treatise on the life of the recluse (*De institutione inclusarum*)[7]. Writing for his own sister, who had asked him for guidance in her vocation as a recluse, Ælred offers a rule and concludes with a *triplex meditatio*, inviting her to reflect upon the gifts of Jesus in the past, present, and future (De inst inc 29). The consideration of the past consists of a reading of the gospel narrative; he urges her to visualize, imaginatively enter, and participate in the series of scenes beginning with the annunciation to the Virgin Mary, continuing through the life of Jesus, and concluding with the passion. The visualization technique he recommends anticipates indeed the *Spiritual Exercises* of Ignatius of Loyola. Thus she should "enter" the Virgin's chamber and join ecstatically in the salutation of the angel: *Ave Maria, gratia plena.* Later, in the house of the Pharisee, she is to join the penitent woman, washing the feet of Jesus with her tears and drying them with her hair, and even if he does not at first accept her service, she should persist (like Jacob wrestling with the angel), and ultimately he will not refuse her, a virgin, what he grants to the sinner. Ælred vividly imagines his sister's reading activity, constantly urging her to "approach," or at least admire from afar, and respond to what she sees: *Quid agis, o virgo?*

[6] Rupert of Deutz, *Commentaria in Canticum canticorum*, prologus 125–36, ed. Hrabanus Haacke, CCCM 26 (Turnholt: Brepols, 1974), 9; Ælred of Rievaulx, *De institutione inclusarum* 31, in *La vie de recluse. La prière pastorale*, ed. and trans. Charles Dumont, SCh 76 (Paris: Éditions du Cerf, 1961), 124. Ælred of Rievaulx, *Treatises and Pastoral Prayer*, ed. M. Basil Pennington, trans. Mary Paul MacPherson, CF 2 (Kalamazoo, MI: Cistercian, 1971), 41-102.

[7] Ælred de Rievaulx, *La vie de recluse*. A similar literal and historical reading of the gospel is proposed in the first part of Ælred's *De Jesu puero*, ed. Anselme Hoste, trans. Joseph Dubois, SCh 60 (Paris: Éditions du Cerf, 2005).

Acurre, quaeso, acurre . . . videsne . . . ? Accede proprius. He does not confine her meditation to the literal level, however. She should not fail to sound the depth of the meaning of each event, translating gospel history into properly spiritual, present experience, as with the gesture of Mary of Bethany breaking open the alabaster flask of ointment: *Frange igitur alabastrum cordis tui, et quicquid habes devotionis, quicquid amoris, quicquid desiderii, quicquid affectionis, totum effunde super Sponsi tui caput, adorans in Deo hominem, et in homine Deum* (De inst inc 31; SCh 76:128: "Break, therefore, the alabaster of your heart, and whatever you have of devotion, love, desire, or affection, pour it all over the head of your Spouse, adoring the man in God, and God in the man").

Ælred's instructions to his sister evoke a silent, solitary reader, presumed to be Latin-literate and in full control of her access to the text. Receptive as she is to spiritual direction, she will be allowed to respond freely to scriptural inspiration, following a rhythm of reading which prompts one's impulse to pray, as it did with the countess Matilda of Tuscany under the guidance of Anselm of Canterbury, and with the Roman ladies who studied with Jerome. This aristocratic textual culture derives in part from the eremitic program, as briefly described, for example, by Peter of Celle, in *On Affliction and Reading.* Reading is "chained," Peter states, to the silence of the cloister. It is the sovereign remedy against the illicit thoughts that may trouble the solitary. Without reading, "the nocturnal and noonday devils assault the idle hermit with as many thrusts of useless and harmful thoughts as there are hours and moments in the day and night. . . . How quickly and easily is the city of one's room captured if it does not defend itself with God's help and the shield of the sacred page."[8]

It is conceded that reading and meditation may take place, as always, in group assemblies as well as in solitude, orally and aurally, under magisterial direction. Guigo II inquires, "How to avoid meditating upon false or idle topics, overstepping the bounds laid down by

---

[8] Peter of Celle, *Selected Works: Sermons, The School of the Cloister, On Affliction and Reading, On Conscience,* trans. Hugh Feiss, CS 100 (Kalamazoo, MI: Cistercian Publications, 1987), 134. Jean Leclercq, ed., *La spiritualité de Pierre de Celle* (Paris: Vrin, 1946).

our holy fathers, unless we have been previously instructed by reading or by hearing? . . . Listening belongs in a certain manner to reading, and that is why we usually say that we have read not only those books that we have read to ourselves or [aloud] to others, but also those that we have heard read by masters" (Scala 13; SCh 163:110).

The customary practices of the classroom, such as those of Bernard of Chartres described by John of Salisbury (above, pp. 204–5), are found in both the monastery and the school: reading aloud and commentary by the master, memorization and recitation by the pupils. In the more academic settings, comparison and collation of texts lead to the formulation of ideas—the *quaestiones* that will form the basis of the Scholastic method. John of Salisbury refers to this process as *doctrina*, "learning," properly the first phase of *meditatio* immediately following the initial *lectio*. This is a properly intellectual, potentially challenging exercise, guided by one's own reason, *ductu propriae rationis*. Where this activity is not undertaken, where classroom reading devolves into a merely passive, unquestioned text-reception, the result is the form of superficiality described by Abelard in his critique of Anselm of Laon: "Anyone who knocked at his door to seek an answer to some question went away more uncertain than he came. . . . He had a remarkable command of words but their meaning was worthless and devoid of all sense [*sensum contemtibilem et ratione vacuum*]. The fire he kindled filled his house with smoke but did not light it up; he was a tree in full leaf which could be seen from afar, but on closer and more careful inspection proved to be barren."[9] Abelard of course went too far in the opposite, aggressive direction, as a *scrutator maiestatis*, in the remainder of his tragic career.

"Reading and meditation are common to both good and evil people," Guigo II concedes. "Even the pagan philosophers discovered, by the use of reason, what the truest good consists of" (Scala 5; SCh 163:92). The concept of *meditatio*, in particular, has widened by this time, reaching well beyond the memorization and recitation prescribed by the early monastic rules. *Meditatio* now mainly denotes the voluntary struggle to understand, without which reading

---

[9] Peter Abelard, *Historia calamitatum*, trans. Betty Radice, in *The Letters of Abelard and Heloise*, (Harmondsworth, Middlesex, England: Penguin Books, 1974), 62.

would be valueless. But the term acquires a still further extension of meaning, one approaching modern "meditation," as the name given to the new literary genre of *meditationes*. In this increasingly important category of writings are found Anselm's *Orationes sive meditationes* described above, the *Meditationes* of two Carthusian priors, Guigo I and Guigo II, the *Meditativae orationes* of William of Saint-Thierry, and other associated writings. Hugh of Saint-Victor offers theoretical descriptions of *meditatio* in *Didascalicon* and in a short treatise, *De meditatio*, to which I shall return shortly.[10]

The defining characteristic of the genre is the freedom enjoyed by the writer. A literary *meditatio* is not bound to the exposition of a given text, as is a commentary; it does not develop a logical argument, as does a treatise; it does not usually address a named reader, as does a letter, nor speak to a present, responsive congregation, as does a sermon. It is still essentially an extension of reading based, however, on no single text but rather on a free-association of any number of scriptural references. In the weaving together of quotations and reminiscences, in the flow of reading into writing, a *meditatio* can become an exercise in high verbal artistry. It is typically presented as the utterance of a solitary individual in prayer addressed to God, following the great example of Augustine in the *Confessions*. The voice that speaks in the first-person singular belongs to a generalized exemplary *persona* derived, we presume, from the self-vision of the actual identified author. His *meditatio* departs from the reading of texts, proceeds from the experience of the book to the "book of experience" (*librum experientiae*), and returns to testify to the valid pertinence of the Scriptures to what has been felt and done in non-textual life. Written down, a *meditatio* becomes a text in its own right, to be read and "meditated" by another reader in turn.

By way of an example, I turn to a passage from the second of the *Meditativae orationes* by William of Saint-Thierry. Here he proceeds from self-confrontation— evoking Jeremiah, Job, and the psalms—to a struggle to conceive the Trinity:

---

[10] For a history of "meditation," see the article in the *Dictionnaire de Spiritualité*, s.v. "méditation," 10: 906–34.

Si, te donante, inuenio fontem lacrimarum, qui in humiliatae et contritae animae uallibus cito solet exoriri, lauo manus operationis et faciem deuotionis. Deinde, sicut extendit accipiter alas suas ad austrum ut plumescat, expando manus meas ad te, Domine, et anima mea sicut terra sine aqua tibi, et sicut terra deserta, inuia et inaquosa, sic in sancto appareo tibi, ut uideam uirtutem tuam et gloriam tuam. Cumque oculos mentis, sensum rationis ad te erigo, o sol iustitiae, contigit mihi quod contingere solet ebriis a somno uel infirmis oculis, ut unam rem aspicientes, duas aut tres esse arbitrentur, donec uidendi processu incipiant intelligere uitium esse oculorum, non rei quae uidetur.

Propter quod, cum a somno negligentiae expergefactus, subito respicio in Deum, de quo me lex diuina instruit dicens: Audi, Israel, Dominus Deus tuus Deus unus est, et in eum a quo sum illuminandus, quem sum adoraturus uel oraturus, dirigere omnino habeam mentis intuitum: occurrit mihi Trinitas Deus, quam fides catholica a progenitoribus mihi incantata, usu ipso inculcata, a te ipso tuisque doctoribus commendata, mihi demonstrat. (Med Or 2.8–10; SCh 324: 56–58)

If by your gift I find a fount of tears such as is wont to spring up speedily in lowly ground and in the valleys of a contrite soul, I wash the hands with which I work and the face I lift in prayer. Then, as the falcon spreads his wings towards the south to make his feathers grow, I stretch out my two hands to you, O Lord. My soul is as waterless ground in your sight, and as desert land, unwatered and untrodden. I appear before you in your holy place, that I may see your power and your glory.

And when I raise to you, O Sun of Righteousness, the eyes of my mind and the perception of my reason, it happens to me as is wont to happen to persons drunk with sleep or of weak eyes. Seeing one thing, they think that they are seeing two or three, until in the process of seeing it dawns upon them that the defect is in their sight, not in the thing seen.

For this reason, therefore, when on awaking from the sleep of negligence, I suddenly direct my gaze on God, concerning whom the divine law instructs me, saying: "Hear, O Israel! The Lord your God is one God," and while I fix my soul's regard entirely on him from whom I look for light and whom I am about to worship or implore, I am confronted with the fact of God as Trinity. This mystery the Catholic faith, rehearsed by my forebears, impressed upon me by long use, and commended to me by yourself and those who teach your truth, declares to me.[11]

Here as elsewhere, William's writing conveys theological reasoning in a highly dramatic prose poetry, balancing intellectual inquiry with affective expression in a felicitous exploration of the *meditationes* genre. Two authors frame the twelfth-century discussion of reading theory. The first, Hugh of Saint-Victor (d. 1141), appears today as one of the most admired figures of the period and is among the most often quoted by students of intellectual history.[12] He was among the last to attempt to hold theology and spirituality together; the split between them, already visible in his lifetime, has lasted to the present time. Hugh's *Didascalicon* (late 1120s) orients an inclusive survey of the arts and sciences toward scriptural study and contemplation as their ultimate goal.[13] The relationship between reading and meditation forms the central theme of that work, and it is also treated in several of his other writings, notably in *De scripturis*,[14] in *De meditatione*,[15] and in the first of his homilies

[11] Guillaume de Saint-Thierry, *Oraisons méditatives*, ed. and trans. Jacques Hourlier, SCh 324 (Paris: Éditions du Cerf, 1985), 56–58; William of Saint Thierry, *On Contemplating God. Prayer. Meditations*, trans. Penelope Lawson, CF 3 (Kalamazoo, MI: Cistercian Publications, 1970), 98–99.

[12] The exhaustive, if not definitive, study of Hugh is that of Roger Baron, *Science et sagesse chez Hugues de Saint-Victor* (Paris: Lethielleux, 1957). See also the article by the same author, "Hugues de Saint-Victor," in *Dictionnaire de spiritualité* 7, 901–39. An anthology of translated selections from Hugh's writings, accompanied by commentary and notes, is presented by Patrice Sicard, *Hugues de Saint-Victor et son école* (Turnhout: Brepols, 1991). In an influential study, Marie-Dominique Chenu situates the Abbey of Saint-Victor as a monastery open to the urban Paris environment: "Hugues fait d'ailleurs la théologie de cette sociologie" ("Civilisation urbaine et théologie: L'école de Saint-Victor au XIIᵉ siècle," *Annales* 29 [1974], 1260). Ivan Illich, *In the Vineyard of the Text* (see n. 1 above), studies Hugh as a pivotal figure introducing the age of "bookish reading," now perceived by Illich as drawing to a close.

[13] Charles Henry Buttimer, ed., *Hugonis de Sancto Victore Didascalicon: De studio legendi. A Critical Text* (Washington, D.C.: The Catholic University Press, 1939). Parenthetical references by book and chapter numbers refer to this edition and to the translation by Jerome Taylor, *The Didascalicon of Hugh of Saint-Victor: A Medieval Guide to the Arts* (New York, NY: Columbia University Press, 1961).

[14] *De scripturis et scriptoribus sacris*, PL 175:9–28.

[15] In Hugues de Saint-Victor, *Six opuscules spirituels*, ed. and trans. Roger Baron, SCh 155 (Paris: Éditions du Cerf, 1969), 44–59.

on Ecclesiastes.[16] The second writer, Guigo II (d. 1188), the ninth prior of the Carthusian order, penned what has become the classic, authoritative summary of *lectio divina*, the *Ladder of Monks* (*Scala claustralium*),[17] well-known to late medieval spiritual teachers, including the author of the *Cloud of Unknowing* and John of the Cross, and referred to today in all the current manuals. Guigo appears to cite Hugh in various contexts, but he belongs more exclusively to the culture of the cloister. Both writers follow in the Gregorian tradition, concerned as they are with linking intellectual and spiritual formation. Between them they summarize the traditional notions of reading discipline in the final phase of the "monastic Middle Ages" on the eve of the Scholastic revolution.

Hugh of Saint-Victor

Hugh's *Didascalicon* outlines a complete curriculum of reading (*lectio*), taken here in the wide sense of academic studies: what to read, in what order, and in what manner. Part 1 (books 1–3) proceeds from basic philosophical definitions to survey the *artes*, divided into four categories: the theoretical, the practical, the mechanical, and the logical (1.11). Part 2 (books 4–6) is devoted to Sacred Scripture. This organization is indeed "scientifically differentiated and academically coordinated."[18] But Hugh's proposal is precisely not one of defining and segregating specializations in stasis (the phrase often quoted by modern readers should alert us here: *coartata scientia iucunda non est* [Did 6.3; Buttimer 115:

---

[16] *Homiliae in Ecclesiasten* 1, PL 175:115–27.

[17] Guigues II Le Chartreux, *Lettre sur la vie contemplative (L'échelle des moines. Douze méditations*, ed. Edmund Colledge and James Walsh, traductions par un chartreux, SCh 163 (Paris: Éditions du Cerf, 1970). Parenthetical references by chapter number are to this edition, and to the translation by Edmund Colledge and James Walsh: *The Ladder of Monks, A Letter on the Contemplative Life, and Twelve Meditations,* CS 48 (Kalamazoo, MI: Cistercian Publications, 1981). Tugwell offers a study of the *Ladder* in chapters 9–11 of *Ways of Imperfection*, 93–124. See also Keith J. Egan, "Guigo II: The Theology of the Contemplative Life," in *The Spirituality of Western Christendom*, CS 30, ed. E. Rozanne Elder (Kalamazoo, MI: Cistercian Publications, 1976), 106–15.

[18] McGinn, *The Growth of Mysticism*, 367.

"confined knowledge is no fun"]). Rather, constantly and on all levels of consideration, he observes the movement or flow of each discipline and each intellectual operation into the next. He is concerned practically with nurturing the progress of his students; more generally, his curriculum reflects and adopts the dynamism that propels studies spontaneously and progressively toward *divinitas*. The act of reading naturally models this movement. In the following pages, I shall refer mainly to books 3, 5, and 6 of *Didascalicon*, where Hugh discusses the reading process most specifically, and adduce the other writings by him that treat the same theme.

In the preface to *Didascalicon*, and again in the last paragraph of the work, Hugh distinguishes reading proper (*lectio*) from *meditatio*, reserving discussion of the latter for a separate work.[19] He does not maintain this distinction, however. He is concerned throughout the treatise with the extension of reading into interpretation and spirituality, outlined as a five-step process: *lectio*, *meditatio*, *oratio*, *operatio*, and *contemplatio* (Did 5.9; Buttimer 109). The operations of *meditatio* are found to be integral to reading, both sacred and secular, and inseparable from it in practice. *Didascalicon* thoroughly surveys the whole development that begins with intellectual and moral predispositions, continues into reading itself, and necessarily proceeds into *meditatio*. Rather than isolating the term *lectio*, he extends his discussion in both directions, before text-reception and after. He alludes, furthermore, to *oratio*, *operatio*, and *contemplatio*, but these higher spiritual levels lie mainly beyond *Didascalicon*'s range.

Among the predispositions to reading, Hugh includes *natura*, from which comes *ingenium*, natural ability; *exercitium*, practice; and *disciplina*, the way of life. (Did 3.6–7; Buttimer 57). He develops the latter concept in Did 3.12–19 into separate discussions of humility, eagerness to inquire, quiet, scrutiny, parsimony, and exile (i.e., the view of this world as temporary exile from our real, permanent heavenly home). These terms, first defined in the section of *Didascalicon* devoted to secular learning, recur throughout the discussion

---

[19] *De meditatione*, ed. and trans. Roger Baron, in *Hugues de Saint-Victor, Six opuscules spirituels* SCh 155 (Paris: Éditions du Cerf, 1969), 44–59, offers only a brief summary, rather less than the comprehensive study he seems to envision in the preface to *Didascalicon*.

of Scripture as well. For Hugh as for Gregory, they refer equally to intellectual techniques and to moral values.

The most general notion, and the most traditional in Christian discourse, is perhaps humility. As a moral quality it is the opposite of arrogance; the student should hold no knowledge, no writing, and especially no person in contempt (Did 3.13; Buttimer 61–64). Intellectually, the attitude of humility is related to patience in the process of learning fundamentals. With humility and patience, the student progresses steadily, step by step, while the impatient or arrogant person will tend to leap forward prematurely and stumble. Hugh associates humility also with the reverent open-mindedness that should attend learning in general and the study of scriptural obscurities in particular (Did 6.3–4; Buttimer 113–122). Lacking this stable disposition, one will tend to change one's opinions daily, with each new difficulty one encounters (Did 6.4; Buttimer 121). The virtue of humility needs, however, to be counterbalanced by discretion. One should not scorn any writing or teaching, but one cannot actually read everything (Hugh comments on the sheer quantity of books available in his time). *Magno uti moderamine oportet, ne quod ad refectionem quaesitum est sumatur ad suffocationem* (Did 5.7; Buttimer 107: "It is necessary to use great discretion, lest what was sought for our recovery may be found to stifle us"). Judgment is called for in the choice of what to read and in negotiating levels of interpretation, lest one lose one's way in the "forest of Scripture" (Did 5.5; Buttimer 103–04). Reading must not develop into an unhealthy preoccupation with arcana; from time to time, Hugh advises, it is good to return to saints' lives "and other such writings dictated in a simple style" (Did 5.7; Buttimer 106).

Reading (*lectio*) "consists of forming our minds upon rules and precepts taken from books" (Did 3.7; Buttimer 57). Here as in the preface, the term *lectio* is ambiguous, referring in Hugh's usage both to reading proper and more widely to academic studies (compare modern British usage, as when one "reads history"). Hugh defines three types of reading activity: that of the teacher, who reads to someone; that of the pupil, who reads under the teacher's instruction; and that of the independent reader, who reads to himself. (John of Salisbury makes the same distinction in *Metalogicon* 1.24 and gives a fuller description of the classroom milieu in which it arises.) Hugh seems mainly concerned with the reception of the solitary, independent reader who might be guided by his treatise, rather than with the activity of the teacher or of pupils reading under the teacher's supervision.

The next chapters (Did 3.8–11; Buttimer 58–61) continue to discuss reading as technique and reading as academic study, without distinction between the two meanings. Concerning the "method of reading" (Did 3.9: *de modo legendi*), he describes the general thought process of "analysis" (*divisio*) as a movement from finite, well-defined, more knowable things (preferably universals), to less well-defined or less knowable particulars. Complementary to the separation work of *divisio* is the action of memory (Did 3.11, *De memoria*), which gathers items together and ideally synthesizes them into "brief and dependable abstracts," whence they can be efficiently recovered as needed.

Exposition is defined as an "order of reading" (*ordo legendi*) in three steps: the letter (*littera*), the sense (*sensus*), and the inner meaning (*sententia*). As he develops this structure elsewhere in *Didascalicon*, it becomes clear that reading proper includes only the first two steps—the third, *sententia*, really belongs to *meditatio*—which he further specifies here: *Littera est congrua ordinatio dictionum, quod etiam constructionem vocamus* (Did 3.8; Buttimer 58: "The letter is the fit arrangement of words, which we also call construction"). *Sensus est facilis quaedam et aperta significatio, quam littera prima fronte praefert* (Did 3.8; Buttimer 58: "The sense is a certain ready and obvious meaning which the letter presents on the surface"). *Littera* for Hugh means mainly grammar (declension and conjugation), producing a "construction" which it will be the first task of the reader to elucidate. This first step is viewed as separate and preceeds the lexical understanding (*sensus*) of the meanings of the words. In Hugh's terms, *littera* and *sensus* together produce the first "reading," which commentators on Scripture often designate by the term *littera* alone.

Hugh's system of exposition overlaps the traditional system of exegesis accepted since Gregory: *historia, allegoria,* and *tropologia*. *Historia* means not only biblical "history," he notes, but also more broadly the *litteralis sensus*, "the first meaning of any narrative which uses words according to their proper nature" (Did 6.3; Buttimer 115–16). His apologia focuses mainly on the apparent inconsequentiality of *littera/historia*—the "littlest things" (*minima*), "stories" (*fabulae*). Seemingly, these are the concerns of children and beginners. Here Hugh recalls, in a precious autobiographical aside, his own experiments as a schoolboy in which he was able to learn much from what seemed to be "games" (*ioci*) or "nonsense" (*deliramentum*) to others. He would retain something of that playful spirit in adult inquiries. He warns that the arrogant pseudo-philosopher who skips over the elementary levels will risk falling headlong. Many things in the Scripture, taken literally, seem to have no importance in themselves but reveal their true meaning and necessity when they are considered in context. "Learn everything," he concludes in a famous line (quoted above, p. 213), "you will see afterwards that nothing is superfluous. Confined knowledge is no fun" (Did 6.3; Buttimer 115: *Coartata scientia iucunda non est*). In exploring literal/historical reading, Hugh will trust open-minded curiosity and accept the "joy" of learning as a reliable guide.[20] *Iucunditas* is the word he uses also to describe the mystical joy of contemplation.[21] Confined, blinkered science, on the contrary, is indeed a joyless thing, and, he implies, joyless science is a wrong thing.

Hugh's system of exposition insists on a careful movement from the recognition of words to the perception of their first (proper) meanings, to be followed, only then, by the discovery of allegory. He denounces, on the contrary, the tendency in certain commentators to move directly from the word to the allegorical interpretation, skipping over the middle term, the *litteralis sensus*. This is an impiety as well as an error in interpretive technique. Words signify things; things in turn may signify other things, as "spoken" by the voice of God in nature (Did 5.3; Buttimer 96). In *De scripturis et scriptoribus sanctis*, he further develops this theme and concludes: neglect of the middle term would amount to a failure to understand the process by which the Holy Spirit informs the carnal senses, proceeding from visible things to *invisibilia*, "as though it were uselessly or in vain that the Holy Spirit had interposed in Scripture the figures and similitudes by which the soul is taught, and led to things spiritual."[22]

---

[20] Bernard of Clairvaux likewise praises the *iucundum eloquium* of the Song of Songs that entices and rewards the reader (SC 1.5).

[21] See, for instance, *Homiliae in Ecclesiasten* 1 (PL 175:118C).

[22] *De scripturis et scriptoribus sacris* 5 (PL 175:14D): *Quod si, ut isti dicunt, a littera statim ad id quod spiritualiter intelligendum est, transiliendum foret, frustra a Spiritu sancto*

Meditatio is the next step:

Meditatio est cogitatio frequens cum consilio, quae causam et originem, modum et utilitatem uniuscuiusque rei prudenter investigat. Meditatio principium sumit a lectione, nullis tamen stringitur regulis aut praeceptis lectionis. Delectatur enim quo-dam aperto decurrere spatio, ubi liberam contemplandae veritati aciem affigat, et nunc has, nunc illas rerum causas perstringere, nunc autem profunda quaeque penetrare, nihil anceps, nihil obscurum relinquere. Principium ergo doctrinae est in lectione, consummatio in meditatione. (Did 3.10; Buttimer 59)[23]

Meditation is sustained thought along planned lines; it prudently investigates the cause and the source, the manner and the utility of each thing. Meditation takes its start from reading but is bound by none of reading's rules or precepts. For it delights to range along open ground, where it fixes its free gaze upon the contemplation of truth, drawing together now these, now those causes of things, or now penetrating into profundities, leaving nothing doubtful, nothing obscure. The start of learning, thus, lies in reading, but its consummation lies in meditation.[24]

This definition merits careful attention. Hugh's emphasis on the freedom of *meditatio* to depart from the base text, to explore digressive ideas, and to fearlessly question obscurities perfectly corresponds to the literary *meditationes* genre, exemplified by the *Meditativae orationes* of William of Saint-Thierry (quoted above, pp. 210–11). As chapter 3.10 of *Didascalicon* continues, Hugh divides *meditatio* into three types: "consideration of morals," "scrutiny of the commandments," and "investigation of the divine works."[25] Elsewhere in *Didascalicon*, *meditatio* figures as the second of five steps—*lectio, meditatio, oratio, operatio, contemplatio*—as we have noted (Did 5.9; Buttimer 109, as also in *De meditatione* 2.1; SCh

figurae et similitudines rerum quibus animus ad spiritualia erudiretur, in sacro eloquio interpositae fuissent. Henri de Lubac compares the discussion in *De scriptoribus* with that of *Didascalicon* 6.3 in *Exégèse médiévale*, 2.1:287–301.

[23] Cf. John of Salisbury, *Metalogicon* 1.23, trans. McGarry, 64.

[24] Taylor, trans., *Didascalicon*, 92–93.

[25] In *De meditatione* 1 (SCh 155:44), he divides the concept somewhat differently into "meditation on creatures, on texts, and on morals."

155:46). In this connection, it is seen not as a distinct activity but as a "consummation" of reading, a transformation that reading undergoes without a break in continuity. In the terms of Hugh's system of exposition, *meditatio* makes the step from the *litteralis sensus* to the *sententia*, the "deeper understanding which can be found only through interpretation and commentary" (Did 3.8; Buttimer 58), that is, the allegorical and tropological levels of Scripture. It is true that Hugh does not explicitly assign this task to *meditatio* as distinct from *lectio*, but his stated association of *meditatio* with the discovery of hidden meanings, obscurities, and ambiguities does strongly imply such a distribution of roles.

Meditatio, for Hugh, begins in a moment when the reader lifts his or her eyes from the words in order to apprehend the meanings of the things that the words signify. It retains something of the unconstrained spirit of adventure described earlier. At the same time, it is described as an intense, voluntary, and focused "scrutiny" of causes and meanings (Did 3.17; Buttimer 67: *Scrutinium autem, id est meditatio*). As such, it is distinguished in the preface to Hugh's *Homilies on Ecclesiastes* on the one hand from mere "thought" (*cogitatio*), defined here as an occurrence of something in the mind, and on the other hand from "contemplation" (*contemplatio*, the clear vision, finally obtained).[26] In the progress toward contemplation, *meditatio* is a phase of struggle between ignorance and knowledge in which the light of truth as yet barely glimmers through the fog of error. It is, Hugh continues in an epic simile, like a green log thrown on the fire: at first the fire catches it only with difficulty, with much noise, smoke, and steam; but eventually the fire takes hold, draws all into itself, and appears in purity and silent splendor.

---

[26] *Homiliae in Ecclesiasten, praefatio* PL 175: 116D–117A: *Cogitatio est, cum mens notione rerum transitorie tangitur cum ipsa res sua imagine animo subito praesentatur, vel per sensum ingrediens vel a memoria exsurgens. Meditatio est assidua et sagax retractatio cogitationis, aliquid, vel involutum explicare nitens, vel scrutans penetrare occultum. Contemplatio est perspicax, et liber animi contuitus in res perspiciendas usquequaeque diffusus. . . . Et ita quodammodo id quod meditatio quaerit, contemplatio possidet.* A little later in this same text (PL 175: 118C) Hugh subdivides *contemplatio* into *speculatio* (*novitas insolitae visionis in admirationem sublevat*) and *contemplatio* proper (*mirae dulcedinis gustus totam in gaudium, et jucunditatem commutat*).

In meditatione quasi quaedam lucta est ignorantiae cum scientia, et lumen veritatis quodammodo in media caligine erroris emicat, velut ignis in ligno viridi primo quidem difficile apprehendit, sed cum flatu vehementioris excitatus fuerit, et acrius in subjectam materiam exardescere coeperit, tunc magnos quosdam fumosae caliginis globos exsurgere, et ipsam adhuc modicae scintillationis flammam rarius interlucentem obvolvere videmus. . . . Tunc victrix flamma, in omnem crepitantis rogi congeriem discurrens, libere dominatur, subjectamque materiam circumvolitans, ac molli attactu perstringens lambendo exurit ac penetrat; nec prius quiescit quam intima penetrando succedens totum quodammodo traxerit in se, quod invenit praeter se. . . . Primum ergo visus est ignis cum flamma et fumo, deinde ignis cum flamma sine fumo, postremo ignis purus sine flamma et fumo. Sic nimirum carnale cor quasi lignum viride, et necdum ab humore carnalis concupiscentiae exsiccatum, si quando aliquam divini timoris seu dilectionis scintillam conceperit, primum quidem pravis desideriis reluctantibus passionum et perturbationum fumus exoritur; deinde roborata mente cum flamma amoris, et validius ardere et clarius splendere coeperit, mox omnis perturbationum caligo evanescit: et jam pura mente animus ad contemplationem veritatis se diffundit. (*Homeliae in Ecclesiasten* 1, PL 175:117C–118A)

In *meditatio* there is a sort of struggle between ignorance and knowledge, in which the light of truth gleams in the midst of a fog of error. It is like a fire which takes hold of a green log with difficulty at first, but then if it is excited by a strong gust of air, it begins to burn the piled material more keenly; we see clouds of smoke come out of it, and here and there small flames appear surrounding it. . . . Then the victorious flame, running over all the pile of crackling wood, freely masters it; surrounding the material and grazing it with a soft touch, it licks, consumes, and penetrates it, not ceasing until it has penetrated into its heart and drawn all that it finds into itself. . . . First we see fire with flame and smoke, then fire with flame but without smoke, finally pure fire without either flame or smoke. Likewise, whenever the carnal heart catches a spark of the fear or love of God, like a green log from which the humor of carnal desire has not yet been dried out, it produces at first a smoke of disturbances and passions, as it struggles to expel wicked desires; then with a strengthened mind it begins to burn more strongly and clearly with the flame of love, and soon all the mist of disturbance is dispelled; finally with a pure mind the soul pours itself into the contemplation of the truth.[27]

The struggle he describes is both voluntary, as when the mind applies itself to elucidating obscurities, and mystical, as when the "spark" of inspiration comes from the Holy Spirit. On the first level, thought is applied as a flame to *subjectam materiam*; on the second, it is the spirit that enflames the mind. The intellectual and emotional process he describes includes dialectical argumentation—the conscious, rational consideration of ideas that we observed also in Anselm's "meditations" (especially in "On Human Redemption"; see above, pp. 154–55)—and it takes place also in the emotional domain. Like Anselm again, Hugh seeks self-knowledge through a penitential purification of desire. In both the rational and the affective dimensions, *meditatio* extends reading beyond consideration of the *wording* of a text, without, however, losing the recollection of the textual encounter as its point of departure.

The sense of connection between reading, argumentation, and spirituality emerges in Hugh's discussion of another traditional metaphor, derived from Gregory, that of comparing scriptural exposition to architectural construction: "First we put in place the foundations of history; then, with the typical meaning we build the superstructure of the mind as a citadel of faith; finally, by the grace of the moral allegory, we clothe the building with a coat of paint" (*Moralia in Iob*, dedicatory letter *Ad Leandrum*, 3).[28] Hugh quotes this passage (Did 6.3; Buttimer 116) and elaborates the simile in the next chapter (6.4; Buttimer 117–18): the foundation, history, is below the surface of the earth; it does not have always smoothly fitted stones—the literal reading of Scripture contains many incongruities—but its solidity bears the weight of the whole edifice. He then places on it a "second foundation" of allegory,

---

[27] This simile is taken up by Saint John of the Cross, *Dark Night of the Soul*, 2.10.1–2, ed. and trans. E. Allison Peers (New York NY: Image Books, 1990), 127–28.

[28] Grégoire le Grand, *Morales sur Job*, ed. Robert Gillet, trans. André de Gaudemaris, SCh 32 (Paris: Éditions du Cerf, 1952), 118: *Nam primum quidem fundamenta historiae ponimus; deinde per significationem typicam in arcem fidei fabricam mentis erigimus; ad extremum quoque per moralitatis gratiam, quasi superducto aedificium colore vestimus.*

which both carries what is placed upon it and is itself carried by the first; unlike the first, the second is composed of stones carefully fitted together and leveled with a taut cord. "The spiritual meaning can have no opposition; in it, many things can be different from one another [*diversa multa*] but none can be in conflict [*adversa nulla esse possunt*]." From there Hugh proceeds to add doctrinal "courses": the Trinity, creation, original sin, redemption, the Law, the incarnation, the mysteries of the New Testament, and finally the mysteries of man's resurrection.[29]

As Hugh continues this discussion, it emerges that the building metaphor functions on three levels simultaneously. It is, first, the structure of the objective meaning contained in a given scriptural text that is to be discovered by exegesis (not every level is to be found in every passage, as the commentators always concede, but the structure is everywhere implicit). Secondly, the building metaphor describes the activity of exposition performed by the reader-interpreter, which takes place in order through time: *Primum littera, deinde sensus, deinde sententia inquiratur. Quo facto, perfecta est expositio* (Did 3.8; Buttimer 58: "The order of inquiry is first the letter, then the sense, and finally the inner meaning. And when this is done, the exposition is complete"). Thirdly, the same metaphor pertains to the architecture of the reader's mind (*fabrica mentis* is Gregory's term), to be built by good education. In this dimension, history, allegory, and tropology are instituted as separate fields of study (Did 3.8; Buttimer 58; and 6.1; Buttimer 113: *disciplinae*).[30] In terms of curriculum, history is foundational, as are the basic articles of the orthodox faith. He notes that history

---

[29] Peter Cantor (late twelfth century) proposes another reading of the building metaphor: "Learning sacred Scripture consists in three things—reading, disputation, and preaching. . . . Reading [*lectio*] is the foundation, as it were, and basis for all that follows, because through it the other occupations are fitted together. Disputation [*disputatio*] is like the wall in this work, because nothing is fully understood or faithfully proclaimed unless it has first been broken up with the tooth of disputation. Preaching [*praedicatio*], which these serve, is like the roof that covers the faithful from the heat and storm of vices." Quoted by Bernard McGinn, *Growth of Mysticism*, 370.

[30] Hugh's usage of the term *disciplinae* in the plural has a meaning different from that of the singular, *disciplina*, which refers to the general moral predisposition to study, as described above, pp. 213–14.

follows the order of time; allegory, however, follows the order of knowledge, beginning with the clear truth of the New Testament and continuing with the elucidation of the figures in which it is shrouded in the Old. In all studies, the student is advised to proceed patiently, under supervision, beginning with clear, finite matters and continuing to things which are more obscure or less well-defined. Exegesis, exposition, education: these three contexts are seen as homologous in Hugh's discussion, which reposes on the non-distinction among them. The structure of the educated, morally purified mind will ultimately mirror the objective structure found in the scriptural text, and it will also reflect, as a result or recapitulation, any and all individual acts of exposition that the learner will have undertaken along the way.

Surveying Hugh's theory of reading as a whole, one needs to fit together the competing analytic systems that he offers. The traditional sequence, *historia/ allegoria/ tropologia*, overlaps, not quite dovetailing, with the expository order of *littera/sensus/sententia*. *Historia* means biblical history and also the *litteralis sensus*, "the first meaning of any narrative which uses words according to their proper nature" (Did 6.3). *Historia* is also associated with *lectio*, the initial stage of *lectio divina*. The following steps in exegesis, *allegoria* and *tropologia*, and the third step in exposition, *sententia*, belong all to *meditatio*. This is the phase in which spiritual interpretation mainly takes place, and the description of the activities associated with it occupies a large proportion of *Didascalicon* (even though he proposes initially to exclude discussion of the term from that volume) and of other associated writings. *Meditatio* is eventually transcended in *lectio divina* by *oratio* and *operatio*, leading to *contemplatio* as its final term.

These terminological distinctions mask, I believe, the non-definitive, exploratory character of Hugh's formulations. More essential than the systematic surface of his writing is the sense of dynamism, the unbroken continuity of phases in process, that underlies Hugh's undertaking throughout: *littera* flows into *sensus* and *sententia*; *lectio* into *meditatio* and beyond; and, most generally, intellectual growth into spirituality. Hugh's discussions constantly spill over the borderline between one term or one chapter and the next. The same aesthetic of movement leads him to insist on orderly, gradual progressions and to denounce the stumbling over gaps that he finds in the systems of the "pseudo-philosophers." Hugh's temperament is fundamentally Gregorian. Themes of spiritual pedagogy, nurture, and growth constantly illuminate his hermeneutical discussions. He emphasizes the literal/historical level of reading not so much as a matter of "scientific" method (as Smalley argued), but rather because he is concerned throughout with beginners, with his students and their needs, with the *parvuli,* as Gregory called them. No system that excludes the *parvuli* or fails to take their progress into account can be accepted as valid.

Gregory had criticized severely the tendency among advanced readers to scorn the "lesser precepts" given to weaker minds and to attempt to change their meaning; it is absolutely needful, rather, to respect the *linkage* between the levels which is realized when the *parvuli* "grow incrementally in understanding as though by certain steps of mind, and so eventually arrive at greater truths."[31] Spiritual progress is not a movement in one direction; as one advances, one will need to look backward occasionally to retain earlier insights as well those more recently acquired. Hugh writes, "The man who looks down on the smallest things slips little by little . . . there are some who want to play the philosopher right away. They say that 'stories' [*fabulae,* i.e., history] should be left to pseudo-apostles. The knowledge of these fellows is like that of an ass. Don't imitate persons of this kind" (Did 6.3; Buttimer 114). It is not in vain or uselessly that the Holy Spirit interposed figures and similitudes in the *sacro eloquio* by which the soul is taught and led to spiritual truths.[32] For Hugh as for Gregory, the ultimate result of exegesis,

---

[31] Gregory the Great, *Hom. in Hiez.* 1.10.1; SCh 327:382. *Solent quidam, scripta sacri eloquii legentes, cum sublimiores eius sententias penetrant, minora mandata quae infirmioribus data sunt tumenti sensu despicere, et ea velle in alium intellectum permutare. Qui si recte in eo alta intellegerent, mandata quoque minima despectui non haberent, quia divina praecepta sic in quibusdam loquuntur magnis, ut tamen in quibusdam congruant parvulis, qui per incrementa intellegentiae quasi quibusdam passibus mentis crescant, atque ad maiora intelligenda perveniant.* This passage is quoted by Henri de Lubac, *Exégèse médiévale* 2.1:315.

[32] *De scripturis et scriptoribus sacris* 5 (PL 175:14D): *Quod si, ut isti dicunt, a littera statim ad id quod spiritualiter intelligendum est, transiliendum foret, frustra a Spiritu sancto figurae et similitudines rerum quibus animus ad spiritualia erudiretur, in sacro eloquio interpositae fuissent.*

the highest level of allegory, actually matters less than the integrity and continuity of the reading-interpretation process that leads to it.

Guigo II

Two works have been attributed to Guigo II, the ninth prior of the Carthusian order, who died in 1188: a collection of twelve *Meditations* and the classic *Ladder of Monks* (*Scala claustralium*). They belong to the context of the third quarter of the twelfth century, but they cannot be dated more precisely. From stylistic considerations the recent editors infer that the *Meditations* precede the *Ladder*.[33] In both works, echoes of ideas and phraseology suggest that the author was familiar with writings by Hugh of Saint-Victor, with the *Sermons on the Song of Songs* by Bernard of Clairvaux, and also possibly with works by William of Saint-Thierry and Ælred of Rievaulx. The following pages will be devoted mainly to the *Ladder*; this treatise marks a kind of terminus in the history of monastic reading, appearing, as it were, after the fact as a didactic summary of the whole *lectio divina* tradition.

Guigo II's *Ladder* has something of the reductionist quality that we might associate with the handy small-format meditation manuals found in the religion section of modern bookstores. Dedicated to a Brother Gervais, unidentified today, the treatise proposes considerations "on the spiritual way of life of monks" (Scala 1; SCh163: 82: *de spiritali exercitio claustralium*). Translators have noted the singular *exercitio*, not plural as in the Ignatian *Spiritual Exercises*; the *Ladder* is not yet a practical prayer method, but it does offer a systematic conceptual introduction, presumably aimed mainly at novices in the Carthusian order. Guigo II shows in the opening paragraphs an indisputable flair for short, memorable definitions:

> Est autem lectio sedula scripturarum cum animi intentione inspectio. Meditatio est studiosa mentis actio, occultae veritatis notitiam ductu propriae rationis investigans. Oratio est devota cordis in Deum intentio pro malis removendis vel bonis adipiscendis. Contemplatio est mentis in Deum suspensae quaedam supra se elevatio, eternae dulcedinis gaudia degustans. . . .

[33] Colledge and Walsh, in the introduction to the edition, SCh 163:25–26.

Beatae vitae dulcedinem lectio inquirit, meditatio invenit, oratio postulat, contemplatio degustat. (Scala 2–3; SCh163: 85–86)

———————

Reading is the careful study of the Scriptures with the concentration of the mind. Meditation is the studious application of the mind seeking knowledge of hidden truth, led by one's own reason. Prayer is the turning of the devout heart toward God in order to drive away evils and obtain what is good. Contemplation is a certain elevation of the mind suspended above itself, tasting the joy of eternal sweetness. . . . Reading seeks the sweetness of the blessed life, meditation finds it, prayer asks for it, contemplation tastes it. (Ladder, 68–69)

The terms are richly evocative of the tradition: *intentio*, an "intent" concentration of a mind seeking knowledge/understanding, fused with the emotional drive or desire to possess the object; the progression from "investigation" (*investigans . . . inquirit*) to the "tasting" of "sweetness" (*dulcedinem . . . degustat*). The concepts will be restated at prudent intervals in accordance with good pedagogy, and the distinctions between them will be consistently maintained.

Having named the four occupations or steps of the ladder, Gugio II proceeds to describe and distinguish the role (*officium*) of each in turn in an initial, systematic portion of his treatise. Each is demonstrated in application to a single gospel verse: "Blessed are the pure in heart, for they shall see God" (Matt 5:8). Most searching is the *meditatio* Guigo II performs, based on this very short verse. Evoking other scriptural associations, he considers the meaning of "purity" in heart and of the beatific vision, which the verse proposes not merely as something to be understood but as something to be attained for oneself. Metaphors reminiscent of Gregory come to mind: "Do you see how much juice has come from one little grape, how great a fire as been kindled from a spark, how this small piece of metal has been stretched on the anvil of meditation?" (Scala 5; SCh163:90).

Guigo II confirms here the conviction shared by all teachers of *lectio divina* concerning the value of in-depth reflection on a preferably minimal scriptural text, as opposed to scanning a quantity of reading material *in extenso*. Unreflective reading is fruitless. "Reading seeks, *meditatio* finds"; *Meditatio* is the activity of human reason voluntarily applied (*ductu propriae rationis*), and it is an indispensable, necessary step toward understanding and retention. *Meditatio* penetrates the literal "surface" of the text to discover the "hidden" or "interior" meaning, that is, the allegorical sense. Guigo II also delineates, however, more clearly perhaps than any other commentator, the limitations of *meditatio* as a procedure that has no spirituality in itself, one that is available to pagan philosophers as well as to mystics, and even to evil minds as well as to the good. *Meditatio* reveals what is contained in the "little verse," but it cannot enable us to take possession of what it has found; having broken the alabaster flask, we perceive the aroma but do not actually taste the sweetness.

It is then the task of *oratio* (prayer) to ask for what the reader now perceives and has learned to desire. Guigo II's prayer is a voluntary petition not for specific goods but for a knowledge of God beyond intellectual understanding, no longer merely in the outer "bark" of the letter but in directly felt experience (*non iam in cortice litterae sed in sensu experientiae*). The beatific vision belongs, of course, to the life to come, but some preview or foretaste of it may be granted on earth as a gift of grace; such would be the moment of *contemplatio* in which the text responds to the reader and God answers prayer. Guigo II's initial definitions of prayer and contemplation are relatively succinct by comparison to his consideration of meditation, but he does return to the two higher phases of reading development later in his treatise. Notably absent from the initial scheme is Hugh of Saint-Victor's fifth term, *operatio* (action), which Hugh places between prayer and contemplation. The omission appears to be intentional, as Simon Tugwell suggests, and tends to "tighten up the sequence, meditation-prayer-contemplation."[34] Guigo II does touch on *operatio* later in the treatise, noting that it is God who accomplishes in us our works, but we are to cooperate with him, opening to him our consent and our will (Scala 13; SCh 163:110).

Like Hugh of Saint-Victor, Guigo II is especially concerned with the linkage, the inseparable "coherence" that holds the four phases of the spiritual exercise together. His first formulation of

---

[34] Tugwell, *Ways of Imperfection*, 115.

this unity is that of a sequence: *Videre potes quomodo praedicti gradus sibi invicem cohaereant; et sicut temporaliter, ita et causaliter se praecedant* (Scala 12; SCh 163:106: "You can see how the degrees mentioned above are joined to each other, preceding each other in causality as well as in time"). Each term depends absolutely on the one before it. Reading necessarily precedes meditation, which digs beneath the letter to find and show the "buried treasure" for which prayer may then ask and contemplation finally receive. But on further reflection, Guigo II perceives not merely a linear progress in one direction but rather an interdependence; the earlier steps are of no value without those that follow—reading and meditation without spirituality will be arid or erroneous—and the following steps "rarely or never" can be taken without those that prepare them. (Guigo II concedes that spiritually privileged individuals—Saint Paul, for example—have received divine communications directly, but for most people, the way must be found through reading in the four steps he outlines.) Guigo II's final formulation looks backward as well as forward and provides for descent as well as ascent of the ladder. One must, of course, resist the forces that would return us to worldliness even after one has reached a height of contemplation. But with due intellectual humility one needs to remember the earlier stages of one's own development and not scorn to revisit these as needed:

> Sed caveat sibi iste post contemplationem istam, qua elevatus fuerat usque ad coelos, ne inordinato casu cadat usque ad abyssos. . . . Cum vero mentis humanae acies infirma veri luminis illustrationem diutius sustinere non poterit, ad aliquem trium graduum per quos ascenderat leniter et ordinate descendat, et alternatim modo in uno, modo in alio, secundum motum liberi arbitrii pro ratione loci et temporis demoretur, cum ut mihi videtur Deo tanto vicinior quanto a primo gradu remotior. (Scala 14; SCh 163:114–15)

> But let such a man beware, after having reached contemplation, in which he was raised to the heavens, lest he fall back in disorder into the depths. . . . But since, indeed, the human mind's eye is not strong enough to bear the illumination of the true light for long, let him descend gently and in orderly fashion to any of the three steps by which he made his ascent. Let him remain

alternatively on one for a time, or on another, following the movement of his free choice, taking into consideration the time and the place; although, as it seems to me, one is closer to God the farther one climbs from the first degree. (Ladder, 83–84)

Guigo II wisely provides here for rereading and rethinking. The higher or more advanced stages of intellectual and spiritual development do not at all invalidate the earlier ones, which remain always in place as a firm foundation on which the superstructure of the building (in Hugh's metaphor) must continue to rest.

Gregory had emphasized care for the learning experience of the "little ones," the beginning readers, as a corrective to the arrogance of the heretical mind seeking to advance beyond its real capacities. In the same spirit, Hugh repeatedly warns against presumption—"Hold no learning in contempt" (Did 3.13)—and he particularly cautions against jumping over intermediate stages, those that link the literal reading of a text to its mystical meaning (*De scripturis* 5). Guigo II provides for careful recapitulation of the reading-meditation-prayer sequence, and he himself frequently recapitulates the development of his treatise (Scala 3, 12, 14). In this manner is maintained the "coherence" in which the four constituents are held together (*sibi cohaerent*).

Two traditional metaphors envision that coherence not only as a sequence but as a simultaneity: the building (in which each higher storey rests on the lower ones) and the chain (whose links are bound together, *catenati*, each inseparable from the others, the whole dependent upon the strength of each one). Surveying twelfth-century authors with these images in mind, we should perhaps hesitate to join historians who have perceived a modernizing "renewal of interest in the literal meaning of Scripture" at this cultural moment, with the Victorines leading the way.[35] Hugh does not propose a scientific exegesis in opposition to traditional allegorism. He does stress literal/historical reading as an indispensable component of a holistic understanding, but as Henri de Lubac argues, he does not ever *limit* exegesis to the literal level. Hugh, Bernard, William of Saint-Thierry, Guigo II, and the others—varying considerably in their emphases on one or another aspect—do all affirm the integ-

[35] E.g., Bernard McGinn, *Growth of Mysticism*, 369, following Beryl Smalley.

rity of the whole reading-contemplation process, that is to say in psychological terms, the unity of intellectual, affective, and spiritual faculties engaged in the reception experience of a scriptural text.

In *lectio divina*, the devout mind should follow, in principle, a sequential order, *sicut temporaliter, ita et causaliter*, advancing by stages from the first reading to contemplation. Hugh of Saint-Victor and Guigo II both value systematic, unhurried procedure, *leniter et ordinate*. They have taken that preference from the pre-Scholastic masters of the period, but they seek at all costs to avoid what they perceive as the superficiality and impatience and arrogance of the schoolmen, profoundly antithetical to true spirituality. In monastic practice, however, the sequence must often yield to simultaneity. For with Scripture, rereading is the norm; the psalms and much of the New Testament have been memorized along with passages from Genesis and the major prophets, and these are constantly repeated in the liturgy. The rereading of a familiar text could engage a lifetime's overlay of meditations and levels of insight achieved and superseded, brought together in the present moment. The first few words of a psalm would immediately evoke the whole, and, in effect, the passage from reading to contemplation could be at times instantaneous.

All spiritual writers value, accordingly, inspired interruptions in the orderly process. We recall once again Anselm's advice to the Countess Matilda, the reader of his *Prayers and Meditations*, that she should not attempt to read the whole, "but only as much as will stir the mind to prayer."[36] The fulfillment of reading begins in the moment the reader lifts her eyes from the page and takes an active part in what is now a dialogue. The impulse to pray does not at all impede the reading, according to William of Saint-Thierry, but rather "returns the mind to a more lucid understanding of the text" (*Epistola ad fratres de Monte Dei* 123; SCh 223:240). The preacher, following Gregory's advice, should likewise expect interruptions leading to digressions, and it will be his duty to share them with the congregation.[37] Religious writers since Augustine have not

---

[36] Ward, *Prayers and Meditations*, 90.

[37] See above, p. 68. Gregory develops an image of a sermon as a river filling adjoining valleys as well as retaining its principal course, in the introductory letter to the *Moralia on Job*, "Ad Leandrum" 2; cf. Bernard of Clairvaux, SC 82.1.

hesitated to insert exclamations prompted by inspiration in the middle of even the most formal written discourse. That rhythm is felt again on the higher level as prayer opens into contemplation; Guigo II, following many others, observes that God does not need to wait until we reach the end of a sentence but often intervenes and immediately answers, showering "sweetness" on the soul, irrigating, anointing, and restoring the weary mind (Scala 7; SCh 163:96). The same thought guides the understanding of the first verse of the Song of Songs, in which the Bride shifts in reference to her Bridegroom from the third person (*Osculetur me osculo oris sui*) to the direct address of the second person (*Quia meliora sunt ubera tua vino*). Ever since Origen's *Commentary*, this movement has been interpreted as a recognition that the Bridegroom is answering her prayer and is now suddenly present and appearing to her.[38]

Lectio divina, as summarized by Guigo II, is in the first instance a discipline. Its orderly sequence ensures thorough accounting for the text, even its tiniest details, and instills the attitude of intellectual humility, proof against arrogance and superficiality. The methodical pedagogy enables, however, its own self-transcendence; at key moments the sequence is seen to resolve into simultaneity, as its discrete constituents become present dimensions of the experiential moment in a flash of spiritual inspiration or an enthusiastic élan.

---

[38] Origen, *Commentarium in Cant.*, 2.1, in Origène, *Commentaire sur le Cantique des cantiques*, ed. and trans. L. Bésard, H. Crouzel, M. Borret, SCh 375–76 (Paris: Éditions du Cerf, 1991–2), 190; *Homiliae in Cant.*, 1.2, in *Homélies sur le Cantique des cantiques*, ed. and trans. Olivier Rousseau, 2nd ed., SCh 37bis (Paris: Éditions du Cerf, 1966), 72; Gregory the Great, *Expositio in Cant.* 13, SCh 314:88; Bernard of Clairvaux, SC 9.4.

Chapter Eight

The Book of Experience

Bernard: *Hodie legimus in libro experientiae* (SC 3.1; SBOp 1:14).
We read and go out into the world; there we find again and recognize what we have read; returning to the text we recognize
what we have experienced. The Scripture becomes clearer, then,
according to Cassian, when it is not only explained by exegesis
but confirmed by all that we have personally seen, felt, and heard.
"Having been instructed in this way . . . we shall feel things in
our grasp rather than hearing them, and from the inner disposition
of the heart we shall bring forth not what has been committed to
memory but what is implanted in the very nature of things. Thus
we shall penetrate its meaning not through the written text but
with experience leading the way" (*Conferences* 10.11.5–6; SCh
54:93). "We shall feel things in our grasp": the medieval religious
writers would have us take outright possession of what we read, as
coming to us not from outside, or secondhand, or from a chance
encounter. One cannot read the psalms as a third party overhear-
ing someone else's prayer. Bernard: "Only the singer can hear the
Song of Songs, and the one to whom she sings" (SC 1.11; SBOp
1:8). It is ourselves that we have to read when we read "with experience leading the way."

What does this monastic pedagogy have to do with reading in
the modern world? Frank Smith, summarizing the thirty-year "in-
terminable controversy" over "phonics" versus "whole language"
methods of literacy instruction, emphasizes the necessary work
of prediction and contextualization in the process whereby the
reader actively constructs, rather than passively decodes or receives,
the meaning of the text in hand.[1] The discussion turns, most profoundly perhaps, on contrasting notions of freedom. Systematic

---

[1] Smith, *Understanding Reading*, 156–77, 291–92.

phonetic study eventually enables us to read even unfamiliar words, with or without understanding; thus, children may be asked to read nonsense sentences to hone this capability. Quintilian (first century) and the earlier classical authorities had given children gibberish texts and exotic proper names to decode for the same purpose. This scientific approach liberates us from context but enslaves us to the texts; when, however, we can bring extratextual, contextualizing resources into play—pictures, imagination, memory—a wholly natural, spontaneous, and reciprocal interaction ensues, rising above the surface of the page. Children read stories in this effortless manner; it is a first step toward *contemplatio*.

But what, then, is the proper role for the adult intelligence? The early monastic authorities advise that understanding may (or may not) come later, as a gift of the Spirit, in sleep perhaps, but we find that we cannot continue to indefinitely repeat "It is good to be here" (Matt 17:4) without struggling to understand the words; something urges us not to abdicate that struggle until our voluntary rational faculties have been engaged to the fullest. Human effort must collaborate actively with grace. Accordingly, the theoreticians of the twelfth century give special attention to *meditatio*, the indispensable second step in the sequence leading from reading to contemplation. The term no longer means merely memorization-recitation, as it did for the earliest monks. For Hugh of Saint-Victor, *meditatio* is bound by none of reading's constraints; it is free to break through the surface of the wording in order to find hidden meanings, and it freely ranges outward to open ground, far from the textual immediacy. It is led solely by the authority of one's own intellectual acumen (*ductu propriae rationis*), in Guigo II's phrase.

It is not enough. *Meditatio* is the sputtering wet log on the hearth, in Hugh's vivid image (taken up years later by John of the Cross); it gives off smoke and steam until eventually, purified, it becomes nothing but the very fire that consumes it. In and of itself, however—where the spiritual dimension is lacking, where *meditatio* fails to transcend itself—even the most earnest, focused study of texts will tend fatally toward academic inanity.

"When I was a child, I spoke like a child, I thought like a child . . . when I became a man, I gave up childish ways" (1 Cor 13:11).

As we become adults, we discharge our tutors (Gal 3:23-24; 4:1-7). The Bride in her impatience cries out, in the first verse of the Song, to do away with intrusive mediations by prophets, teachers, literary critics, etc. The Scripture itself is a screen—or a dark mirror—interposed between the reader and the Author, concealing as much as it reveals. Reading spiritually would, however, free us (at least partially, for now) from dependence upon the wording, as we transform passive text-reception into active dialogue and reciprocity.

Modern literary theorists moved toward this realization when they revolted against the previously prevailing New Critical/Formalist imprisonment of the text in self-enclosed objectivity and began to explore the reader-response experience. The movement hesitated, however, to proceed through the doorway it had opened, blocked apparently by a felt need to restrain interpretations (lest "interpretive anarchy" reign); it ended in the 1980s, overwhelmed by a politicization of the interpretive community, having failed to reach the conception of reading toward which, I believe, it ideally tended: spiritual freedom. That is to say, *fiducia*, boldness, interpretive confidence, licensed by a spiritual rather than political consciousness of community; an energy impelling the reader to venture beyond the inert *littera* (the New Critical/Formalist textual object) into a fullness of active, affective, intellectual, and creative literary participation.

These avenues have been closed off for some time now to the modern reader. My belief is that the study of medieval spiritual literature could lead to their rediscovery and reopening.

Select Bibliography

A. Editions and Translations

Abelard, Peter. *The Letters of Abelard and Heloise.* Translated by Betty Radice. Harmondsworth, Middlesex, England: Penguin Books, 1974.

Ælred of Rievaulx. *De institutione inclusarum.* Edited and translated by Charles Dumont as *La vie de recluse. La prière pastorale.* SCh 76. Paris: Éditions du Cerf, 1961. Translated by Mary Paul MacPherson as *A Rule of Life for a Recluse. Treatises and Pastoral Prayer.* CF 2. Kalamazoo, MI: Cistercian, 1971.

———. *De Jesu puero.* Edited by Anselme Hoste and translated by Joseph Dubois. SCh 60. Paris: Éditions du Cerf, 2005.

Alcuin (attributed). *De psalmorum usu.* PL 101:465–508.

Anselm. *Orationes sive meditationes.* In *S. Anselmi Cantuariensis archiepiscopi opera omnia,* Tomus 2:2–91. Edited by Franciscus Salesius Schmitt. Stuttgart: Frommann, 1968. Translated by Benedicta Ward as *The Prayers and Meditations of Saint Anselm.* Harmondsworth, Middlesex, UK, and New York, NY: Penguin Books, 1973.

Augustine. *Confessions.* Edited by James J. O'Donnell. Oxford: Clarendon Press, 1992. Translated by R. S. Pine-Coffin. New York, NY: Penguin Books, 1961.

———. *De catechizandis rudibus liber unus.* Translated with an introduction and commentary by Joseph Patrick Christopher. Catholic University of America, Patristic Studies vol. VIII. Washington, D.C.: The Catholic University of America, 1926.

———. *De doctrina christiana.* Edited by J. Martin. CCSL 32. Turnhout: Brepols, 1972. Translated by D. W. Robertson as *On Christian Doctrine.* Upper Saddle River: Prentice Hall, 1958.

———. *De Genesi ad litteram.* PL 34.

———. *De magistro.* In *Aurelii Augustini Opera* 2.2. Edited by W. M. Green. CCSL 29:157–203. Turnhout: Brepols, 1970. Translated by Whitney J. Oates as *Concerning the Teacher.* In *Basic Writings of St. Augustine,* 1:361–95. New York, NY: Random House, 1948.

————. *De spiritu et littera.* Edited by William Bright. Oxford: Clarendon Press, 1914.

————. *De utilitate credendi.* PL 40. Translated by Whitney J. Oates as *On the Profit of Believing.* In *Basic Writings of St. Augustine,* 1:399–427. New York, NY: Random House, 1948.

Benedict. *Rule of Saint Benedict 1980.* Edited by Timothy Fry. Collegeville, MN: Liturgical Press, 1981.

Bernard of Clairvaux. *Sermones super Cantica canticorum.* Edited by Jean Leclercq, Charles H. Talbot, and Henri M. Rochais. Vols. 1–2 of *Sancti Bernardi opera.* 7 vols. Rome: Editiones Cistercienses, 1957–74. Translated by Killian Walsh, Irene Edmonds, and M. Corneille Halflants as *On the Song of Songs.* 4 vols. CF 4, 7, 31, 40. Kalamazoo, MI: Cistercian Publications, 1971–80.

————. *Treatises II: The Steps of Humility and Pride, On Loving God.* Translated by Robert Walton. CF 13. Kalamazoo, MI: Cistercian Publications, 1980.

Caesarius of Arles. *Regula ad monachos.* PL 67.

————. *Regula ad virgines.* PL 67.

————. *Sermones.* Edited by Germani Morin. CCSL 103–104. Turnhout: Brepols, 1953.

Cassiodorus Senator. *Cassiodori senatoris institutiones.* Edited by R. A. B. Mynors. Oxford: Clarendon Press, 1937.

Defensor of Ligugé. *Liber scintillarum.* Edited by Henri Rochais. CCSL 97. Turnholt: Brepols, 1957.

Gregory the Great. *Commentaire sur le Cantique des cantiques.* Edited and and translated by Rodrigue Bélanger. SCh 314. Paris: Éditions du Cerf, 1984. Translated by Denys Turner in *Eros and Allegory: Medieval Exegesis of the Song of Songs.* CS 156:215–55. Kalamazoo, MI: Cistercian Publications, 1995, *Gregory the Great: On the Song of Songs.* Translation and introduction, Mark DelCogliano. CS 244, Collegeville, MN: Cistercian Publications, 2012.

————. *Homiliae in Hiezechihelem prophetam.* Edited by Marcus Adriaen. CCSL 142. Turnhout: Brepols, 1971. Edited and translated by Charles Morel as *Grégoire le grand, Homélies sur Ézéchiel.* 2 vols. SCh 327, 360. Paris: Éditions du Cerf, 1986, 1990.

————. *Moralia in Iob.* Edited by Marcus Adriaen. 3 vols. CCSL 143, 143A, 143B. Turnhout: Brepols, 1979, 1979, 1985. Edited by Robert Gillet and translated by André de Gaudemaris as *Morales sur Job: Livres 1 et 2.* SCh 32. Paris: Éditions du Cerf, 1952. Edited and translated by

A. Bocognano as *Morales sur Job, Livres 11–14*. SCh 212. Paris: Éditions du Cerf, 1974. Edited and and translated by A. Bocognano as *Morales sur Job, Livres 15–16*. SCh 221. Paris: Éditions du Cerf, 1975.

Guigo II. *Lettre sur la vie contemplative. L'échelle des moines. Douze méditations*. Edited by Edmund Colledge and James Walsh and translated by "un chartreux." SCh 163. Paris: Éditions du Cerf, 1970. Translated by Edmund Colledge and James Walsh as *The Ladder of Monks, A Letter on the Contemplative Life, and Twelve Meditations*. CS 48. Kalamazoo, MI: Cistercian Publications, 1981.

Hugh of Saint-Victor. *Hugonis de Sancto Victore Didascalicon: De studio legendi. A Critical Text*. Edited by Charles Henry Buttimer. Washington, D.C.: The Catholic University Press, 1939. Translated by Jerome Taylor as *The Didascalicon of Hugh of Saint-Victor: A Medieval Guide to the Arts*. New York, NY: Columbia University Press, 1961.

————. *De scripturis et scriptoribus sacris*. PL 175:9–28.

————. *Homiliae in Ecclesiasten*. PL 175:115–27.

————. *Six opuscules spirituels*. Edited and translated by Roger Baron. SCh 155. Paris: Éditions du Cerf, 1969.

Isidore of Seville. *Regula monachorum*. PL 83.

————. *Sententiae*. Edited by Pierre Cazier. CCSL 111. Turnhout: Brepols, 1998.

Jerome. *Select Letters*. Translated by F. A. Wright. Loeb Classical Library 262. Cambridge, MA: Harvard University Press, 1933.

John Cassian. *Conférences*. Edited by E. Pichéry. SCh 42, 54, 64. Paris: Éditions du Cerf, 1955–59. Translated by Boniface Ramsey as *John Cassian: The Conferences*. New York: Paulist Press, 1997.

John of Fécamp. *Confessio theologica*. Edited by Jean Leclercq and Jean-Paul Bonnes in *Un maître de la vie spirituelle au XIe siècle: Jean de Fécamp*. Paris: Librairie Philosophique J. Vrin, 1946. Translated by Philippe de Vial as *Jean de Fécamp: La confession théologique*. Sagesses chrétiennes. Paris: Éditions du Cerf, 1992.

John of Salisbury. *Metalogicon*. Translated by Daniel D. McGarry. Gloucester, MA: Peter Smith, 1971.

La Règle du maître. 3 vols. SCh 105–07. Paris: Éditions du Cerf, 1964–65. Vol. 1 (prologue–chap. 10) edited and translated by Adalbert de Vogüé; Vol. 2 (chap. 11–95) edited and translated by Adalbert de Vogüé; Vol. 3 (concordance) edited and translated by Jean-Marie Clément, Jean Neufville, and Daniel Demeslay. Translated by Luke Eberle as *The Rule of the Master*. CS 6. Kalamazoo, MI: Cistercian Publications, 1977.

Origen. *Commentaire sur le Cantique des cantiques.* Edited and translated by L. Bésard, H. Crouzel, and M. Borret. SCh 375–76. Paris: Éditions du Cerf, 1991–92.

———. *Homélies sur le Cantique des cantiques.* Edited and translated by Olivier Rousseau. 2nd ed. SC 37bis. Paris: Éditions du Cerf, 1966. Translated by R. P. Lawson as *The Song of Songs: Commentary and Homilies.* Ancient Christian Writers 26. Westminster, MD: Newman Press, 1957.

———. *Traité des principes.* Edited by H. Crouzel and M. Simonetti. Vol. 3. SCh 268. Paris: Éditions du Cerf, 1980. Translated by G. W. Butterworth as *Origen: On First Principles.* Gloucester, MA: Peter Smith, 1973.

Pachomius. *Regula sancti Pachomii.* Translated by Jerome. PL 23.

Peter of Celle. *Selected Works: Sermons, The School of the Cloister, On Affliction and Reading, On Conscience.* Translated by Hugh Feiss. CS 100. Kalamazoo, MI: Cistercian Publications, 1987.

Quintilian. *Institutio oratoria.* Translated by H. E. Butler. 4 vols. Loeb Classical Library. London: Heineman, 1920–22.

Rupert of Deutz. *Commentaria in Canticum canticorum.* Edited by Hrabanus Haacke. CCCM 26. Turnhout: Brepols, 1974.

Smaragdus of Saint Mihiel. *Expositio in regulam S. Benedicti.* Edited by A. Spannagel and P. Engelbert. Corpus Consuetudinum Monasticarum 8. Siegburg, Germany: F. Schmitt, 1974. Translated by David Barry as *Commentary on the Rule of Saint Benedict.* CS 212. Kalamazoo, MI: Cistercian Publications, 2007.

———. *Diadema monachorum.* PL 102:593–690. Translated by David Barry as *The Crown of Monks.* CS 245, Collegeville, MN: Cistercian Publications, forthcoming.

Vatican Council II: The Basic Sixteen Documents. Translated by Austin Flannery, OP. Northport, NY: Costello Publishing Co., 1996.

William of Saint-Thierry. *Epistola ad Fratres de Monte Dei.* Edited and translated by Jean Déchanet as *Lettre aux Frères du Mont-Dieu (Lettre d'or).* SCh 223. Paris: Éditions du Cerf, 1975. Translated by Theodore Berkeley as *The Golden Epistle: A Letter to the Brethren at Mont Dieu.* CF 12. Kalamazoo, MI: Cistercian Publications, 1971.

———. *On Contemplating God. Prayer. Meditations.* Translated by Penelope Lawson. CF 3. Kalamazoo, MI: Cistercian Publications, 1970.

B. Secondary Sources

Astell, Ann W. *The Song of Songs in the Middle Ages.* Ithaca, NY, and London: Cornell University Press, 1990.

Baron, Roger. *Science et sagesse chez Hugues de Saint-Victor*. Paris: Lethiel-leux, 1957.

Bennett, Andrew, ed. *Readers and Reading*. London and New York, NY: 1995.

Bianchi, Enzo. *Praying the Word: An Introduction to* Lectio Divina. CS 182. Kalamazoo, MI: Cistercian Publications, 1998.

Bouyer, Louis. *Introduction à la vie spirituelle. Précis de théologie ascétique et mystique*. Paris: Desclée, 1960.

Brésard, Luc. "Bernard et Origène commentent le Cantique." *Collectanea Cisterciensia* 44 (1982): 111–30, 183–209, 293–308.

Brown, George Hardin. *Bede the Venerable*. Boston, MA: Twayne, 1987.

Calati, Benedetto. "La 'lectio divina' nella tradizione monastica benedit-tina." *Benedictina* 28 (1981): 407–38.

Calinescu, Matei. *Rereading*. New Haven, CT, and London: Yale Univer-sity Press, 1995.

Carruthers, Mary. *The Book of Memory: A Study of Memory in Medieval Culture*. Cambridge: Cambridge University Press, 1990.

Casey, Michael. *Sacred Reading: The Ancient Art of* Lectio Divina. Liguori, MO: Liguori/Triumph, 1996.

Catry, Patrick. "Lire l'écriture selon saint Grégoire le grand." *Collectanea Cisterciensia* 34 (1972): 177–201.

Clanchy, M. T. *From Memory to Written Record: England 1066–1307*. Lon-don: Edward Arnold, and Cambridge, MA: Harvard University Press, 1979. 2nd ed. Oxford and Cambridge, MA: Blackwell, 1993.

D'Ambrosio, Marcellino. "*Ressourcement* Theology, *Aggiornamento*, and the Hermeneutics of Tradition." *Communio* 18 (Winter 1991): 530–555.

Dagens, Claude. *Saint Grégoire le grand: Culture et expérience chrétiennes*. Paris: Études Augustiniennes, 1977.

De Lubac, Henri. *Exégèse médiévale: Les quatre sens de l'écriture*. 4 vols. Paris: Aubier, 1959–64. Translated by Mark Sebanc and others as *Me-dieval Exegesis: The Four Senses of Scripture*. 3 vols. Grand Rapids, MI: Eerdmans, 1998–2009.

———. *Histoire et esprit: L'intelligence de l'Écriture d'après Origène*. Paris: Aubier-Montaigne, 1950.

———. *Mémoire sur l'occasion de mes écrits*. Namur, Belgium: Culture et Vérité, 1989.

———. *Résistance chrétienne au nazisme*. Edited by Renée Bédarida. Paris: Éditions du Cerf, 2006.

———. *Surnaturel: Études historiques*. Paris: Aubier-Montaigne, 1946.

De Vogüé, Adalbert. "Les deux fonctions de la méditation dans les Règles monastiques anciennes." *Revue d'Histoire de la Spiritualité* 51 (1975): 3–16.

———. "*Orationi frequenter incumbere*: Une invitation à la prière continuelle," *Revue d'Ascétique et Mystique* 44 (1968): 3–9.

———. *The Rule of Saint Benedict: A Doctrinal and Spiritual Commentary.*
Translated by John Baptist Hasbrouck. CS 54. Kalamazoo, MI: Cistercian Publications, 1983.

———. "*Sub regula vel abbate*: A study of the Theological Significance
of the Ancient Monastic Rules." In *Rule and Life: An Interdisciplinary
Symposium*, edited by M. Basil Pennington. CS 12. Kalamazoo, MI:
Cistercian Publications, 1971.

Dumont, Charles. *Praying the Word of God: The Use of* Lectio Divina.
Oxford: SLG Press, 1999.

Egan, Keith J. "Guigo II: The Theology of the Contemplative Life." In
The Spirituality of Western Christendom. Edited by E. Rozanne Elder.
CS 30:106–15. Kalamazoo, MI: Cistercian Publications, 1976.

Elder, E. Rozanne, ed. *The Joy of Learning and the Love of God: Studies in
Honor of Jean Leclercq*. CS 160. Kalamazoo, MI, and Spencer, MA: 1995.

Fish, Stanley. "Interpreting the *Variorum*." *Critical Inquiry* 2 (Spring 1976):
465–85.

———. "Literature in the Reader: Affective Stylistics." *New Literary History* 2, no.1 (Autumn 1970): 123–62.

Gilson, Etienne. *La théologie mystique de saint Bernard*. Paris: Vrin, 1947.

Hall, Thelma. *Too Deep for Words: Rediscovering* Lectio Divina. New York,
NY: Paulist Press, 1988.

Holub, Robert C. *Reception Theory: A Critical Introduction*. London and
New York, NY: Methuen, 1984.

Illich, Ivan. *In the Vineyard of the Text. A Commentary to Hugh's* Didascalicon. Chicago and London: University of Chicago Press, 1993.

Iser, Wolfgang. *The Act of Reading: A Theory of Aesthetic Response*. Baltimore,
MD, and London: Johns Hopkins University Press, 1978.

Kelly, J. N. D. *Early Christian Doctrines*. San Francisco, CA: Harper Collins,
1978.

———. *Jerome: His Life, Writings, and Controversies*. New York: Harper
and Row, 1975.

King, J. Christopher. *Origen on the Song of Songs as the Spirit of Scripture: The
Bridegroom's Perfect Marriage-Song*. Oxford: Oxford University Press, 2005.

Leclercq, Jean. *The Love of Learning and the Desire for God: A Study of
Monastic Culture*. Translated by Catherine Misrahi. New York, NY:
Fordham University Press, 1961.

———. *Recueil d'études sur saint Bernard et ses écrits*. 3 vols. Rome: Edizioni di Storia e Letteratura, 1962–69.

———. "Les Sermons sur les Cantiques ont-ils été prononcés?" *Recueil* 1:193–212. Translated by Killian Walsh in *Bernard of Clairvaux: On the Song of Songs*. Vol. 2. CF 7. Kalamazoo, MI: Cistercian Publications, 1976. vii–xxx.

———. "Les étapes de la rédaction." *Recueil* 1:213–44.

———. "Aux sources des sermons sur les Cantiques." *Recueil* 1:275–78.

———. "Smaragdus." In *An Introduction to the Medieval Mystics of Europe: Fourteen Original Essays*. Edited by Paul E. Szarmach. Albany: SUNY Press, 1984.

———. *Histoire de la Spiritualité Chrétienne*. Vol. 2, *La Spiritualité du Moyen Âge*. Paris: Aubier, 1961.

———. *Memoirs: From Grace to Grace*. Petersham, MA: St. Bede's Publications, 2000.

———. *Monks and Love in Twelfth-Century France: Psycho-Historical Essays*. Oxford: Clarendon Press, 1979.

Magrassi, Mariano. *Praying the Bible: An Introduction to* Lectio Divina. Collegeville, MN: Liturgical Press, 1998.

Marrou, Henri. *Histoire de l'éducation dans l'antiquité*. Paris: Editions du Seuil, 1948. Translated by George Lamb as *A History of Education in Antiquity*. New York : Sheed and Ward, 1956.

———. *Saint Augustin et la fin de la culture antique*. Paris: E. de Boccard, 1938; 2nd ed. 1949.

Matter, E. Ann. *The Voice of My Beloved: The Song of Songs in Western Medieval Christianity*. Philadelphia, PA: University of Pennsylvania Press, 1990.

McGinn, Bernard. "Jean Leclercq's Contribution to Monastic Spirituality and Theology." *Monastic Studies* 16 (1985): 7–23.

———. *The Presence of God: A History of Western Christian Mysticism*. Vol. 2, *The Growth of Mysticism*. New York, NY: Crossroad, 1999.

——— and John Meyendorff, eds. *Christian Spirituality: Origins to the Twelfth Century*. New York: Crossroad, 1985.

Milbank, John. *The Suspended Middle: Henri de Lubac and the Debate Concerning the Supernatural*. Grand Rapids, MI: Eerdmans, 2005.

Moorhead, John. *Gregory the Great*. London and New York: Routledge, 2005.

Mundó, A. "*Bibliotheca*, Bible et Lecture de carême d'après S. Benoît." *Revue Bénédictine* 60 (1950): 65–92.

Ohly, Friedrich. *Hohelied-Studien: Grundzüge einer Geschichte der Hoheliedauslegung des Abendlandes bis um 1200*. Wiesbaden: Franz Steiner, 1958.

Ong, Walter J. *Orality and Literacy: The Technologizing of the Word*. London and New York, NY: Routledge, 1982.

Parkes, Malcolm B. "The Contribution of Insular Scribes of the Seventh and Eighth Centuries to the 'Grammar of Legibility.'" In *Scribes, Scripts and Readers*. London and Rio Grande: The Hambledon Press, 1991.

———. *Pause and Effect: An Introduction to the History of Punctuation in the West*. Berkeley, CA: University of California Press, 1993.

Pennington, M. Basil. Lectio Divina: *Renewing the Ancient Practice of Praying the Scriptures*. New York, NY: Crossroad, 1998.

Pope, Marvin H. *Song of Songs: A New Translation and Commentary*. The Anchor Bible. New York: Doubleday, 1977.

Riché, Pierre. *Écoles et enseignement dans le haut Moyen Âge, fin du Ve siècle–milieu du XIe siècle*. Paris: Picard, 1979.

———. *Education and Culture in the Barbarian West: Sixth through Eighth Centuries*. Translated by John J. Contreni. Columbia, SC: University of South Carolina Press, 1976.

Saenger, Paul. "Silent Reading: Its impact on Late Medieval Script and Society." *Viator* 13 (1980): 366–414.

———. *Space Between Words: The Origins of Silent Reading*. 2nd ed. Stanford, CA: Stanford University Press, 1997.

Senn, Frank C. *Christian Liturgy, Catholic and Evangelical*. Minneapolis, MN: Fortress, 1997.

Harper, John. *The Forms and Orders of Western Liturgy from the Tenth to the Eighteenth Century*. Oxford: Clarendon, 1991.

Sicard, Patrice. *Hugues de Saint-Victor et son école*. Turnhout: Brepols, 1991.

Smalley, Beryl. *The Study of the Bible in the Middle Ages*. Notre Dame, IN: University of Notre Dame Press, 1964.

Smith, Frank. *Understanding Reading: A Psycholinguistic Analysis of Reading and Learning to Read*. 6th ed. New York: Routledge. 2011.

Southern, R. W. *Saint Anselm: A Portrait in a Landscape*. Cambridge: Cambridge University Press, 1990.

Stewart, Columba. *Cassian the Monk*. New York and Oxford: Oxford University Press, 1998.

Stiegman, Emero. "A Tradition of Aesthetics in Saint Bernard." In *Bernardus Magister: Papers Presented at the Nonacentenary Celebration of the Birth of Saint Bernard of Clairvaux*. Edited by John Sommerfeldt. CS 135. Spencer, MA: Cistercian Publications; Cîteaux: Comentarii Cistercienses, 1992.

————. "The Literary Genre of Bernard of Clairvaux's *Sermones super cantica canticorum.*" In *Simplicity and Ordinariness: Studies in Medieval Cistercian History IV.* Edited by John R. Sommerfeldt. CS 61. Kalamazoo, MI: Cistercian Publications, 1980.

Stock, Brian. *After Augustine: The Meditative Reader and the Text.* Philadelphia: University of Pennsylvania Press, 2001.

————. *Augustine the Reader: Meditation, Self-Knowledge, and the Ethics of Interpretation.* Cambridge, MA and London, England: 1996.

————. *The Implications of Literacy: Written Language and Models of Interpretation in the Eleventh and Twelfth Centuries.* Princeton, NJ: Princeton University Press, 1983.

————. *Listening for the Text: On the Uses of the Past.* Baltimore, MD: Johns Hopkins University Press, 1990.

Straw, Carole. *Gregory the Great: Perfection in Imperfection.* Berkeley: University of California Press, 1988.

Studzinski, Raymond. *Reading to Live. The Evolving Practice of* Lectio Divina. CS 231. Collegeville, MN: Cistercian Publications, 2009.

Suleiman, Susan R., and Inge Crosman, eds. *The Reader in the Text: Essays on Audience and Interpretation.* Princeton, NJ: Princeton University Press, 1980.

Tompkins, Jane, ed. *Reader-Response Criticism: From Formalism to Post-Structuralism.* Baltimore, MD, and London: Johns Hopkins University Press, 1980.

Torjesen, Karen Jo. *Hermeneutical Procedure and Theological Method in Origen's Exegesis.* Berlin: de Gruyter, 1986.

Tugwell, Simon. *Ways of Imperfection: An Exploration of Christian Spirituality.* Springfield, IL: Templegate, 1985.

Turner, Denys. *Eros and Allegory: Medieval Exegesis of the Song of Songs.* CS 156. Kalamazoo, MI: Cistercian Publications, 1995.

Urs von Balthasar, Hans. *The Theology of Henri de Lubac: An Overview.* Translated by Joseph D. Fessio and others. San Francisco: Ignatius Press, 1991.

Voderholzer, Rudolf. *Meet Henri de Lubac.* Translated by Michael J. Miller. San Francisco: Ignatius Press, 2008.

Wagner, Jean-Pierre. *Henri de Lubac.* Paris: Éditions du Cerf, 2001.

Wilmart, André, ed. *Precum libelli quattuor aevi karolini: Nunc primum publici iuris facti cum aliorum indicibus. Prior pars.* Rome: Ephemerides Liturgicae, 1940.

Wogan-Browne, Jocelyn. *Saints' Lives and Women's Literary Cuture: Virginity and its Authorizations.* Oxford: Oxford University Press, 2001.

Index